ALL I WANT
IS OUT
OF HERE

BY

ROB CHAPMAN

DEDICATED TO ALL THE HEADS.

"choose to choose/choose to go"
Lou Reed

Danny (honey brown hair) and Me (dark hair) Oct/Nov 1971

Contents

Chapter 1

HEY DANNY. REMEMBER THAT TIME THE ROOM TURNED INTO A CHURCH AND ANGELS RAINED DOWN FROM THE CEILING?

Never drop a purple microdot on a multi-coloured carpet. The intricately patterned weave will swallow it whole and give you static shock when you comb it. I only unwrapped the little piece of silver foil to see what Steve Sangster had sold us that afternoon. It pinged out onto the living-room floor and now look what's happened. Mum, Dad, brothers and sister sound asleep upstairs. Me and Danny giggling nervously as we combed in vain, the Numbskulls in our heads fetching fire buckets to quell the mirth.

– What if your cat eats it?

– Shut up Danny.

– No, seriously.

Scenarios envisaged. Giant mice.

– There it is!

Just call me Microscope Eyes. Laughter subsiding. Palpable relief. Anyone could have fallen face first into that carpet and inadvertently gone on a heaven and hell trip, according to what the more lurid newspaper exposés told me on a weekly basis.

– And we'll get a trip out of something as tiny as that?
– Trust me.

Danny Hanson had turned up unexpectedly on my doorstep in the October of 1971. Apart from one ill-fated visit to the last of that year's Hyde Park free concerts in early September I hadn't seen him since we'd left Grammar school in July. Danny had arrived during that final school year and carried the disconsolate air of someone who had been evicted from a much happier life elsewhere in order to be somewhere he didn't want to be. He immediately gravitated towards others who felt the same way. We bonded in mutual captivity, back-of-the-class GCE rejects, refuseniks, recalcitrant little fuckers, sneering at all we surveyed. Teachers, prefects, rock bands we didn't like, anyone who wasn't us basically. We condemned them all as "hype".

Hype was our all-purpose rub-out word. Supergroups. Hype. Sixth-form pretend hippies. Hype. All the music liked by sixth-form pretend hippies. Hype. Dylan's motorbike accident. Hype. "Beatles to reform" headlines in the music papers. Hype. Progressive groups who weren't really that progressive. Hype. One wave of the word-wand banishes all phonies and pseuds. Hype.

We saw out our schooldays in simmering cynical contemplation and then went our separate ways. Apart from that dismal September Saturday in Hyde Park, that was it, until one October afternoon a few weeks after I'd started Tech college Mum called into the living room from the kitchen in her best mock-posh: "Robert, there's someone at the door for you." And there was Danny standing on my back doorstep, long honey-brown hair, uncertain smile. We sat in my front room for a bit chatting, playing records, catching up. Then we arranged to meet in Bedford that coming Saturday. The weekend that followed set into motion a chain of events which would determine the course of my life for the next year.

I'd only gone to the second of that year's Hyde Park free concerts out of a sense of obligation. I'd enjoyed all the previous ones. They were necessary initiation ceremonies for any young questing Home Counties head. The sun mostly shone. The music was good and the vibe pleasurable. This one was different. The weather was overcast and the atmosphere oppressive. King Crimson were at their most intense and Jack Bruce at his most uncompromising, performing material that I would later recognise when I heard his contributions to Carla Bley's *Escalator over the Hill* LP. To compound the unease, I'd gone with my ex-girlfriend Cindy. Those two Hyde Park concerts bookended our summer. We'd met at the Grand Funk Railroad one in July. We split just before the September one. We were joined at the second concert by Danny and Dickie Dangerfield. Dickie was the weirdest weirdo of my schooldays. The kid who had long hair before anyone else. The kid who owned blues anthologies at 13. He also possessed a malevolent sense of humour, even by our coruscating standards. At Hyde Park he seemed to revel in my discomfort as I stood there next to the girl who had been my summer.

I don't even know why Cindy came. Perhaps she just wanted the albums back that she'd lent me a couple of weeks before we split. That hung-up afternoon in Hyde Park played out as a carnival of grotesquery – staged, it seemed, purely to annoy me. Roy Harper annoyed me when he played a version of *The Lord's Prayer* that went on so long the trees started shedding their leaves. The PA annoyed me by playing a lengthy extract from Frank Zappa's recently released live *Fillmore East* LP. Zappa aficionados in the crowd annoyed me by laughing along with Flo and Eddie who were no longer the fun boy two in the Turtles. "Hype Park," pronounced Danny whenever he saw musicians stepping out of their limos in the cordoned-off backstage area.

In the Kings Cross station bar afterwards, everything I said turned numb on my tongue. On the train going home everything stuck stupid to my lips. Things that would have made Cindy smile in July made her wince in September. She looked at me through dismayed disappointed eyes. Dickie Dangerfield, who I had never seen kiss a girl, was fucking loving it. It was regular teenage tragicomic turmoil stuff. Everything I said or did merely compounded my new-found status as an ex. Danny, Dickie and Cindy decided we should all get off the homebound train at Hitchin and head into town for something to eat. By now the earlier clouds had lifted and the evening was filled with the kind of later summer light that seems to taunt you with its melancholy beauty. I trailed along behind the three of them, sullen and silent.

We walked over a hump-backed bridge. A railway cutting ran beneath. A narrow footpath, overgrown with brambles, ran parallel with the track and led to a small industrial estate. I peeled away into its privacy, stumbled down a winding incline and was soon hidden completely from the road. Eventually, in the distance, I heard muffled shouts.

– Rob.
– ROB!

It really is that easy just to walk away. I learned that pretty quickly over the following months.

The shouting didn't last. I waited till they'd given up on me, then shuffled back up that dusty narrow track to the station to complete my journey home. When I walked onto the platform there was a train already standing there, which I soon recognised as the one I'd stepped off half an hour earlier. Must be engine failure. Just waiting for a tow. I walked the length of the platform towards the coaches at the back-end of the train. A policeman stepped forward and barred my way. Red paint ballooned in thick splatters alongside one of the carriages, ebbing to drips and specks. British Rail officials were in attendance, and I noticed a couple more cops further up the platform. So not engine failure then, probably football hooligans returning from an early season game and vandalising the train. No, not football hooligans either. Much grimmer than that.

"Sorry son, you can't get on," said a man in overalls. "There's been an accident. Some kids were fooling around. They held their mate out of the window and that's what's left of his head."

The horror-show made the Sunday papers the next day. It brought my summer to an end.

****

That Saturday Danny and I met in Bedford as arranged and wandered around aimlessly for a bit. Eventually we drifted back to the bus station. It was late afternoon; the floodlights were going out all over the football hemisphere. The usual gathering of men congregated at the TV Rentals shop window to watch the teleprinter and final scores. Mothers, arms limp with shopping, herded platoons of kids homewards. Buses came and went. Queues formed and dispersed in the bays. The resident alkies sat sipping Strongbow on their regular seat by the photo-booth. Danny and I squatted on the back of a bench in front of the multi-storey car park and watched the dusk light fade. Waiting for something to happen.

Warding off the moment when we would be able to think of nothing better to do than go home. Then something did happen. A crowd in front of us parted and out of the throng of shoppers emerged Jeremy Carr, resplendent in greatcoat, billowing frayed flares and grimy pumps. He had a battered acoustic guitar slung round his neck, adorned in Ban the Bomb and Jesus smiley stickers. He wore, as always, an ingratiating grin on his face. "I know him," I muttered apologetically. Jeremy Carr was one of the resident fixtures of the college canteen, regularly holding court, rarely attending lectures, forever strumming chord sequences that never quite turned into tunes.

They were everywhere, the Jeremy Carrs. There was at least one in every town. Ours was omnipresent, standing by the college lift as you got out, strumming away. Standing in the college lift when you got in, strumming some more. If you were desperately unlucky he might attempt a Bob Dylan song, whining along to whichever fragment of *Visions of Johanna* he could remember, like infinity really was up on trial and he, Jeremy, was presenting the case for the defence.

I knew what was coming. If we were lucky we might get away with a brief bout of string-tuning or capo-tightening while Jeremy waited for the muse to attend. But no, on that late October afternoon in the last of the light Jeremy Carr gave us his rendition of *Alice's Restaurant* by Arlo Guthrie. Not the cool electric version called *Alice's Rock and Roll Restaurant*, that I had on a single, with *Coming into Los Angeles* on the B side. Nor the tight acoustic version which Arlo, son of Woody, may or may not have sung at Woodstock – Danny and I couldn't agree on this at our subsequent inquest. No, in the unrelenting glare of the Saturday gathering, with us allocated front-row seats, Jeremy Carr attempted the full 18-minute version which Arlo performed in the film of the same name, replete with rambling introductory monologue, and authentic to the very last quip. Compared to his usual college efforts this sounded rehearsed, a party piece even. Every ad lib, every aside, every cosmic non sequitur, every inference and intonation cribbed faithfully and rendered near verbatim to his captive audience that autumn afternoon with the dusk glow forming a funeral shroud around Greyfriars Police Station, a facility which lay tantalisingly close, yet so far away.

For once I wished for someone from the local constabulary to make an intervention. But not one copper heeded my silent plea. To make matters worse, because yes, they did get worse, less than a minute or two into Jeremy Carr's shtick a group of girls appeared behind us and greeted him warmly by name. The two parties, Carr with his guitar, and now his fan club with their Chelsea Girl bags, lingered uncomfortably adjacent to our bench with us as unfortunate stuck-betweens. Danny and I bowed our heads in purgatorial shame as Jeremy Carr gave his best straight-faced rendition of all 119 verses of Alice's fucking Restaurant. The girls listened attentively, not in awe but appreciatively enough, as if this was something they did every Saturday. They seemed oblivious to our muttered sarcasms, as did Jeremy Carr, who sailed on through his borrowed song without a stutter – although if there had been a stutter in the original version Jeremy would have had it off pat.

I watched my five o'clock bus come in and go out again over his right shoulder and rued all those missed opportunities we'd had to flee the scene. Eventually Jeremy Carr ran out of inspiration and drifted away, his troubadour work done for the day. The girls sort of started to drift away too. Then they sort of drifted back. It was as if an unspoken bond had developed in our shared proximity, and they now perhaps wished to be humoured further by these long-haired boys who had suffered so visibly in the name of Jeremy Carr's art.

Casual conversation ensued. Mostly about Marc Bolan, as I recall. One of us must have asked them what groups they liked. Danny and I feigned enthusiasm with an insincerity that amazed us both, given that we had banished T Rex to the hype bin since they'd shortened their name and become pop stars, thus forcing us to share them with the very teenybop types we were now engaging in polite conversation. "I'd love to see them live," said the straw-haired one in the Biba smock. Harriet. I mentioned that T Rex were playing at Fairfield Hall Croydon tomorrow. "Probably sold out weeks ago," said the one whose thick red lips parted slightly and formed a perfect O. Michelle. The group consensus was it probably had sold out, what with them being so popular now. I can precisely date our initial encounter with the girls from that one snippet of conversation. The Fairfield Hall gig was on Sunday October 24th, the following day.

As they talked they edged inquisitively closer. It gradually became apparent that they weren't teenybop types at all. They were confident, assertive, never giving too much away. The epitome of cool girls, not gushy girls. None of that you-ask-him-no-you-ask-him giggly stuff. They told us they were sixth-formers at the local Grammar school. Same age as us then, but obviously far more enthusiastic about staying on for A levels. The tall one had long dark hair that tumbled down over a high forehead. She occasionally ran her fingers through her locks, looked amused, and said little. Tessa. I asked her what she'd been buying. "Booble bath," she said in a Yorkshire accent. I immediately fell in love with the way she said "booble bath" and wanted to ask her again just so she would say "booble bath" again. The last of the quartet was called Veronica. She had a Cheshire Cat grin, fussed the most and bossed the others a bit, but her gaze I noticed never strayed far from Danny. Perhaps that was the reason they had drifted back in the first place, compelled by the pack leader's desire. Danny and Veronica would later marry and later still divorce, but on that October evening we were all still novices, with our young lives spread out ahead of us – beguiled by each other's presence and keen not to let this moment pass. Eventually the girls said they had to be going and somehow magically, in the seconds before running for buses, we arranged to meet here again, same spot, tomorrow.

Tomorrow was more mooching about without purpose. Window-gazing. The shopping arcades shut and the window grills down. Smaller than small talking. Crappy joking and half-hearted laughing. The things you do in a provincial town on a Sunday when nothing's open. All routes leading back to the bus station should we become bored with each other's company, and there were often moments during the conversational pauses when it seemed that we were. Tessa, the tall one, wasn't there. "She's just joined our school this year. She's from Sheffield." Mildly snarky comments were made in her absence. Girls do that. To Danny and I they mostly offered cool-girl detachment, interspersed with the occasional conversational crumb, like we had just been sitting in the right place at the right time yesterday and so we would do, for now. Michelle was the most amiable. Big brown eyes, bangles clanging, pretention-pricking scoff never far from that perfect O bow of those deep red lipsticked lips. Straw-haired Harriet seemed a bit otherworldly. Away with her thoughts. Smiling. But not at you. At some private joke maybe. More freckled in the sunlight than I'd noticed the evening before. Veronica was still the organiser, let's go down this alleyway, let's see if this café is open, eyes for Danny only.

It was Harriet and Michelle who broke the autumn ice. Steve Sangster was feeding pigeons in Church Square. "He deals," said one of the girls. I knew that much from hanging around the college canteen. He and his associate Eugene moved nefariously about the place, occasionally dropping discreet packages at high table, where the long-haired freaks gathered. In the precious seconds it takes, Harriet and Michelle were suddenly asking us to empty our pockets.

"How many shall we get?"

"How many can we afford?"

"Will two be enough between six of us?"

"No, let's get one each."

"Tessa won't want to do it."

"Never mind her. Five then. When are we going to drop it?"

"Next Sunday."

The two of them marched briskly up to Steve Sangster, who stopped feeding the pigeons and rummaged around in his pockets.

That night Danny stayed at my house on the front room put-you-up. Curious to see what had been purchased on our behalf, we waited till everyone in the house had gone to bed, then opened the little piece of silver foil. Out popped Nirvana. Never drop a purple microdot on a multi-coloured carpet.

The following Sunday Tessa was absent again. Harriet, Veronica and Michelle declined to dine electric and opted instead to babysit our trip. This was probably wise in the circumstances. They shepherded us out of town and harm's way, along the river embankment and up to Russell Park where on a golden October afternoon we watched endless shorelines ripple and melt into the sea. Autumn dripped down on us. Blood-red scars raked a stained-glass sky. Nature dug nails in deep to get that effect. Danny and I were endlessly entranced and the girls were greatly amused.

– Yes, Rob. The sky is, now you draw our attention to it, truly amazing.

All we did, Danny and I, was bob up and down on a bench, bounce around on the spongy moon grass and point at the sky show.

– Lookskylandseaallatonce.

– There isn't any sea.

But there was. Measureless oceans of milky blue. Did I tell you about the sky yet?

Later, when the day began to fray we retired to the bus station, much to the enjoyment of the Bedford heads who congregated in the seven-day café. Ex-public-school boys mostly, they all seemed to have flats in and around Albany Road where half a century earlier millennarian devotee Mabel Barltrop had founded the Panacea Society, based on the teachings of Devon prophetess Joanna Southcott. It seemed appropriate that the heads should also gravitate towards Albany Road, engaged as each of them was in their own search. Some were having what would now be called gap years. Others were having gap lives. Some were on their way to the ashram, others no further than council jobs in the parks and gardens, others still to psychiatric institutions or degree courses. For now though they were all biding their time, surreptitiously smoking charge on the bus-station benches or making woo-woo faces and hypno-hands at us through the steamed-up glass of the café window. Danny and I earned our waxwork wings that Sunday as we provided the heads with a little late-afternoon cabaret. We were persona grata after that, worthy of their time and attention spans, those who had attention spans.

"Do we know them?" Danny kept asking as we did yet another circuit of the bus station block seemingly intent on walking the trip out of our systems before we dare go home, whatever home was.
"I do, yeah. Some of them. Don't look in their eyes."
Later, whatever later was, when the girls had gone and the bus-station heads had dispersed, when the sky was just a sky and there was no one flying there, we sat on the steps of the dry cleaners in Allhallows and Danny asked me if the effects of this would last forever. It was Danny's first trip, and so from the vantage-point of my second one I had to sit there with him and explain that no Danny it won't always be like this.

Marks & Spencer won't always look like a marble temple and all those alabaster people, they'll look normal in the morning. In fact, it will all look normal in the morning, disappointingly normal.

– What, even the sky?

– Especially the sky.

– Look at everyone walking round. Can't they tell?

– Not from looking at us. No.

– Even when you hugged that tree in the park?

I felt sorry for it. It looked so lonely.

The first time I'd taken acid, a week before we went back to school for my final year, I'd assumed it to be a one-off, a cosmic ceremonial. It never occurred to me that I might take it a second, or a third time. After that glorious autumn day, peaking euphorically in Russell Park, then enjoying a comic afterlude with the bus-station heads, Danny and I took to LSD like smarties. During the year that followed I don't remember so much as a toke on a joint or a sniff of speed. Barely an underage pint was supped in a pub, but tripping became a regular sacrament.

A few days after our voyage Danny and I sat in the bus station waiting room flicking through the local paper. Danny needed a job. "Look. Sales assistant wanted for record shop," I said. Kerry's was a music shop of the old school. An entrance in the shopping arcade led you past TV and hi-fi displays and upstairs to musical instruments, sheet music and accessories. A separate entrance out on the main road led straight into the record department. The walls were lined with racks and there were old-style listening booths by the counter.

Danny needed to be convinced that working there would be a good idea. Having to listen to other people's music tastes all day didn't appeal to him, and I had to persuade him to apply. He was offered an interview and he got the job. Not only did I have an acid buddy, I now also knew someone who worked behind a record counter. The first weekend he worked there *Jeepster* by T Rex was released and a life-size cardboard cut-out of Marc Bolan in *Electric Warrior* pose was placed just outside the shop doorway for promotional purposes. It vanished within hours. Veronica, Harriet, Michelle and Tessa had chatted to Danny at the counter that day, but denied having anything to do with its disappearance. They did however admit that they had some idea of its whereabouts, and conceded that their presence at the counter might have somehow unwittingly acted as a diversionary tactic.

With the girls we did all the goopy lovelorn and lust-struck stuff that all teenagers do when they haven't got anywhere to go and be more intimate. Sitting in the Cadena café in the High Street eating brazil-nut and banana pancakes with maple syrup. Pouring thick cream slowly down the back of a silver spoon onto hot black coffee. Danny after work. Me after college. The girls after school. Sometimes, if there was room, we went and sat upstairs in a tiny café opposite the side entrance to WH Smith in Lime Street. All the cool kids congregated there. If you were one of the first dozen or so to arrive, you might even get a seat. It's a wonder they ever made any money. They must have done though, because in 1997 Toby Litt mentioned the place in his debut novel *Beatniks* and described the cramped "three tables eight chairs" ambience and provincial bohemianism of the place perfectly.

We never seemed to have much money, and after the cafés closed we had nowhere to go in the evening. We were too young to be legally served in pubs, and although plenty of landlords were happy to take the money of underage drinkers, we weren't exactly what you would call "nursing a half of mild in a snug bar" kind of kids, so mostly we sat in shop doorways, much like the homeless do now. In the high street there was a furniture

store with a labyrinth of alcoves and window displays, and in the days
before shutters and locked entrances became obligatory we used to go
and sit in there out of the wind and rain, watching the car lights gleam,
talking our small talk until a passing copper would move us on, again
much like they do the homeless now.

Harriet, Michelle and Tessa lived out in the adjoining villages. Veronica
was the only one who lived in town, and on Saturdays we were often
permitted back to hers for supper at a respectable table. This was
utterly novel to me. I'd never been part of a boy/girl clique like this. It
was all very cosy and warm and womblike, and Veronica's parents were
always welcoming. There was a Bovril advert at the time featuring Sally
Thomsett. After being stood up outside the cinema she goes home and
her Mum makes her a nice warm drink. "He's got big ears anyway," she
says to herself consolingly. Eager for an audience I reprised the punchline
one night as we sat at the table and received warm approving laughter.
Danny and I would take the pleasant piss out of the girls' music tastes as
we sipped our soup: Carole King and her patchwork thing, Marc Bolan and
his hot new single Electric Corkscrew Up My Arse c/w You Can't Really
Hear Mickey Finn Can You? James Taylor and All You Godda Do Is Call
(But I Won't Be In) c/w Nasal Clench Blues. The only progressive groups
they liked were Genesis because Peter Gabriel was cute and Curved Air
because Sonja Kristina was indisputably one of their own.

Danny and Veronica entwined like ivy and quickly became a serious
fixture. I gave Harriet my copy of Marc Bolan's *Warlock of Love* because
I'd fallen out of love with him and in love with her. We went out for a
bit (well, sat in shop doorways), but it didn't last long because none of
my relationships did then. I'd put my cold hands inside her warm coat
on winter nights, pull her close to me and ward off all thoughts that this
would ever end. I'd wave her off on the last bus back to her village and go

and get mine. Danny would repeat the ritual with Veronica. "We must get a flat," said Danny one night. "We need to have somewhere to go." Until such a moment arose we sat huddled in department-store doorways or in the Cadena or round Veronica's kitchen table. It was all very halcyon and idyllically, innocently adolescent and I remember every second of it as if it was yesterday.

Danny and I flew a freak flag for Lol Coxhill. Everything else was hype. Why Lol? Because Lol was the saxophone player in Kevin Ayers and The Whole World who were my dream band, and because I'd seen him busking on Hungerford Bridge for stare-faced tourists and fat-gutted commuters, but mostly of late because he played on John Kongos' Top Ten hit *Tokoloshe Man*. We fervently hoped that one day Lol would appear on every record in the charts and the world would go Lol-shaped. Little Lol saxophone pendants would rain René Magritte-ly from the sky. It would be the fashion to perm one's pubic hair into sax-shaped twists. We used to giggle this stuff out while we walked around town during Danny's lunch break. "Tugging the tenor" would become the new slang for mastur-

– Give us your money.

I was walking out of college at 4.30 on a late November's evening. I was away with my dream thoughts and carrying a copy of Lol Coxhill's newly released Dandelion LP *Ear of the Beholder* under my arm. My assailant moved quickly, pushing me into the stone wall of the river bridge before I had time to activate my sense of self-preservation. He had long, greasy, matted black hair and a beard and gave every indication of being a stranger to a regular bed and washing facilities. He wore a crumpled suit that looked like it had been slept in, and possibly only purchased from a charity shop in the first place for a court appearance. He spoke quietly so as not to arouse suspicion from passers-by, of which there were many, and menacingly asked for my money and my LP. I emptied my pockets of small change but convinced him that the sell-on value of an improvised jazz LP probably wouldn't bring him much money, so he let me keep it. I reasoned afterwards that he would probably have had to throw me in the River Ouse before I released my grip on that record.

We laughed about it later in the Cadena, but the girls could tell I was shaken up. "Mugged by a tramp, eh?" said Danny sympathetically. It remains to this day the only time I have ever been forcibly relieved of money on the street. The next day at college a couple of A level students told me they'd passed me on the bridge but had assumed I was talking to the guy, so skilled and low-key was his technique. A day or two after that Danny and I were sitting in Church Square on his lunchbreak when my mugger went walking past. He looked even poorer and more crumpled in daylight. He turned left just before the shopping arcade and walked down a narrow alley. We briefly thought of following him, but for what? Thirty-two pence and headlice?

I'd left school that past summer with two O Levels, English Literature and History, which was two more than anyone, with the possible exception of my History teacher, thought I would get. From the moment I walked out through those gates for the last time I don't think I saw more than half a dozen of my old schoolmates ever again. But I didn't settle at college the way I perhaps should have done. Five years of failure at Grammar school had left me with baggage, a wayward and unruly intellect, and a lax attitude towards the formalities of attendance and punctuality.

The day before I was due to start college in September I went to a free concert in Grantchester Meadows with Jimmy Dunn, an older mate who lived in my street, who had taken me to my first Hyde Park Free Concert, the Blind Faith one, and introduced me to the person who first offered me acid. Grantchester Meadows looked dewy green and glistening that sunny September day. It was my *Umma Gumma* myth world come to life. Donovan's Open Road (minus Donovan), Carol Grimes' Uncle Dog and assorted raggle-taggle harlequins and buskers got up and performed. After their set, Carol Grimes and a couple of members of her band came and sat adjacent. We shared their spliff. It came to me last. I sucked ferociously on a cardboard cylinder wind tunnel containing little but cinders. I tried to look meaningful and groovy but it's hard to act hip when you've got a mouth full of hot ash and air.

When the bands weren't playing there was little to hear but birdsong and the restrained cool chatter of the gathering. The only time the tranquillity was broken was when a young woman on a bad trip got up and ran around screaming. First, she did it with clothes on. Then she did it with clothes off. At one point she dived into the Cam and tried to drown in two feet of water. After a while everyone sort of decided that attention-seeking was the name of her game, and she was left to her paddling and her shallow madness. It was not the done thing to make an intervention in those days. I soon learned that. In fact, half the time it was not cool to speak at all. I learned that too but found it much harder to adhere to.

We departed the festival with the sun nestling in the lower branches and church bells pealing in the distance. When we reached the edge of the meadow, at a point where a dusty track led up to the picture-postcard cottages of Grantchester, early leavers came running back up the path towards us hastily cramming polythene bags and balls of foil into hedgerows and the hollows of tree trunks, and warning everyone to hide their stash. Up on the main street the local constabulary were randomly stopping and searching. "Don't meet their eyes," said Jimmy. We hitchhiked the 20 miles back to Sandy, Jimmy nudging me awake in a warm nocturnal van when we reached our destination. I went to bed with bird song in my head and set off for college the next morning on little more than four hours sleep.

At 9 am I found myself sitting in a classroom full of strangers who all seemed a little older than me. For a first day at college they all appeared to know each other remarkably well. I soon discovered that I'd read my timetable wrong and was sitting in a second-year English A level class. Mine didn't start till ten so I went and sat in the common room with another bunch of random strangers. It was while sitting there that I thought once more about just peeling off and walking away, as I had down that track-side path at Hitchin a few weeks earlier. I could leave right now, I irrationalised. Just get up and walk out of here. I don't have to be here. In the afternoon I fell asleep in an Environmental Studies class. I didn't even know what Environmental Studies was. I opted for it simply because it was suggested as a time-table filler to go with the English and the O Level retakes.

"I've got my eye on you already, Chapman," said a stern lecturer called Williamson who called everyone by their surnames. Suddenly it seemed just like school again. Apart from that one class, I liked college in general. I liked the inclusive shabby ambience of the place. I liked the long-hairs who sold their magazines full of confessional poetry and druggy Furry Freak inspired cartoons with names like Tab Man (an airborne superman figure dispensing acid from a little bag). I liked the girl called Marianne – older, posh, privately educated – who used to turn to me in English A level and go: "Slightly all the time Rob, eh? Slightly all the time," believing me I suppose to be permanently high. This was far from the truth, but I assume the dining electric had given me a certain Ready Brek zing which always took time to wear off. On December 10th Marianne told me she was off to the Rainbow Theatre in London with her boyfriend to see Frank Zappa. She had tickets for the second performance that night, and unfortunately never got to see him play as an aggrieved fan pushed him off the stage at the end of the first set and he landed in the orchestra pit.

I liked Marianne and all the other willowy ingenues like her, girls who had older boyfriends or were dating their lecturers, Bridget St John or Sandy Denny lookalikes who were warm and wistfully approachable but way out of my league as far as dating went. I liked the English tutors too, especially the A Level ones. I particularly liked my O Level Language retake lecturer, a painted china doll with hair piled high called Henrietta, a woman who seemed so brittle she might break. I learned that she had an actress past which made her even more alluring. When I wrote an essay for her in yellow felt-tip she called me "prissy and fey" which was very astute of her. I was indeed in the process of becoming very prissy and fey, as I discovered when I looked up what both of those words meant. In 1972 I would go prissy and fey in a big way.

I had to look up "mezzanine" too. The college canteen was on a mezzanine floor between the ground and first floor. No one ever referred to it as the canteen. You said "I'll meet you in the Mezz". I learned that a mezzanine is a half-floor, midway between the ground and the first floor, but not quite either. It soon became my favoured college location, an appropriately in-between world, neither high or low, everyone in limbo. The hippie heads distributing their Xeroxed magazines full of street politics and variable verse. Jeremy Carr, killing you softly with his half songs. The Malloy sisters talking about Free Derry and collecting for the Irish Republican Army with a green plastic bucket, all this several weeks before Bloody Sunday. All the throw-outs and drop-outs who hadn't made the grade at Grammar school or public school or convent school. All the miscreants and misfits, gay and straight, to whom Tech college threw a lifeline. All those who had disgraced or disappointed Daddy. All us avant-garde proles, a new tribe in the making. We all gathered in the Mezz.

Ian Pinner worked in the bus-station caff, washing crockery out the back or wiping tables while dispensing hot drinks and literary criticism. Short curly black hair and mutton chops. Looked a little like Roger McGough, which was appropriate. One day he gave my Penguin *Liverpool Poets* anthology a derisory glance. Sat himself on a stool next to the steamed-up window and told me why.

– They're so twee, aren't they? Adolescent love juice the lot of it. You'd get more poetry out of...

Out of what, I may never know because he goes off collecting plates and trays. But he returns in a while and elaborates.

...Oh, it's just the dirty old men aspect of it all that I can't stand. All that navy-blue knickers stuff. I can see them in 20 years, sitting on park benches or flashing at schoolgirls from the bushes.

At that moment Veronica and Michelle walk in, resplendent in their school uniforms. Ian Pinner does a double take and confronts his hypocrisy. He smiles a sinner's smile and asks the girls, "What can I get you?"

He was always good for an educated chat was Ian Pinner. He had erudite thoughts about what other erudite people thought and was happy to pass them on. In doing so he helped me locate my own early stirrings of something that resembled an intellect. He was yet another one of those ex-public school, university-material types, who were just passing through. The café was full of them. All those bus-station heads who were there that Sunday as Danny and I skipped the light fandango on purple microdots, they were the regular clientele. Starry-eyed and laughing fixtures among the old dears sipping tea and the alki tramps and registered junkies taking a hot meal. Andy Gardner was there, a walking straw-blond shag in a sheepskin coat. Looked like Kevin Ayers. Always smelt of exotic scent, not the cheap acrid head-shop patchouli we dabbed on. When he walked past our table, the girls would stop talking and drool over him. I saw him years later and he had turned to pudgy alcoholic fat, but in the early 1970s he was in his hippie Adonis prime. Pat and Mick, the Irish brothers, were there. They both wore moustaches but rarely at the same time. Pat was the first Bedford head I ever encountered. Brendan Brotherson, another public-school throw-out who had joined our school in the fifth year and introduced me to Allen Ginsberg's *Howl*, came into class one day and told those of us who cared about such things that Tony Palmer's *Goodbye Cream* film was showing at Bedford Teachers' Training College.

So, one evening after school a bunch of us trooped up several flights of stairs, crammed into a small lecture theatre and watched Cream's farewell concert at the Albert Hall. I was bored with all the permajamming within half an hour. When it came to technical proficiency in popular music, I wasn't buying all this ego-driven rockaboogie riffing. I was already through with that shit by the time *All Right Now*, *Black Night* and *Paranoid* appeared in the charts. I much preferred studio Cream to live Cream. Songs with cellos and hand bells, not gargantuan egos thrashing it out like their reputations depended on it.

Gazing around that small viewing room, I remember seeing Pat there, and I seemed to see him at every Bedford event after that: at the showing of *Woodstock* at the Granada Cinema, at an Edgar Broughton Band gig at the Corn Exchange, always standing by the lip of the stage (sometimes on the stage), or in front of the cinema screen posing. Doing that "surveying the room" thing but really just waiting to be adored, which he was by many. He was also there in the Tech college common room that first day when I arrived an hour early. Pat was a professional looner and ligger, a full-time poser. His brother Mick was more serious. He was studying for an astronomy degree in London, the only one in the country at the time. "Ask my brother about the Universe. He knows everything," said Pat proudly. Mick would indicate modestly that that wasn't strictly true.

Another bus station regular was Rosalyn. Rosalyn Rip-Off we learned to call her after purchasing some of her window-pane acid. This particular LSD variant rarely aided our enlightenment. It usually contributed to our continued endarkenment, or indeed befuddlement, because as often as not you couldn't tell if the stuff was actually working. Steve Sangster sold microdots or White Lightning. Rosalyn dispensed erratically priced orange shards from a little black Kodak film canister. Occasionally you got the full kerblammo. Mostly you just coasted on the runway for a bit, waiting for a take-off moment that never came. She was selling her dud stuff to the local bikers too, and we fully expected her to wind up dead in a ditch one day. Surely the only feasible outcome, we figured after one too many shards of nothingness had been purchased by a leather-clad greebo who might subsequently take a dim view of being duped.

One November evening in the bus-station caff I was getting up to go and catch my bus. Rosalyn Rip-Off reached over from an adjacent table, tugged the bottom of my jacket and yanked me back.
– I love that V neck. Where did you get it?
– My Gran gets them from her Mum.
– And where does she get them?
– Off the market I think. I don't know.
– Is it Italian? It looks Italian.
– Yeah. (I had no idea if it was Italian or not. Underneath the duffel coat I dressed as a hippie/mod hybrid. Granny cardigans and sharp tops.)
She told me her older brother used to wear stuff like that when he was a mod. Then she tried to sell me her shards of brittle orange from a Kodak film canister.
– You can have them cheap because I don't know how old they are. They might have gone off so shall we say...
She was with this guy called Guy. Slit eyes. Bandito moustache. Malicious grin. Stinking Afghan coat.

– Hey mod boy, how you doing?

– Gotta get my bus.

– Hey mod boy, dog is god backwards.

So what?

– And evil is live backwards.

Likewise. This passes for a "hey man" revelation among the heads and Rosalyn is stroking his cuffs like he's the Mahabloodyrishi.

So, I told him you could get high smoking dandruff.

– What?

– I said that dandruff contained this chemical secreted from your scalp that –

 – And he believed you?

– Yeah.

Danny let out a giggle that only dogs could hear.

– I told him that there's a chemical in the scalp that's hallucinogenic and when it reacts to sweat...

Danny pretends to scratch drugs out of his head.

– Hey man, wanna score?

What I wasn't expecting was that Guy would tell all the other heads and that some of them bought it. My dandruff scam went all round the bus station. I pushed my luck by telling certain fascinated parties that brunette was stronger than blonde and it was best to dry it first. Some realised I was bullshitting straight away and offered a sceptical grin, others – as with the great dried-banana-skin hoax in America – willed themselves into belief. Some of those bus-station freaks would have hollowed out a turnip and used it as a bong if you'd told them a turnip had hallucinogenic properties. Steve Sangster's sidekick Eugene asked me if you could mainline it and I said: "No, Eugene. Christ no! For God's sake don't mainline it." When I admitted I'd made it all up Guy thumped my shoulder. Not a playful thump. A "Don't make a fool out of me" thump. – I'll fucking mess you up for that.

He fucking did too.

I can't remember if it was Harriet or Michelle who told me about Steve Sangster's "Buy six get one free" scheme. The idea was you bought six acid tabs off him at a quid each, then sold five of them for 24 bob each (LSD currency, pounds, shillings and pence) thus paying for your free tab. It seemed a good deal so I approached him at High Table in the Mezz. We went into the toilets where he sold me purple microdots in a little matchbox and I passed on two of them that same evening in the bus-station café. One quiet lunchtime, a week before the end of term I was sitting on the fifth-floor stairwell of the main Tech college building safely out of harm's way. I was in the process of exchanging goods for currency with Jack and Paula, a couple of second-year Sociology students, when I became aware of a lingering presence behind me.

"I think we both know what's going on here, don't we?" said a very senior lecturer. As I was at the point of the transaction where Paula was leaning in for a closer inspection of the openly displayed microdots I agreed that we probably did. Jack and Paula were invited to make themselves scarce very quickly, which they did and I was invited – in my own interest – to leave college, which I also did. I can't remember if I ever sent in the formal covering letter which was requested of me, but from that day onwards I stopped attending lectures and only went back after Christmas to resit my English Language O Level exam. My one and only foray into the murky world of drug-dealing had effectively fucked up my post-school education and left me £3.20 down on the acid deal.
"What will you tell your parents?" asked fussy, concerned Booble Bath

Tessa.

"I don't know," I answered honestly.

It was Christmas Eve. I hitched early into Bedford looking for last-minute presents. Smellies for Mum. Smellies for Tessa who I was really beginning to fancy. And why can't I find Harriet a ring with crescent moons and stars on it? All those hippies called Julie making jewellery, they just shake their heads at my sketch.

– Like that.

– No, sorry.

Oh well, smellies for Harriet as well then. Walking through the arcade. The burnt bitter coffee-roast aroma drifting through the air, the best smell in Bedford. The alki-tramps feed pigeons from the benches by Woolworths. Abandoned Dads stand vacant and forlorn outside shops, tethered to gift bags. I hear one old dear say to her friend: "Leave him there the daft sod, we'll go and have a cup of tea." In the bus station bays 12-year-old girls are learning how to smoke, and 13-year-old boys are learning how to smoke and gob while chatting up 12-year-old girls.

E.P. Rose's department store is rammed. The lone blatantly detectable security guard can't be everywhere at once and it's just as easy to nick the soaps and talc as it is to pay for them. Money saved means more for tonight's booze. We're all heading for Tessa's on a Number 51 bus ride to her village. Her parents are going out. I walk into Kerry's. *Gypsys, Tramps and Thieves* is playing and it reminds me of Harriet. To this day it still reminds me of Harriet.

Later, I meet up with the girls. We walk around concealing unwrapped presents from each other. Into Chelsea Girl as usual. I'm the only male in the shop. Customers wander unselfconsciously in and out of changing rooms. Clothes go on. Clothes come off. "Do you think Gary will like this?" Danny joins us on his dinner hour and we watch Steve and Eugene, junked out of their heads, weaving in and out of the Salvation Army band that plays for the shoppers. The band launches into a brisk *Ding Dong Merrily on High*. Steve and Eugene providing the "in excelsis" bit, crouch-walking and waving their shaky hands like they've got old-time religion. Guy comes over and sells me a handful of Mandrax for 20p each.

– Have you taken them before?

– No, but I've read about them. They make you go a bit dreamy, don't they?

– They make your alcohol go further as well. A pint and one of these is like drinking four pints, so you only need to take a couple.

Great, think of the money we'll save on booze.

I remember Danny smashing his head on the corner of the record player and I think I remember the girls crying, but maybe they told us that afterwards. I remember someone shaking the carpet and making the room go all wavy – no not wavy, drowny. But I kept blacking out so it's difficult to say or slur or anything at all and fuck me, what was in those tablets? Sherry, wine, beer, just add two mandies and fade to black. We'd waved Tessa's parents off at the door and looked forward to a sociable Christmas Eve. Then Danny and I took those pills and waved ourselves off too. By the time Tessa's parents got back me and Danny were well gone. Heads bowed over us, concerned, crying, Harriet holding me under the chin, going, going, no it's gone again. I came to at the bus station, near to the bench where we all first met. Now the pavement is coming up to greet me. Now it's headbutting me.

Veronica's Dad arrived in his car to put Danny up on their sofa for the night. There was no way he could get on a bus in that state. I'm sure there was a moment where I extended an arm towards them and said, "Please let me sleep on that sofa too," but they left me there at the bus station with all the other celebrators and sad clowns, wheeling in a circle, spilling my change. Someone helped me onto the last bus home. Someone may have even paid my fare and nudged me awake at my stop. Nobody steered me across the A1 though. I must have done that myself, sleep-walking through four lanes of late-night drivers. The ground came up to greet me again, softer now, as I staggered home. I hit a mossy bank by a hedgerow and should have had the sense to sleep it off there or crawl into someone's shed. It was a mild, mizzly night, I wouldn't have died of exposure, but something kept propelling me forward. Must get home. Must get home. Black out – back in – black out – back in – till I'm suddenly fumbling open the back door and walking into the searchlight glare of the living room where a voice that sounds like Mum says: "You look like death warmed up, boy." Then she screams, then she slaps my face with a wet flannel, then she dispenses with the flannel. Dad helps me to bed, but not before I've rambled a lot of incriminating stuff about Rosalyn and Guy and the night I've just had or should I say just had me. "You'll have a hell of a headache in the morning, boy," is all he says. Is all I remember. Brain waves ripple until I flatline into sleep.

I trance-walk and mumble through a frosty Christmas dinner which I've pretty much ruined for everyone. In the afternoon I sit alone in an unheated front room and wonder what happened the bag of presents the girls gave me, and my V neck Italian jumper which I know I was wearing last night but now can't find anywhere. My little brother, seven, and my sister, 11, come in the room to see me. I ramble out a tale. I took these tablets, see, and I didn't know how strong they were. Being only seven and 11 they relay this information to Mum thinking they are being helpful. "Oh, he did, did he?" says Mum in the kitchen. She tells me she's thrown my V neck out because it was covered in mud and sick and that she would be more than willing to throw me out too, having brought disgrace... etc etc. Thinking back, it was probably the vomiting that saved me, otherwise

I'd have been communing with Hendrix, Brian Jones and the heavenly angels right now rather than standing in my kitchen receiving another hard slap from my Mum and she might have to slap me harder than that because I still can't feel a fucking thing. I stutter out more stupidity from a mush mind that isn't mine and by Boxing Day I decide to take her at her word and move out.

Danny says I can stay at his house for a few days and we really should get that flat sorted out. Danny's Mum cooks dumplings on my first night there and on my second night too. I'm probably the only person in the Western world to lose weight over Christmas, so this is nourishment. A couple of days later I get the village bus to Harriet's. It's lightly snowing and my brain still feels blanketed and immune. Harriet is on her own when I get there. Her Mum is out. I've never met her Dad and never will.
– Hi.
Harriet opens the door to her cosy little gingerbread cottage. I'm halfway in, already telling her about getting a flat and won't that be great Harriet before I notice the hesitancy in her voice and the panic in her eyes. She's holding a letter.
– This arrived from your Mother. I don't know how she got this address.
Nor do I but Mums are very resourceful.
– What does it say?
Dear mother of my son's girlfriend, your daughter has been taking drugs with my son. That kind of thing.
– You can see why I've moved out, can't you?
– But...
– She was pretty freaked out when I got home, but look, things will be OK now, forget it.
– But...

I'm continuing to be "Yes it will be all right" but Harriet's face says "No

34

it won't. It can't be after this."

– What if my mum had read this letter? It's lucky she was out when the post came.

Silence. A long time.

– I'm sorry Rob. I can't... We can't...

I'll just sit at this kitchen table for a few minutes. My legs are suddenly very tired. Outside the cottage window, a pale winter sun is shining on the snow-coated everywhere.

I walk a long walk from gingerbread cottage back to main road. It didn't seem that far a few minutes ago with the snow sparkling on the hedgerows and holly. Now it seems like an endless, weary trudge. A car slows down to pick me up and I hadn't even realised I was hitchhiking. This young guy opens the passenger door, looks not much older than me, picks up on a certain stare that doesn't quite reach the windscreen.
– You OK?
So, I tell him. Hollow-hearted and open-veined. At the traffic lights I notice how the roadside slush trickles towards a drain. My driver was comforting and kind, rationalised his own life a little and said yeah, it's happened to me too, and he didn't once say plenty more fish in the sea mate, plenty more fish in the sea. And all the time this heartache was happening the morning was beautiful. Snow softly drifting down and me with it.

The next night we got the bus back to Danny's after he had finished work. We walked in to the smell of stew, and Danny's Mum says: "You've had a visitor." There's a letter which I open and it's from Dad. I don't know how he got the address. Dads can be very resourceful. It starts off hesitantly.

"I usually know what to say and how to say it but I'm finding it hard to find the right words here." It opens up my guts a mile wide to read it. The short letter ends with something reconciliatory along the lines of "The door is always open if you want to come back". I lay and face the bedroom wall for a while and it's some time before I can compose myself sufficiently to go through for stew.

The next evening after Danny has finished work we go to Veronica's for something to eat and then we wander around Bedford Park for a bit. Dee and Vee canoodle on the swings, snuggle in the windbreak by the keeper's hut, feeling each other's warmth in the ice-cold night. The part of gooseberry was played by me. I feel like I'm 13 again. The park seems like a vast, unlit runway. On the playground tarmac I have a bumpy turbulent touchdown. Marooned in the grassy dark I stare into acres of empty blackness and feel an overwhelming loneliness envelop me. Time to go home.

"Yes, I think you should," said Veronica.

"Yes, I think you should," says Danny's Mum when we go back to his house. She hasn't been judgmental once. She's provided a free bed, food and lodgings for a week, but it's time for me to mend things now.

When I walk in the back door the following evening my little brother is in the kitchen. He looks somewhat startled and runs into the living room without greeting me. I head straight upstairs and lay on my bed exhausted. Dad follows me up within minutes and I tell him that I hope Mum is happy with her detective work now that Harriet has finished with me. "Don't be so hard on her," he says and proceeds to tell me what a genuinely wicked mother is like, i.e. his own. His mother was the first of her gypsy family to "go gaujo", i.e. move out of a caravan into a house. She had a bit of a local reputation as a white witch and as a dealer in herbal remedies. Another of her special gifts was to flay the living shit out of my dad with the inner tube of a bicycle tire when he was young. There was history there far beyond what little he told me that night and he carried the inner scars for the rest of his life. His Dad died just weeks after he and Mum were married, and he told me he still thought about him all the time. When his Mum died he had to be talked into going to the funeral. I only have vague memories of her. She was entering the long, dark tunnel of dementia by the time I was ten: putting her purse in the oven, laying a table for her eight boys "who are all coming home from the War".

Anyway, he told me all this, and a few other family secrets too, as I lay on the bed bemoaning my lot. As we were in confessional mode I told him I had taken LSD. I even called it LSD, not acid, out of courtesy to Fleet Street terminology. Dad blinked, stared, looked at first like he was going to cry, but didn't. All he did was retell a few well-aired cautionary tales about the Egyptians he saw wedded to hash pipes, comatose with lethargy, when he did his National Service in 1946. We traded truths for a bit, the bleakness of the occasion allowing us this brief moment of soul-baring intimacy. I told him not to worry. I hadn't taken any other drugs. I didn't even like smoking pot, which was basically true at that point. He told me again how much he had loved his Dad. "And there hasn't been a day since when I haven't..." His voice trailed off. I could hear the telly downstairs. "Is Mum still angry with me?" I asked. "You gave her a fright," he said. "She'll come round." New Year came and went. I sat in our unheated front room, not feeling the cold, still numb with everything. I was listening to Loudon Wainwright's second album. Its sparse arrangements and anguished sense of emotional isolation complemented my mood perfectly. It was 1972. I'd had a shit Christmas and put a dampener on everyone else's. Mum came in and said: "Why on earth are you listening to this dreary music, boy? Put something happier on."

All this and I still hadn't told them I'd been kicked out of college.

All I Want is Out of Here

Chapter 2

DIVE DEEP

I was sitting at the foot of the stairs in the hall putting on my shoes when the morning post came through the letter box. There on the carpet in front of me was a brown envelope bearing the unmistakeable logo stamp of the Tech college. I knew what the letter would contain and swiftly intercepted it.

In the Daily Mirror just before Christmas there had been a news story about the effect unemployment was having on the middle classes. Previously immune to a downturn in the economy, the white-collar job loss currently being experienced under Heath's government was a relatively novel phenomenon. The article talked about the pride of male breadwinners when faced with the new situation. There were stories about men who daren't tell their wives and left the house every morning pretending they had a job to go to. Stuffing the incriminating letter in my pocket and leaving my parents none the wiser, I left the house and pretended to go to college. It's what I did for the next seven months. At first, I still went into Bedford, but as time went by I ventured further afield, to Cambridge, to London, to wherever a lift might take me. Initially though, I'd hitchhike to Bedford, but instead of going to college I'd head for the County Library.

The short walk from Tech to Library took me round the back of the main college building and past a row of derelict prefabs which had recently made way for a brand-new engineering block. Most of the windows in the prefabs had been smashed and the entrance doors were boarded up. The workbenches and chalk boards hadn't been removed yet, so the buildings looked like ghostly remnants of some nuclear fall-out scenario, or a location set where an episode of *The Avengers* might have taken place: The School that Never Was. Behind the abandoned buildings was a small wood-built public convenience. Despite its isolated location it still seemed to be doing a regular trade for those in need of its facilities.

At this cottage rendezvous point I'd head on down a narrow riverside path, the Ouse to my right, the stagnant green waters of a civic pond to my left. From there I'd climb a concrete stairwell that looked like something out of *Clockwork Orange*, which had just that month had its UK premiere. At the top of the stairwell I'd hurry across a bleak, windswept concourse and into the warm, plush-carpeted sanctuary of the County Library. The facility was part of the newly built County Hall complex, an imposing neo-Brutalist structure that rose like a dystopian monolith and dominated the flat Bedford skyline for some distance. Work had started on the infrastructure in the mid-1960s, but there were problems from the outset. At one point the whole thing started sinking and the basement flooded, which meant that everything had to be razed to the ground and rebuilt. The building that became my initial day-time retreat was less than three years old when I started going there. Everything about the place smelt brand-new and felt under-utilised. When an equally brand-new Central Library opened in town in April 1972, the County became even less busy. It gradually became more of an archive facility and local-history establishment, but I remained loyal to the County. It was discreet and out-of-the-way for starters, and it was stocked with the treasures that became the building blocks of my new alternative curriculum.

Each day I'd pack a lunch, walk through the derelict college lot and up that dystopian stairwell to spend several hours feeding my head. I scaled an imposing edifice of Romantic poetry. Blake, Keats, Shelley and Coleridge mostly, a fool persisting in his folly until he became wise. I knew nothing of Blake other than the fact that there was a copy of his *Complete Works* next to Marc Bolan on the back of the Tyrannosaurus Rex *Unicorn* album. Grappling with Keats and Shelley I would grope from Grecian god to Grecian Urn, learning that zephyr was a wind as well as a car and that winged could have one or two syllables depending where it fell. I worked my way through *Prometheus Unbound*, *Epipsychidion*, *Hyperion* and *Endymion*, barely understanding a fraction of what I read but drowning drowsily in the opiated scent of antiquity.

I plucked a copy of *The Soft Machine* from the shelves assuming that it was a biography of the band and in doing so inadvertently discovered the writing of William Burroughs. I was familiar enough with Burroughs through the Underground press to know that it wasn't the same guy who wrote *Tarzan of the Apes* and also knew that the Soft Machine had taken their name from a book, but here it finally was on a library shelf, a hardback volume at that. I immersed myself in the unethical experimentation of Dr Benway and marvelled at his propensity to turn people into scorpions. I rapidly got to grips with the ways in which structure and plot were permanently up for grabs as characters metamorphosed and language folded in on itself. I was amused by the dry colonial interventions of the narrator and hung on in there as the action shifted from Mexico to South America to linguistic interzones I'd never encountered before.

The ever-present imagery of junk-sick boys, gay fucking, carbolic soap and the smell of stale sperm was novel too, although the latter was not that new to a 17-year-old with backed-up spunk to spare. I'd seen Burroughs' work described as "pornographic" but this all constituted a different kind of arousal. The language and structure in *The Soft Machine* were an assault on everything I'd previously assumed fictional narrative to be. It was alien but not alienating, and I took to the Burroughs cut-up method intuitively. It felt a like a very natural way to think, a very logical way to perceive the world. I felt I knew this world already, partly through the ellipsis and elisions of Syd Barrett on his solo albums, but also because of exposure to the experimental poets I was starting to read. There were other Burroughs novels on the shelves – *The Naked Lunch* and *The Ticket that Exploded* – and I hungrily devoured those too.

Reading became a sensual pleasure, the library an erotic emporium full of promise and possibility. I would cruise the Dewey rows, eagerly seeking out the new and the unknown, tiptoeing tentatively but willing to be seduced by the thrill of a sudden encounter. The sheer voracious sensuality of the experience was enhanced by the librarian who wafted past me, as she returned books to their shelves. She was curvaceous, smartly dressed, hair worn in a bun, and her scent drove me wild. I would often smell her before I saw her, and there were mornings when her presence drove me to distraction. One day I plucked up the courage to ask her what her perfume was. "Musk," she said, unsmiling, aloof, barely acknowledging the tremulous 17-year-old who dared to whisper at her as she went about her work. I have associated her scent with libraries ever since, no matter how drably municipal or dimly lit. Musk is my synaesthetic aroma of learning. Early 1970s dab musk, not the cheap sprays you could get which smelt of civet.

There was nothing methodical about any of this learning. I had all the attributes but none of the purposeful drive of the autodidact. I simply followed my nose. Occasionally my instincts led me up blind alleys, to dull leaden prose and stuff that wasn't any good. I would persevere with books to the very end, even when I knew within a couple of chapters that they weren't going to inspire me or lead to anywhere new. Lacking both the necessary nimble faculties of critical judgement and the assurance of intellectual confidence it simply didn't occur that I could just stop reading and ditch the book for something else. Some deeply embedded legacy of school failure had instructed me that learning was an obligatory chore and that literature was cod-liver oil, good for you even when your first instinct was to gag and spit it out. It was some time before I dared apply to literature what I had already learned in other aspects of my life – that you could just get up and walk away.

This is how I spent my mornings, reading until hunger or eye-strain took over. All through that sunless January and much of February I'd sit in a comfy chair at the end of the book rows with only a carousel of magazines and periodicals for company. On the rare occasions the comfy chair was occupied, I'd seat myself in the sparsely populated desk area by the windows. There were never many people in there, just the occasional researcher poring over court records or local-history archives. I rarely saw another student, and never anyone I knew from college. On drizzly days I would sit and watch the wind cutting up rough on the River Ouse, defiant ducks bobbing on the water, Bedford Modern schoolboys rowing in eights, instructions shouted through a loud-hailer from a well-swaddled games master riding his bicycle along the towpath.

Steve and Eugene would sometimes go tumbling by having fixed up in the Library toilets. I'd see them sneak in and sneak out, staggering down to the waterside, wires all tangled as if some inept invisible puppet master was operating them from the bare trees. How they never fell in the river... At lunchtimes I would visit Danny at Kerry's before returning to the library for a couple of hours, then I would head home pretending I had put in a shift at college.

Danny's co-workers at Kerry's were Clifford, a quietly radical Afro-Caribbean guy in his mid-20s who dispensed political wisdom to me between bouts of selling records, and store manager Adrian, who was pleasant and gay in both senses and remarkably tolerant of people like me who hung about at the counter and bought little. The first record Clifford made me listen to was the newly released *This Is Madness* LP by The Last Poets. This baptism of fire alerted me immediately to the fact that Clifford was not your average Tamla and Stax soul brother. Nothing I'd ever heard before could have prepared me for the sheer verbal assault of that album. To hear Tom Jones being taken down like that and Diana Ross described as "hoof-and-mouth disease" was a revelation.

Ten years further down the line that legacy would manifest itself in rap music, but in early 1972 The Last Poets sounded utterly incendiary and original to me, verbal grenades going off in my head. Clifford's political views were also way ahead of anything I'd ever encountered before. His take on Enoch Powell was that the "send them back" brigade should get together with those of a Marcus Garvey/Black Star Liner persuasion to see if they might find common ground, or at least agree a fee regarding what constituted ample compensation. Clifford handed me a Free Angela Davis badge and explained who Angela Davis was. When Bloody Sunday happened on January 30th he lent me a copy of Ink magazine which put out a special issue about the background to the events of that day. I added Ink to my inventory of Underground mags to read on a regular basis. As was so often the case, Ink folded a few months later.

Another of Clifford's methods of cultural dissemination I noticed was to hand the occasional free LP to a buddy who came into the shop to check out the new releases. Cautiously and discreetly taking his lead from his co-worker, Danny began to provide me with the same complimentary service. When the annual stocktaking loomed (an event that would see the shop closed for the entire day), Danny switched from dispensing free records to handing over free record tokens. As a result, I barely paid for a new album for the next year. As I had no money whatsoever, I was more than grateful for the service.

At the end of January, I returned, briefly, to Tech college to re-sit my English Language O Level. I sat by the huge windows at the side of the hall and studied a black-and-white plate of the River Styx boatman. Invited to write a composition about it I improvised something suitably trippy with a requisite amount of recently learned polysyllabic words, few of which were correctly contextualised, I'd imagine, but I obviously utilised them competently enough because a few weeks later a letter arrived to tell me I was now the proud owner of a third O Level to go with my English Literature and History. Henrietta, the English lecturer who thought me prissy and fey, must have been quietly pleased too, because an ex-classmate came up to me at the bus station one afternoon to inform me she had told the O Level group of my achievement. To her I suppose I was just another errant pupil gone astray, but not before I had absorbed enough of what she taught me to pass an exam.

It was also during this period that I saved the NME from extinction. OK, approximately 200,000 other people were cut in on the deal over the next couple of years, but I like to feel that if Danny and I hadn't given the new-look New Musical Express our seal of approval one Thursday lunchtime on his afternoon off, who knows what might have happened? By 1972 the NME had become a bit of a joke and I hadn't so much as glanced at a copy since 1969, having long since decamped to the more serious and in-depth reportage of Melody Maker and Sounds. When Danny and I saw that relaunch issue with Marc Bolan sitting cross-legged on the cover, our initial reaction was a sneering: "Oh look, NME's gone heavy."

"Going heavy" had been all the rage for a few months at the tail-end of the 1960s. It quickly became a derisory term aimed at mainstream pop bands who wanted to sidestep the light-entertainment graveyard by demonstrating their musical chops. Love Affair, minus Steve Ellis, became LA. Andy Fairweather Low ditched Amen Corner and formed Fairweather. Dozy, Beaky, Mike and Tich, minus Dave Dee, became DBM&T and began featuring synthesisers on their records. All over the British Isles, cabaret-friendly groups with neatly coiffed hair and ruffled shirts suddenly discarded their cuff-links, grew hirsute and "went heavy". The most notorious exponents of the trend were The Tremeloes who issued a couple of "mature" (and actually half-decent) singles, (Call Me) Number One and Me and My Life, and then gave an interview where they claimed to piss themselves laughing at their teenybop fans who lapped up the chart drivel. As a result, the chart drivel dried up almost immediately and the Tremeloes never had another Top 10 hit. Now, two years after the fashion had died out, and despite editor Alan Smith's protestations to the contrary in a front-page editorial, the New Musical Express did indeed look like it was going heavy. It was certainly bulkier than the old NME, 36 pages rather than the 12 it had been reduced to by the time IPC sounded the death knell, but when I handed over my 6p in the newsagents it was more out of curiosity than expectation.

That Thursday as we sat amidst the heady stench of disinfected vomit in the bus-station waiting room we found our scepticism turning into something resembling begrudging respect as we flicked through the pages. "Not that bad," was our overall judgement. Meaning it could have been an awful lot worse. It took a few months before my praise became less qualified, but I continued to buy it – if not religiously, then certainly fairly regularly, while still remaining broadly loyal to Melody Maker.

Tessa and I sort of dated for a bit. We went to see Ken Russell's *The*

Boyfriend at the Granada, probably my idea. A few weeks later, again at my suggestion, we went to see *Cabaret*. If Tessa thought these were strange choices from her little cosmic plaything she didn't say anything. I liked Tessa a lot, she had a no-bullshit Northern manner about her which I found refreshing. She took the gentle piss out of me as well which I also warmed to. Unfortunately, it all came crashing down when she agreed to do an acid trip with me and Danny one Sunday afternoon. Veronica came along to babysit. It was virtually a rerun of our inaugural blast-off that weekend after we met the girls. We went back to the same location, Russell Park, and tried to enact all the same circus tricks, but acid doesn't work like that.

You can try to find your way back to the same headspace with the same good intentions, only to discover that the LSD has decided not to play ball. It's just one of the many reasons why that whole Timothy Leary "set and setting" approach is unreliable. Acid is too combustible for house rules, it throws up too many psychological variables. Our previous golden October Arcady suddenly seemed a long time gone. A steady drizzle made the park cold and uncomfortable and the benches wet to sit on. We sipped tea in Russell Park café in the vain hope that the rain would ease off and our trip would take flight. My acid was working. Danny's was working. Tessa said, "Why can't I see anything?"
– Look, can't you see the faces forming in the window mist?
– Look, can't you see the patterns in the Formica?
– Look at the coffee stains.

We are badgering Tessa with all this and Tessa is just getting confused and more than a little agitated. "No, I can't see any patterns in the Formica and why is any of this important anyway?" And she's right. Why are we so superficially impressed with the drab and dismal visuals? Our empty words suddenly sound hollow even to us. Me and Danny become increasingly dispirited. There's nothing much to see and Tessa can't see it anyway. She goes and sits on a wet bench with Veronica while Danny and I see-saw in silence in the children's playground. The whole thing is a massive downer. A disconsolate atmosphere curtails our giggling. There are no cosmic jokes and japes to indulge in. Things go sullen for what seems like an extraordinary length of time. We eventually give up and trudge back into town. Later, as I was coming down, I wondered if she was in fact tripping as much as we were but was just warding it off with her brusque Northern logic. Is that all there is to a trip? Is that all there is? I phoned her up one filthy rainy evening from a call box after I'd been to see Grummar and Grandad. "Let's not do that anymore," she said without rancour. Another shrug. Another logical decision.

It was around this time that I decided many of my troubles might be solved if I went and lived on a commune just outside of Paris with Daevid Allen and Gong. Daevid Allen had been an almost mythical figure to me in the late 1960s, the pre-history mystery man of the Underground. To discover as I did that there had been this member of the original Soft Machine who had been and gone before I heard their debut session on John Peel's *Top Gear* was intriguing in itself. The fact that he spelt his name Daevid was also alluring. He looked beatifically cool as he and Gilli Smyth bathed in a heavenly fireside glow on the sleeve of his *Magick Brother* solo album – Magick with a K, a literary affectation I rapidly adopted. And he radiated insolent cool on the sleeve of the *Banana Moon* album, leaning languidly and seemingly eight-foot aloft next to the diminutive Robert Wyatt and Archie Leggett, while pretending to smoke a banana. Kevin Ayers was also prone to throwing in the occasional banana when things looked like they were getting too serious.

Bananas rapidly became an essential motif in my own absurdist repertoire too. Inspired by Allen's cartoon doodles, I took to sketching them in notepads and exercise books, even inking them onto my jeans. On that awful Mandrax Christmas Eve, shortly before I lost contact with reality, Tessa had given me a banana as a joke Christmas present. She'd even felt-tipped a seasonal greeting on the skin. Like everything else in my goody bag that night it got lost, mashed to a pulp I expect, like my head was. Hearing Allen's *Banana Moon* LP for the first time was a revelation. Musically it sounded raw, rough-edged and raucously intelligent. Allen clearly possessed the kind of nimble, twinkly mind that was rarely evident amongst the more dour and earnest Underground acts. My kind of acid warrior. He did an immaculate low-pitched impression of Kevin Ayers on *White Neck Blooze*, and played some of the most inspired freak-out music I'd ever heard on *Stoned Innocent Frankenstein and His Adventures in the Land of Flip*. *Banana Moon* also contained the best of the numerous versions of Hugh Hopper's *Memories* that were recorded over the years. The opening track *All I Want Is Out of Here* seemed like the living embodiment of my entire mission. As Burroughs put it at the end of *The Naked Lunch*, "The way OUT is the way IN".

In the autumn of 1971, Kevin Ayers briefly joined Gong, and on October 9th they played at Luton Tech, supported by the Third Ear Band – 50p advance, 60p on the door. I went with Duncan, one of the second-year English students from High Table in the Mezz. We safely negotiated the bandit-country terrain between railway station and venue without attracting the attention of marauding skinheads and Oak Road End thugs, and as a reward witnessed Gong in their spacy prime. They were everything I wanted a stoned troupe of miscreants to be. Genuinely progressive, ramshackle rather than slick, and given to the most splendid interstellar meanderings. They had an anarchic wit about them too, and as many long-haired bands of the time seemed to possess neither anarchy nor wit, I was utterly sold. Gilli Smyth's space whisper floated in and out of the music like a less-abrasive Yoko. Didier Malherbe's sax wafted like hash smoke to the rafters. Daevid Allan presided as master of ceremonies over the whole astro-jazz assemblage. Kevin Ayers stood quietly at the back, playing bass and guitar, only coming to the front for the last two numbers, lengthy and inspired extemporisations on *Why Are We Sleeping* and *We Did It Again*.

Duncan and I got the last train back to Flitwick, and walked jabbering away in roadside darkness all the way to Ampthill where he lived. I spent a comfortable night on the sofa, dreaming in space whispers and saxophone breath, and awoke at an agreeable hour to the sight of Duncan's father, employed at that time by Reuters, spreading out all of the Sunday papers on the living-room floor. This intrigued me greatly. School had managed to suppress much of my enthusiasm for formal learning, but it could never dull my desire for newspapers. Like many working-class households at that time we took two Sunday papers at home, permutations of the Sunday Mirror, People and News of The World. Five years of doing a paper round meant that I came home with ink-stained hands every morning. The previous summer I'd read the daily Oz Trial proceedings in two-paragraph instalments as I walked from door to door. That October morning, in a comfortable heated living room with a crisp sun shining outside and Duncan's Dad spreading out the papers before him, another cerebral seed was sown. Imagine having the resources to be able to spread out all the Sunday papers before you. I aspired to that.

A smattering of music-press interviews accompanied that short Gong tour, and they all mentioned this commune where the band all lived on the outskirts of Paris. What if? What if? I took stock of my situation. I've been thrown out of college and forced to live on my wits. So far, my wits have taken me little further than Bedford Library. The mind tick-tocks and next thing I know I'm drawing on my limited resources, finding an address for Actuel/BYG records and writing a typical teenage angsty letter to someone I've never met to ask if I can come and live with him and his band. I hadn't thought any of this through. I wrote completely on impulse.

By now Danny had moved into a second-floor flat in Bushmead Avenue down by the river. His new pad appeared to be furnished with an unseemly amount of random clutter. Armchairs three. Sofas two. Chest of drawers three. Lampstands numerous. Hostess trolleys two. An obstacle course of pouffes, a nest of tables plus miscellaneous footstools. It was as if all the landlords in Bedford had got together to see how much surplus furniture they could cram into one small property. It was a good place to slip away to though, out of town and just a stroll away from Russell Park where we'd done our inaugural trip. We did a few more at the flat. Usually on Thursday afternoons when it was half-day closing and almost everywhere in Bedford apart from the larger department stores shut up shop at one o'clock.

Steve and Eugene sold us this stuff called White Lightning, tabs as big as aspirins, pure fizzing euphoria they were. It was raining outside, which wouldn't have bothered me but Danny didn't fancy wandering around in the February drizzle. Plus, he saw a policeman through the front window and went into his "Can he tell just by looking??" paranoia thing. This wouldn't have bothered me either, and chemically emboldened as I was, I would happily have breezed past him wielding a brace of bananas in each fist, but out of respect to Danny – who was after all providing shelter, sounds and regular cups of tea for the duration – we stayed in.

I remember the afternoon well because it was the first time I ever tried writing on acid. I found this huge sheet of grey paper, wrapping paper I think, and began scrawling a snaking screed of babble that ran down the page like a river. Spiralling doodles began to appear too, much in the style of Daevid Allen's encryptions on the Gong record sleeves. I think I even drew a board game at one point, a sort of Monopoly set in Middle Earth affair. I would dearly love to be able to present this acid juvenilia as evidence of my state of mind at that time, but Danny – suspecting that I was having a better, and indisputably more self-indulgent, trip than he was – came over and screwed up my twinkling tapestry with a displeased grunt. Subsequently I reverted to the more prosaic pleasures of flicking through Danny's records. Three Quintessence albums glowing in the dust. I counted the people in the centrefold of their first LP just for something to do. Forty-two. The band, plus girlfriends, children, dolls and dogs, in beads and headbands and Vietgrove ashram clothes. I flicked through the rest of Danny's records. John Sebastian. Hot Tuna with Papa John Creach. Jefferson Airplane's scratch-and-sniff Bark album, plus lots more Jefferson Starship, Jefferson Tugboat, Jefferson Paddling Pool, Jefferson Puddle. Jefferson Evaporating Dewdrop Bead of Sweat. Ptoof!

One lunchtime, soon after he had started working at Kerry's, Danny pulled an LP out of the racks and said, "Shall we listen to this?" It had a huge yellow banana on the cover. How could I refuse? By the time I reached the fifth form at school I'd heard the name Velvet Underground on numerous occasions. I'd seen the band name-checked in Melody Maker interviews with John Lennon and Pete Townshend, and by others who seemed to be in the know, people whose recommendations you could trust. However, when I finally heard the band in the spring of 1971 and discovered them to be little more than purveyors of lightweight sappy pop I was more than a little underwhelmed. *Who Loves the Sun*, released as a single and played regularly on Radio One, sounded like a Vanity Fare B side. All that fuss, just for this?

I didn't know then that what I hearing wasn't the real thing, just as David Bowie didn't know either when he first encountered the band in New York, only to discover later that the person he thought he was talking to backstage wasn't Lou Reed but Doug Yule. I didn't know that Doug Yule wasn't Lou Reed either, or that Lou Reed was the only member of the original Velvet Underground line-up on *Who Loves the Sun*. I didn't know this for the simple reason that I had no idea who Lou Reed was in the first place. The name meant nothing to me. For the remainder of my schooldays I filed the Velvet Underground away under F for Forgettable. And then I entered that Kerry's listening booth with Danny. It was one of those old-fashioned glass-doored plywood-panelled booths that always smelt of stale smoke and body odour. A suitably drab and seedy setting for the revelation to come. The moment those first bars of *Waiting for My Man* kicked in I knew I wasn't going to be listening to a Vanity Fare B side.

Oblivious to the band's pedigree, the first thing I reacted to was the noise – not the sound, the noise. The sheer relentless intensity of it, heavy on rhythm, low on conventional virtuosity. There seemed to be an almost contemptuous disavowal of musicianship going on – the guitars conformed to no notion of soloing I'd ever heard before. By the time that glass shattered one minute into *European Son* I had heard the future. That was the Damascene moment for me. The guitar interplay on the remaining six-and-a-half minutes of that track helped me formulate what my own band would sound like should I ever find such like-minded musicians.

Early in 1972 Melody Maker printed a photo of Lou Reed, John Cale and Nico taken at the Bataclan club in Paris where they performed a rare one-off gig, the first time they had been on stage together since the Velvets split. It was also the first time I'd seen them all photographed together. The expressions alone set them apart. To me at the time they looked like rock immortals carved into the face of Mount Rushmore – already legendary, already mythical.

Not hearing the Velvet Underground's debut LP until five years after it was recorded seemed like a long time at the time, but later on it didn't seem like much time at all. It was only years later that I pondered why we'd chosen that day to listen to that particular album and why I'd never noticed it in the racks before. A full decade after the event I saw an article in Record Collector which mentioned that those first three Verve LPs had all been reissued in late 1971. At the time, "How did I not discover this noise until now?" would have been the awestruck summary of my feelings as I stood in that lunchtime record booth, head against the greasy plywood panel, the volume up way loud. A smattering of lunchtime browsers at the counter, indifferent to my epiphany. Someone asking for *I'd Like to Teach the World to Sing* as I listened to *The Black Angel's Death Song*.

As with *Who Loves the Sun*, I wasn't that fussed for Nick Drake either when I first heard him. *Time Has Told Me*, the third track on Side Two of the

Island Records sampler *Nice Enough to Eat* sounded ploddy to me. It had that late-sixties countrified rock sound that I was never particularly fond of. The running order of *Nice Enough to Eat* does the song few favours either, following as it does Blodwyn Pig's brass rock stomper *Sing Me a Song that I Know* and Traffic's eerie, ethereal *Forty Thousand Headmen*, and followed in turn by King Crimson's brain-crunching *21st Century Schizoid Man*. Whatever magic Nick Drake possessed, I didn't hear it then at all. There was no instant troubled cure for a troubled mind. *Time Has Told Me* went on for a minute too long and I regularly used to skip it.

I measured out my gradual appreciation of Nick Drake from Island sampler to Island sampler. *Bumpers*, a double album, was released in 1970 and contained *Hazey Jane*, which I warmed to, but not sufficiently enough to want to hear *Bryter Layter* in full. "From his album to be released autumn '70," it said in parentheses on the liner notes. *Hazey Jane* sat well with the other gossamer-light, semi-jaded serenades on the album: King Crimson's *Cadence and Cascade*; Bronco's *Love*; *Oh I Wept* by Free (I always preferred Free when they were being moody and fragile rather than hard-rocking boogie merchants). *Hazey Jane* sounded nice enough (but not to eat). Nick Drake was still self-contained in those autumn '70 parentheses for me. Something forthcoming.

Cindy, my summer of '71 first true love, played me *El Pea*, the fourth and last in that sequence of cheap Island samplers. This one contained *Northern Sky*, mistitled as *One of these Things First* on the sleeve. As with *Hazey Jane*, I was intrigued as much as enchanted, but only in the same way that I was intrigued by William R. Strickland or Moondog or Amory Kane or any one of a number of one-track curios I encountered during that golden era of cut-price affordable samplers. With *Northern Sky*, though, it's fair to say that I may not have been giving the beauty of the song my full attention, wrapped up as I was in the splendour of Cindy.

And then Melody Maker ran that full-page ad for *Pink Moon*. The one with a photograph of Nick, shot from behind, drifting down to a tow path as an enthusiastic dog comes bowling round the corner and raises a paw in greeting. The day is mist-shrouded, the trees stark and bare. Running down the right-hand side of the photo was a statement from Dave Sandison, Island Press Officer. He talked about how Nick had gone into the studio to record his new album without telling anyone but his engineer, and about how the first two albums "haven't sold a shit". He mentioned that Island were prepared to release anything and everything Nick recorded, because they thought he was special. I gaze at the photo, which I assume, incorrectly, to have been taken in Cambridge. I gaze back at the press-office eulogy and the aura of Nick Drake finally begins to radiate. The Monday after the MM ad, I'm in Cambridge buying *Pink Moon*. My Nick Drake habit begins at what I didn't know at the time (what none of us knew at the time) was the end, and works its way back to the beginning. For the first time in my life I bought an LP purely on trust, based solely on what I've been told by an ad.

A week or so before that, another Thursday, another Danny half-day off, we hitched to Cambridge just for something to do. Found a shop down a narrow alley way called Red House Records. On the counter was a spread of flyers advertising gigs, poetry readings, jam-session nights. One of them reads: "The debut of *Stars*. (Barrett, Alder, Monck)."

"Is that Syd Barrett?" I asked. "Yes, it is," said the record-shop guy.
 "Shall we go?"

And so, by virtue of just happening to be in Cambridge that day, Danny and I get to bear witness to a legendary event, one that like many such events didn't seem that legendary at the time. These days I'm all mythed out as far as that Corn Exchange gig goes. Each time I portion out a little more anecdotage about Syd's performance, witnessed by fewer than 30 or 40 people, it removes my 17-year-old awestruck self just a little further from the ramshackle intimacy of the occasion. It was a night no more shambolic than many others, but in the intervening half-century since I stood, elbows on the lip of the stage gazing in awe at magic that was no longer there, the untogether nature of the occasion and the sheer charisma of the man seem to have gained undue prominence over what was in many ways just another gig. Any untogetherness that has retrospectively been projected onto the event has to be rationalised strictly in the context of the times. There were many occasions when I saw the Edgar Broughton Band take at least 15 minutes before they could negotiate a convincing resolution to *Out Demons Out*. Hawkwind sometimes seemed to conclude a space jam only when the last chemically enhanced musician stopped playing.

Was Syd untogether? No more so than many others were in the early 1970s. Was he outré and totally out there? Not really. His unassuming eccentricity seemed child's play compared with the full-on maniacal assault of a Vivian Stanshall, a Ron Geesin, a Roy Harper. This was 1972. The Syd myth hadn't taken hold yet. The portents weren't writ in stone. Danny and I spoke to him afterwards. He wasn't weird. He was polite.

We hitchhiked back to Bedford well after midnight and Danny put me up on one of his several lumpy sofas. He was snoring loudly within seconds. I made the best of it but lay awake half the night, freezing cold. I watched the early light make scarlet blotches on murky brown curtains having dozed fitfully while having dreams about trying to sleep. I was woken by the clanking of cups and there was Veronica in her school uniform beaming down at me with her Cheshire Cat grin, offering me a mug of tea. She climbed fully clothed into bed with Danny and they sat with the blanket up to their chins sipping tea and making small talk. When

Veronica started nibbling Danny's ear I made my excuses and headed for home.

Halfway up my road I saw our randy tom cat Rusty heading past the front of the house. Rusty had been rescued by a workmate of Dad's whose neighbour had moved house and left a cat and her four tiny kittens locked in a shed to starve. We never had him neutered and as a result he spent most of his short life shagging. He'd come home reeking of pheromones, pausing just long enough to be fed before going off out again to make more little Rustys, the evidence of which we saw regularly in numerous backyards and out-buildings. He'd gone missing a couple of weeks earlier while still woozy on anaesthetic, administered by the vet after he'd been hit in the hind quarters, presumably by a car.

"Whatever you do, don't let him out," said the vet. "He'll be vulnerable and won't be able to defend himself." Rusty slipped out the back door the moment our backs were turned. We consoled ourselves with the hope that he was resting in a field somewhere, but after a week it was noticeable that Mum had stopped mentioning him in front of my younger siblings. I was so glad to see him that I rushed into the house. "Mum, Rusty's back!" I shouted as soon as I got in. "He came back yesterday," she said dismissively. "Where have you been all night?"

It was a sudden sharp reminder that Christmas hadn't been entirely forgotten. An even sharper reminder came in the shape of an awful mawkish record called *Mother of Mine* by a freakishly sentimental child called Neil Reid. The record spent several weeks at Number Two in the Top 30 and was played incessantly on the radio. Reid also turned up with distressing frequency on *Top of the Pops*, resplendent in a double-breasted suit, collar and tie combo and plastered-down hair. "Why couldn't you have turned out more like him?" said Mum one night as I watched the balloon-headed boy wringing the pathos out of his best-selling dirge while making the kind of beseeching gestures towards camera one would normally have associated with an exorcist teasing the devil out of the possessed.

A couple of weeks later I was sitting in the living room contemplating how I might best spend my day at Pretend Tech when the post arrived and Mother of Mine, with another disapproving look, handed me a letter. The address was etched in neat purple felt-tip block capitals (the "Angleterre" seemed an exotic flourish), and the envelope bore the unmistakable imprint of Daevid Allen. On the front, written in barely legible yellow, were the words: "It's the time of the Banana Moon – Wherever yr going yr gonna get there soon. Love from Gong." The message was underscored by a trademark Banana Moon, the kind I had been doodling for months. On the back of the envelope, etched in the same purple felt-tip as the address, was a drawing of a pot-headed pixie and a speech balloon reading: "The real meaning of cool is the wind in this nightingale's face." Next to it was a thought-bubble with the teasing message: "Fate... fate... my steak-and-kidney's on your plate. See p434."

Inside, in a tiny booklet, courtesy of "Gong Management 20 rue Serpente", was a three-page letter from Daevid. It read as follows:

"Robert: Greetings mate. The problem is there is no more room left in the place and we can't invite anybody more 'til we find a bigger place. Sorry! But why don't you just take off and look for a soul family. Soon as yr out of UK you'll soon feel you're being manipulated by uncontrollable fate. You gotta help yourself out there. You don't need a reason. Mutter Mumble.

"Whew! Sorry if that sounds like preaching but somebody gotta say it. There's lotsa communes which unlike ole Gong can welcome with uncomplicated conscience and mutual benefit creative gents like yourself. Bit of research via UK Ug mags – even in South of Engl & Wales also lots of groovy communes that'll welcome you.

"One day when present music cycle is finished for us we'll be back in open community again and just live instead of having to keep a precarious music trip together. Understand? It shur ain't easy but it's intense learning and karma burning 'til yo are high and don't hafta get high any mo... someday soon soooo... lotsa luck

Daevid"

He didn't have to say any of that. And I can't think of anyone else who would have done. He wrote back to a 17-year-old kid living in the sticks. I could have been just another little hippie waster, yet more alternative-society flotsam. I dread to think what I wrote in that original letter, the contents of which I would probably squirm at now (or maybe not, who knows?). But in my reaching out he must have detected a spark of sincerity, perhaps even some sign of intelligent life pulsating away beneath the small-town desperation. He wrote to me. Daevid Allen wrote to me. I still have the letter. In fact, he wrote again a few weeks later with the address of a UK commune guide. He even asked how things were progressing. Imagine that happening now. I no longer have that follow-up letter. But I still have all my follow-up thoughts. This book is part of that very process. And he was right. His advice was sound. "You gotta help yourself out there. You don't need a reason." All I had to do was turn to page 434.

Those Velvet Underground albums were reissued in late 1971. I acquired them, in the order of their original release during February and March 1972. The date of that Melody Maker with the full-page *Pink Moon* ad, February 26th 1972. Delivered to my house and read on February 24th, the same day that me and Danny went to see Syd Barrett's Stars at Cambridge Corn Exchange. The following week's MM featured the Roy Hollingworth review that made Syd jack it all in. The post date on that first letter from Daevid Allan in France, March 8th. All this condensed into just a few short weeks of my life. Reverberative. Transformative. Epochal.

It was around about this time that Dickie Dangerfield reappeared on the scene. I assume he'd been at home with his parents, cultivating what would become a sustained aversion to work and an equally life-long methadone habit. When he walked into Kerry's one sunny spring morning it was the first time I'd seen him since the Hype Park concert where he bore witness to the smouldering ashes of my relationship with Cindy. With a contraband £5 record token in my pocket, courtesy of Kerry's, the two of us caught a bus to Hitchin where I bought *White Light/White Heat* by Velvet Underground and *Bryter Layter* by Nick Drake. Imagine those two albums, nestling side-by-side in a record bag. Necessary yin and yang purchased on the same mizzling, drizzly March afternoon.

We thumbed it back to Bedford in the rain and who should recognise our thumbs but former school bully Gary Brady? By now GB was a police cadet, but I first became aware of him in 1967 in the first year at school. At this time, he was a budding entrepreneur, offering to chalk pastel flowers on girls' shoes in order to exploit the commercial possibilities of the Summer of Love and cop a look up their skirts. Once he got the love and peace thing out of his system he settled down to being a thug. He grew thick-necked and broad-shouldered, and played for the first XV at Rugby. At lunchtimes he led the smoker's club to the bike sheds. By the fourth year he had graduated to beating up the boyfriends of girls who failed to be seduced by his oafish charms and go out with him. As plenty of girls fell into this category, there was usually a lunchtime beating being dished out somewhere. By the fifth year there was a rumour going around that he'd been to the needlework teacher's house – and not just to brush up on his cross-stitch.

And now he'd found his vocation as a police cadet. In between jollying us along with reminders of how enjoyable our schooldays were, and the fun times we all had together, "Eh boys?", he called me and Dickie hippies, drop-outs and cunts all the way back to Bedford. We had to act so straight in the back seat it hurt. Still gave us a lift though.

A couple of weeks later I handed over another Kerry's record token for *Five Leaves Left* and completed the set. My Nick Drake and Velvet Underground appreciation grew in tandem. I found the third VU album, already unloved and available at reduced price, in the sale at Braggins, a Bedford department store. The common denominator in all this was John Cale, who played on *Fly* and on *Northern Sky* – a song which now finally revealed its magic to me. *Time Has Told Me* still sounded ploddy, but the rest of *Five Leaves Left* was as refreshing as the spring rain that dampened the council-tended crocuses in Russell Park.

Nick Drake had enjoyed brief undergraduate tenure in cloistered Cambridge during 1968. (Proximity flash! – Did I ever glimpse a tall young stranger back-lit in an alley? Did I ever catch the eye of a homeward-bound student on a station platform as I scribbled down the number of the train he was about to board?) All this time he was out there living a life at the same time as I was, inhabiting the same days with the same sun rising and setting, only 20 miles away from where I lived. My initial encounters with his music, in reverse chronological order, were like a paper trail scattered from the centre of a maze outwards towards the point of entry.

It's almost impossible now to imagine that there was a time when Nick Drake was just another nondescript name, trying his luck at the song-and-dance game. I was one of Dave Sanderson's legion of "hardly anyone" who bought his LPs while he was still alive. My purchases would have found their way to a balance sheet, a royalty statement, a bank account. Soon enough the evidence of those meagre sales would have been presented to disbelieving Nick, cut to the quick by the realisation that so few people were buying what he had to offer. Pacing Joe Boyd's office like a prima donna. You told me. You promised me. Recriminations met with record-company logic. Why has Cat Stevens sold millions and I haven't? Because Cat Stevens tours, Nick. Because Cat Stevens tours.

Danny, Dickie and I started going to the Century Cinema down by the river embankment, to watch what at the time were not called Blaxploitation movies. Bedford had three cinemas in the early 70s: the Granada, which had hosted all the major package-tour pop gigs in the 1960s and now showed mainstream blockbusters; the Empire ("We put the Sin in cinema"), which showed mostly X-rated skin flicks; and the Century, which showed all the music-related stuff. I'd seen *Woodstock* there when I was still at school – Pat the Bedford head posing at the front.

More recently I'd unsuccessfully attempted to negotiate the entrance to the Century to go and watch the first Monty Python film. I was blitzed on acid and chickened out at the sight of a neon-lit foyer full of glowing radioactive customers. The prospect of my coins turning to cinders in my hand as I attempted to count them was enough for me to turn tail and flee. With Danny and Dickie though I was assured of safety in numbers. Some nights we'd go clear-headed and straight, other nights we'd get chemically enhanced. Rosalyn Rip-Off sold us some shards and we went to see *Zachariah*, the self-styled "first electric Western". It starred Country Joe and The Fish, the James Gang, Elvin Jones and The Firesign Theater, and as far as we could ascertain boasted very little in the way of plot.

Admittedly our abilities to recognise a narrative arc were disassembled somewhat by whatever it was that Rosalyn Rip-Off had sold us. We sat in a state of twitchy agitation, occasionally turning to one another to check if we were taking off yet or still merely taxi-ing on the runway. When fiddler Doug Kershaw appeared on screen we agreed that snakes appeared to be writhing in rivulets all the way down his ancient face, and I was briefly back in the Nile times with pyramids and sphinxes and shit, but then Doug Kershaw looked like that anyway, so none of us were really sure if the apparition set before us was a result of our chemical enhancement or not.

We spent a great deal of the film discussing this under our breaths and not much time paying attention to any plotlines that might have manifested themselves in our absence. We put the exertions of that night down to the imbibing of yet another of Rosalyn's damp squibs and went our separate ways. The next day Dickie walked into Kerry's and announced that he'd gone home, said goodnight to his parents, got into bed, turned out the light and had the full pterodactyls-on-the-ceiling experience. That's how it was with Rosalyn Rip-Off and her window-pane crystals. Lucky dip. Clunk or click every trip.

Inspired partly by reading Daevid Allen's sleeve doodlings on Gong's *Camembert Electrique* album, which was recorded during the full moons of May, June and September 1971, and by whatever nostalgic residue I still had for Marc Bolan's supposed meeting with a wizard in France, I began to take an interest in witchcraft, white magic, lycanthropy and any other paranormal texts I could get my hands on in the County library. This was my moon-worship phase. I'd break off from watching *Play for Today* or *Softly, Softly* or whatever else was on the telly to go outside and commune with the sky. I had a vivid dream one night, clearly Gong-influenced, that I was in a band. I walked up to the mic and announced: "This song's called *Tonight We're Gonna Bomb the Moon*", and there was an audible "Oh wow" in the audience at my wondrous phrasing and cosmic ingenuity.

I started to explain to the adoring crowd that when the song came out on a forthcoming album it would be called *Tonight We're Gonna Bomb the Moon* open brackets *With Love* close brackets. Everything dream-dissolved into a Tanguy painting after that, but I still think how good that song would have sounded in 1972. If Gong had let me go and live on their commune like I'd asked it could have been on their next album. Sensing my burgeoning interest in the supernatural, a member of staff in the County Library – young male, not stereotypically esoteric himself – offered to go and look in the stack to see if there was anything else I might like to read. He walked down a spiralling staircase in the centre of the Library and came back minutes later with fusty hardbound books on Tibetan Buddhism, Shamanism, Celtic lore. I used to watch him disappear down that staircase and pondered what other riches might be down there in his subterranean stack world.

I can't remember if I found George Ivanovich Gurdjieff on the library shelves or if my willing accomplice brought him up from the stack, but I did attempt to wade through an impenetrable tome or two by the Armenian mystic and philosopher. I'd first encountered the name Gurdjieff in an interview with Kevin Ayers, who explained that the Soft Machine song *Why Are We Sleeping?* was directly informed by the philosopher's central belief that human beings are essentially asleep, and in this somnambulistic state are denied their full potential. It was never clearly explained how we might awake, and I was no further forward after dipping into *Beelzebub's Tales to His Grandson* and *Meetings with Remarkable Men*. What I mostly gained from the experience was an understanding that much of Gurdjieff's writing was allegorical.

Kevin Ayers was also a dab hand at the allegorical, and what little I understood of Gurdjieff's thinking was derived in part from Ayers' own songs, which were at times full of unsettling image shifts, detours and teasing asides. *Stop this Train (Again Doing It)* the first track on Side Two of Ayers' solo album *Joy of a Toy*, was central to my Gurdjieffian quest, and I spent much time pondering the journey of the sleeping passengers who rode aimlessly – "going nowhere for the ride". Later I learned that obscuring the message with sleight-of-hand, riddles and ambiguity was half the act as far as Gurdjieff was concerned, but at 17 I was doing little more than faithfully following Ayers' guidance to the end of that song, at which point he is poised precipitously, staring into a blinding light.

Despite having been an enthusiastic hymn singer at Junior school any formal adherence to faith had been drummed out of me during five years of authoritarian assembly at Grammar school. What fleeting empathy I had for the theological rose and fell in accordance with the appearance of gospel pop records like *Oh Happy Day* by the Edwin Hawkins Singers,

Govinda by the Radha Krsna Temple, and *Spirit in the Sky* by Norman Greenbaum in the Top 20.

Any revived stirrings of a spiritual awakening were slow and superficial, and by 1972 were largely gleaned from perusing the covers of Danny's Quintessence LPs. As with Nick Drake, my introduction to the band had been the Island sampler *Nice Enough to Eat*. Their contribution, *Gungamai*, was Track Five on Side Two, and sat between the abrasive assault of *21st Century Schizoid Man* and the pleasantly ludicrous wittering of Dr Strangely Strange. At 14, *Gungamai* might as well have been *Ging Gang Goolie*. It struck me as preachy and preposterous, but that might have been because at 14 I hadn't a clue what they were on about. On first encountering their music, I doubt if I even thought they were English. The follow-up Island sampler, *Bumpers*, featured *Jesus Buddha Moses Gauranga*. By this time I'd at least worked out that they were on a bit of a god trip, although I still didn't have a clue who Gauranga was. Heard in isolation, their devotional music left me cold. It all seemed a bit Kumbaya and happy-clappy but with electric guitars.

It was Danny who was responsible for turning me on to Quintessence, lending me the *Dive Deep* LP while we were still at school and playing their other albums endlessly at his flat. Once I heard their music in context, as a flow rather than as isolated tracks on samplers, the whole vibe of the thing started to make sense. Their creative collaging, live tracks next to studio ones, chants and mantras next to extended freak-outs, reminded me of the way Frank Zappa assembled his records, and I began to dive deeper. I familiarised myself with the iconography. I took the time to learn the difference between dharma and Brahma. I found myself increasingly drawn to the allure of those devotional titles. *Dance for the One. Sea of Immortality. Infinitum.* A growing curiosity about the spiritual realm led to me sitting in the County Library and spending a week working my way through a huge Reference copy (abridged) of the Sanskrit epics *The Ramayana* and *The Mahabharata*. A previous reader had left flower petals pressed between the pages of the book. Something stirred within me. A flame ignited.

Sitting there in Danny's flat I felt like I was embarking on some new voyage. Small talking. Big thinking. Whisper words inside me chanting from a Tibetan mountain-top. Danny said some of the original members had left and he didn't like the new LP, entitled *Self*, as much as the first three. Evening light fought its way through incense smog and dirty curtains. I'd bought these foul-smelling joss sticks from the head shop in town. They smelt like gasoline. The music washed over us like breaker waves. Allan Mostert's guitar sounded like razors wrapped in velvet. Danny told me for the thousandth time that Allan was the greatest guitarist in the universe. I was beginning to believe him, starting to hear what he heard. I said that the singer, Shiva, reminded me of Del Shannon, particularly on that bit in *Dive Deep* where he appears to be quoting *Runaway*. "Shiva Shannon," said Danny.

Chapter 3

REALITY CHECKPOINT

I found myself in the Central Library in Cambridge and then I lost myself again. It happened while I was seated among the old people poring over the daily newspapers. Mine eyes likewise, darting hither, spooling through paragraph shapes and small ads, crossword clues and TV listings, snug amidst the panelling, all buffed up to illuminate the grain and giving off wood-polish fumes in the quietness of a Tuesday evening. My brain oozing memory scent of old pavilions, linseed oil and smoke-kippered panelling. The dusky remains of the day pressed themselves to the window. I chased the football scores down the pages of the Evening Echo (Final) and skidded clean off the edge until I was ragged among brambles. Let me explain what happened as best I can.

The smoke rose from mill stacks and chimney tops as I hovered above Blackpool or Blackburn or Burnley. A nicotine mist clung to everything and made the roof-slates glisten. I parted the sky and dribbled down the wind. Nobody noticed in that quiet library reading-room. Not a soul stirred to observe my strange behaviour. Each time I refocused on the page a new town emerged in a mirage of word shimmer. The railway tracks snaked through industrial estates, freight trucks dangling like beads from a necklace. Diesel perfume dabbed. Battery acid leaking. My brain sweating memory scent of dubbin on hard leather footballs, pages flapping as boys chase their shadows over frost-cracked turf. Villa Park. Molineux. Trafford Park. Turf Moor. Bramall Lane. The five o'clock bell and the factory gates flung open. Crowds teeming through a latticework of narrow streets to corner shops and pubs. The gridlines of the city shone like burnished silver until they brittled and flaked, and all that remained was the embossed after-image of the wood panelling blurring my vision and fading to fog.

Heavy-lidded and lotion-eyed I didn't believe what was happening at first, but let me explain as best I can though thoughts are fleeting and I'm still here in the First Division among tall men in flat caps bent double by wheezing. Starting at the top of the page I rowed down the leagues in a leaky boat, bailing out somewhere around the Industrial Revolution. Floundered in filthy canal backwaters. Soared over respectable red-brick suburbs with trellis and tended roses and children playing out in corporation parks, lasered by sun-rays the colour of butter. An old man poured ink into a beaker, dipped a nib and glanced at me suspiciously. I avoided his gaze by dreaming myself down the divisions, tumbling and plummeting through Plymouth and Portsmouth and Bournemouth until there were no longer any terraced houses only tree-lined semis and I was pacing through genteel neighbourhoods choking my own throat with reddening face and contortionist grip.

I hurtled headlong through the Combination (Reserves) and the Southern League. By the time I had tethered my equilibrium I was back in the Isthmian days. The Lions were triumphantly holding a Cup aloft and the Christians were being relegated, except in those days Relegation meant something else entirely. It's changed its meaning many times as the years have scrolled by. In the Hellenic League players were hitting each other with shields, a practice that has all but died out now. How odd! Somebody playing for Wycombe Wanderers called Royston and somebody playing for Royston called Wycombe Wanderers. That can't be right.

I tried to restore some calm by concentrating on the Midweek Floodlit League. These were the truest words I had read for some time and I thought I could trust them. Towering celestial stacks shadowing every stadium, floodlights illuminating every square of dew-glistened turf, casting a glow on the corrugated tea-hut gathering. Almost tearful about it. Midweek. Floodlit. League. The reassuring essence of those words lulled me. It was indisputably getting on for half-past midweek and the pages were astonishingly floodlit but something still wasn't in league with me. I tried to scrabble back to my previous vantage-point, hovering above Bolton or Bellchester or Bubblewell, but now it was all lizards and rocks among the heating pipes. Where was I any more?

Somebody spoke and the librarian shooshed. A voice told me not to go North young man. In Belper and Matlock, sheep grazed in cable cars, spiteful children goaded silhouettes and old women vandalised garden sheds, rampaging through the flame-ravaged remains of out-houses, stealing mangles, cramming stolen china into handbags, lining their purses with PG Tips. I sought refuge in the Athenian League. I think it was there that I found myself among the brambles. Scratches and scars on my arms that took weeks to heal. All the trophies glistened like treasure trove. The Essex Senior Cup. The Essex Professional Cup. The East Anglian Cup. The Mithras Cup (semi-final first leg.)

"That's roight, it be cup picking season about now," said a ruddy-faced man on a tractor as he chugged down narrow country lanes leaving a trail of spittle on the breeze. "Roip and lovely," he kept repeating. "Roip and lovely. Don't go thieving our harvest now." I hitched myself to his trailer and he gave me a suspicious glance. He seemed wary of my intentions even though I had none, save temporary respite from the word-blizzard and the bracketed half-time scores. A proper storm got up, tearing the roof off the library and leaving the old men in the reading-room coated in cinders and debris dust, then frozen and ice-bound, icicles dripping from noses. Tractor man dropped me in a leafy lane and I walked for hours in the peace-time of a different evening with the roadside poppies waving and a bright red phone box beckoning in the distance. It seemed that all I had to do was reach it and dial and Nick would come and get me, swooping from his high perch on the tallest library shelf. Nick was a knowledge owl now.

I was in Cambridge because Jack Monck, the bass player with Syd Barrett's Stars, had invited me along to Fisher House, the Catholic Mission Hall just off the Market Square where every Tuesday night an informal jam session took place and an arts lab atmosphere prevailed. Jack had responded to a small ad I'd pinned to the wall in Red House Records, where he worked when he wasn't being the bass player with Syd Barrett's Stars. He'd turned up at my door one spring Sunday morning not long after the Stars project had fizzled out, his van parked respectfully at a distance down the road. The van also contained his wife Jenny and a boisterous dog, hence the respectful distance. I failed to recognise him from that Corn Exchange night with Syd and he had to explain who he was. I don't remember being star-struck or overawed when confronted with this realisation – these were different times, more cool and aloof times. It wouldn't have been the done thing to gush, although it did occur to me tangentially that here was a chance to replace Syd Barrett in a band. Jack suggested an informal meet-up at Fisher House.

The first time I went, a few members of Gong turned up, including Didier Malherbe and Pip Pyle, as did the bulk of what was about to become Hatfield and the North. This loose conglomerate got up on stage and

Chapter 3

jammed, with the unshowy ego-free complexity you would expect of a Planet Gong/Canterbury hybrid. I was smitten by the "Hey this isn't really a gig as such" laid-back ambience of the occasion and asked Jack if the next time I came along I might be permitted to read some of my poetry. The fact that I'd cobbled together no more than a loose sheaf of random scribblings at that point didn't deter me.

At that time the psychic fault-line of Cambridge was Parker's Piece, a magical patch of green on the outskirts of the city centre. A network of paths intersected at its apex where a cast-iron lamp post stood. Affixed to the lamp post a small rectangular trade plate honoured the makers, the fittingly celestial Sun Foundry of Glasgow. Directly underneath the plate someone, in the not-too-distant past, had etched the words "Reality Checkpoint". Those words had incantatory resonance for all who paused en-route to read them. On certain days it was easy to believe that Cambridge, perhaps the universe itself, spun on this very axis. To crisscross Parker's Piece in the hallucinatory misty blue haze of dawn was to understand. Wherever you were going, wherever you had been, Reality Checkpoint came looming up like a beacon for ships and souls lost at sea.

I'd been walking across Parker's Piece in the bright spring sunshine when a voice called out to me. I turned around and there was Nick Tate, who I'd been at school with the previous year. He was one of the less obnoxious members of the Lower Sixth, one of the few who was prepared to talk to you on a level, about music usually, which was often the only leveller we had. "How are you Rob? What have you been doing?" He meant since leaving school, I guess. I said I was in Cambridge for the day and there was this gig at Fisher House if he was interested, and knowing he played guitar I asked him if he wanted to come. He told me he had dropped out of the sixth form and was living in Cambridge now, where he spent his time busking outside shops and owing rent to his landlord.

73

We went back to his flat where he offered me some acid, and that's how we ended up in the town library with me navigating the newsprint and Nick perched like an owl ready to swoop down from his vantage point among the County Court Records. I think at some point during the trip he convinced himself that one of his ancestors had been deported to Botany Bay. At the euphoric peak of his acid rush he thought this was a truth worth verifying via the library parchments of old. Consequently, at about 5 pm Nick buried himself in Court records while I tore up and down the quiet country roads of the Fourth Division. I should never have walked across Parker's Piece or accepted his acid tab. That night got very messy.

We did the trip at about midday and in the early afternoon headed back to Parker's Piece where we anchored our senses to the Reality Checkpoint lamp post and spooled out as much lifeline as we dared. The girls from the High School were playing hockey so we sat in cross-legged meditation and watched them click sticks for a while. As the acid came on stronger I kept feeling I was astral-projecting myself several yards onto the field of play. A pot-headed pixie after-image of myself kept whooshing forward, shedding a Vorticist after-trail like a multiple-exposure photo. I knew it was just the acid surging, but it kept happening again and again and each time it unsettled me just a little more. I kept edging backwards, convinced I was on the pitch. Then Nick started doing it too. "Whoa. Too much momentum!" he shouted in panic. Then the grass began to feel damp and we convinced ourselves that we had pissed our pants. Then we started giggling. Then we started to feel self-conscious that we were sitting on the grass watching lithe young girls playing hockey, although I noticed this didn't seem to deter the group of dirty old men in raincoats who had also gathered to watch. Eventually we reached some sort of scrambled consensus that we should get up off the damp grass and find ourselves more agreeable scenery, so we headed back to the sanctuary of Nick's flat. Walking across the market square cobbles, the transistor radio at the tea stall was playing *Runnin' Away* by Sly and the Family Stone. We walked the rest of the way to Nick's flat singing "Ha-ha hee-hee, you're wearing out your shoes," in squeaky wheezy voices.

Nick's flat was two small rooms that smelt of painted-over damp. As soon as we walked in I wished we were back on Parker's Piece. Nick hunched himself over his acoustic guitar and began searching for a tune while I attempted to astrally project myself back to the hockey field. When that didn't work I suggested we eat some food. All Nick had in his cupboards was a small heap of sawdust left by boreholes and a packet of rice. Nick carried on doing his blues "Came down from Bedfordshire B roads" thing while I convinced him that we could lead the kind of good macrobiotic life I had read about in the Underground press by emptying the rice into a saucepan and filling it with water. That was the easy part. After a while Nick put his guitar down and came over to watch the water boil.

"What you have to do," I said, "is keep putting water in until all the rice evaporates." "Are you sure?" said Nick. At this moment I was as convinced of this weird alchemical cooking method as I had ever been of anything. "How long will it take? I'm hungry," Nick asked as we watched the bubbly mess congeal, both of us fascinated by the steam shapes and the primordial glue. "What you have to do," I repeated, "is... you have to wait till the rice turns to steam." Nick added some more water, as we convinced ourselves that our reasoning was good and our quest was sound. To our gradually dawning dismay the rice swelled to fill the entire pan. After a while we forgot about eating and left the pan to burn dry on the stove. By now the place reeked of scorched rice so we went out again.

By the time we drifted into the cloisters of Kings College, everything had begun to freeze to mediaeval tapestry in the pale afternoon sun. For a while we clung to a mossy seat in the shelter of an ivy-clad wall.

"Everything's tangled up here," said Nick. "I know," I nodded. "It's the same everywhere you go. There's just too many tentacles." A flurry of wind shook blossom from the trees. We got up and walked the Backs along the riverbank where further obstacles awaited us. A camouflaged willow branch twanged Nick in the face.

"You can see everything in the smallest detail," he said drily, swatting twigs from his mouth. Our laughter echoed off Gothic stone and ran shrieking down shadowed quadrants all the way back to ghost times. We sat by the water's edge transfixed by the milky stillness of the Cam, but it started to get cold so we walked into town again. I thought the acid had levelled out a bit but it jack-in-the-boxed back to life the moment we walked into the library in search of comfortable seating and indexed periodicals. Nick never did find out anything about his Botany Bay ancestors but he did eventually find me wandering the country lanes of the lower leagues. He prized me away from the inky blackness of the newsprint and led me out into the street again. How we ever made it to Fisher House I'll never know.

There were probably 60 people there, about the same as the first time I'd been. We stood around for a while wringing the acid out of our clothes. Strychnine ripples played havoc with my empty stomach. A bit of formless jamming was going on onstage. I can't remember if Nick got up and jammed with them or whether he played on his own or at all. I thought about getting up and reading my fragments aloud, but poleaxed by the acid I felt the parchment pages turn to cobwebs and memory dust in my pocket and remained rooted to the spot. At one point I wandered off in search of a toilet and found myself in a tiny backyard, groping around in the half-dark. From the midst of the hippie mingling and the hash aroma a soothsayer's voice emerged. "I wouldn't go in there," it said.

But compelled to piss I ignored the advice and before I knew what I was doing I was in a dimly lit cubicle gazing at the kind of interior décor the IRA would later champion during their dirty protest. There was blood and shit everywhere. Such was the force of the action-painting splatter, it seemed that the manoeuvre had only been possible to execute if someone had dropped their pants, and done a handstand while rotating with sufficient rapidity to ensure that the effluence emerged lawn-sprinkler style from their revolving orifice. The cleanest spot seemed to be the enamel toilet pan itself which was lightly flecked with only a hint of reddish-brown discharge. I held my breath, pissed, and backed out gagging. The soothsayer voice spoke again. "Someone must have been right off their conk to do that," he said. His friend stared hard at me as if I might have been the culprit. The shit-spattered khazi incident brought me down somewhat. I looked up at the clear night sky and experienced a piercing surge of the all-alones. I just wanted to be back home in my bed, or at least crashing on Nick's couch till the morning. I went back inside and re-acquainted myself with the comforting warmth of the throng, only to realise after a few minutes that Nick had scarpered.

The music stopped playing, the house lights went on and people began to drift towards the exit. I stared at the alabaster icons on the walls for a bit, transfixed momentarily by the mission hall's regular function. Then survival strategy kicked in and I realised I must find Nick or I was going to be wandering the empty streets of Cambridge all night. I'd taken a few hesitant steps outside before it occurred to me that I hadn't a clue where he lived. I could clearly recall the inside of his flat, reeking of burnt rice and painted-over damp, but hadn't been paying any attention to the direction we'd walked as we pranked about the streets. Cambridge suddenly took on the aspect-defying properties of a Cubist painting, splendidly asymmetric, but in all other respects utterly useless for Ordnance Survey purposes. It was also at this point that I realised I didn't actually know Nick that well. He was just someone who used to sidle up to us at school, guitar round his neck, as we waited for four o'clock buses to take us home. Another of life's Jeremy Carrs, perhaps the first Jeremy Carr I ever met. He'd pick out a few rudimentary riffs in the late afternoon sun and we'd stand around basking meaningfully in the aura of his coolness hoping that girls we fancied were watching us.

I fell in with the flow of the late-night crowd, mostly people pouring out of pubs and University functions. The decaying remains of the acid began to dissolve with a bubble pop way upstream and I felt my survival instincts kick in. I remember consciously listening to the murmur of chatter, and waiting for the moment when I could turn to an empathetic gathering and, with all the will I could summon, ask if they had a sofa I could crash on. I'm pretty sure that the first group I asked offered an apologetic no, but the second small gathering, which almost bumped into the first as I shared my plight said: "Yeah sure, follow us."

And that's how I ended up sleeping on another of life's sofas under a borrowed greatcoat, with someone softly strumming a lullaby guitar in the kitchen and a cardboard box of new-born kittens on the floor beside me. The sofa was uncomfortable and the greatcoat barely adequate for warmth. During the night the kittens clambered all over me and made new beds in the contours of the coat. I slept only fitfully and in the morning a stranger who I hadn't seen the night before made me a cup of tea and told me there had been a spare unoccupied bed upstairs which I could have used. I hitched home bleary-eyed and offered my parents another set of inadequate excuses as to where I'd been the night before.

As the weather got warmer I started hitching into Cambridge more often, forsaking the sanctuary of Bedford County Library for a whole new vista. In the great cultural divide of townies and gownies, I was a ghosty.

Assuming invisibility, I would drift past porter's lodges wherever a gate might be open or a gravelled yard look inviting, and wander the cloisters, quadrants and well-manicured lawns unchallenged. I soaked up the whole medieval-laned, Henry the Third vibe of the place without intruding one iota on the consciousness of its privileged inhabitants. I remained simultaneously a chancer and an innocent abroad. I thought nothing of cadging a bed for the night or soliciting the thoughts of strangers over matters that might concern me. I remember walking up to a guy one day – late 20s, resplendent in eccentric finery, some kind of deerstalker/poncho hybrid festooned with various ivory-based accessories – and asking him if he knew what Syd Barrett was up to. He looked like Steve Peregrin Took's wealthier older brother. He stopped, smiled and pondered Syd's current whereabouts with me if this was the most natural thing he might be asked to do on a bright spring morning, walking down Trumpington Street, going about his business.

Townies, Gownies and Ghosties. King's College Gardens. Photo by Brendan Brotherson. Late 1972. Even in the photos I am ghosty.

Cambridge had considerable symbolic resonance in my young life. My aspirational parents, wanting their children to have more out of life than they'd had, and presumably seeing intelligence and potential in their first-born, took out an insurance policy on me when I was young, with the intention of cashing it in for books and learning materials when I was old enough to go to university. Once I started Grammar school and began to fail at everything, they gave up on that dream and cashed in the policy for our first-ever car, a second-hand Sunbeam Rapier.

I remember a Sunday visit to Cambridge not long before we bought that car. We went on the train and wandered round the streets for no other purpose it seems than to gaze at ivory towers and soak up the atmosphere of privilege and exclusion. I don't think we visited the Fitzwilliam Museum or Botanical Gardens or any other public facility. I was in full-on 12-year-old irritant mode, fluctuating between quiet-behaving boredom and silly voices. I began reading out the names on plaques as we passed various distinguished buildings until Dad snapped at me and I resumed my ennui-ridden sulk. Thinking back, I suspect it was his disappointment in me that inspired the outburst. To see this idiot boy, the vessel of so many of his hopes and dreams, the embodiment of all the life-chances he and Mum had been denied, now doing parodic cripple walks down the street, making spazz faces, blowing his fringe and reciting the names of eminent biologists, zoologists and Latinate professors that I had no more chance of meeting than he did, must have been a harsh reminder of the myriad ways in which your children can fail to fulfil your expectations. All Cambridge meant to me at that time was a railway station, where I sometimes went trainspotting until they closed the branch line at the beginning of 1968.

I still don't know why I thought that photo of Nick Drake in the full-page Melody Maker *Pink Moon* ad had been taken in Cambridge. Bare trees. Still waters. Fog and frosty parkland. Probably for the same reason that I thought the back-cover photo on the Barrett album was taken in Cambridge too. The poorly reproduced black-and-white image of Syd leaning against that car looked to me like the back of the Corn Exchange. It was in fact taken in Earls Court. Because so much of my life suddenly began to revolve around Cambridge, I shrunk the world to its architecture. Initially a fair proportion of that time was spent gravitating towards Red House Records in St Edward's Passage, the shop Danny and I had walked into and spotted tickets that said "Barrett" on them. Red House was frequented by heads and empathetic spirits. The staff were knowledgeable and friendly, and never too hip and sniffy to share their knowledge with a rookie like me. The place was like an ashram with vinyl. Another sanctuary. An Electric Church. A safe haven for lysergic refugees. One day I stumbled in there, tripping my sparks off and asked to listen to Terry Riley's *A Rainbow in Curved Air* on the headphones.

The listening area was a dimly lit alcove at the back of the shop where you sat on what felt like an old church pew. I put on the Major Tom space cans and went on a straight-backed journey to other another galaxy, one that had more forgiving furniture and room to sprawl. Pretty soon the headphones filled with electric bees which began buzzing away as they pulsated in a fizzing mesh of currents and crossed wires. After a while they were joined by a colony of fibre-glass butterflies. Initially beguiled, I rapidly began to find their flutterance distracting. "THESE HEADPHONES ARE FULL OF ELECTRIC BEES," I shouted. "BUTTERFLIES AND BEES." A customer turned and nodded knowingly. When it all got too much I took the headphones off and left the butterflies and bees to fight it out. "I won't bother with that one mate," I said spring-heeling back to the counter. "Was it the bees or the butterflies you didn't like?" the assistant enquired with a smile.

On another less chemically challenged occasion I plucked the Howard

Riley Trio's 1969 album *Angle* from the bargain bins. I'd heard Riley on Radio Three and liked that taut trio sound of his, but mostly I liked the 75p sticker on the sleeve, which placed the record firmly within my financial reach. The previous summer Cindy's parents had taken us to jazz nights at The Bell, an old coaching house pub in Codicote, Hertfordshire. Her father knew Jimmy Skidmore, saxophonist Alan Skidmore's dad, and on Sunday nights Skidmore senior had a residency at the pub. Alan would sometimes join them for a blow at the end of the night. I'd be sitting there with my permitted half a shandy and the guy whose CV at that point already included Soft Machine Fourth, Nice's *Five Bridges* suite, and numerous collaborations with the heavyweights of British jazz would be blowing his tenor inches from my face.

At the time I thought this was going to be my life from now on, my entrée into a whole new musical world, but I hadn't counted on Cindy ditching me for an apprentice gas-fitter with prospects. I'd blown my chance there, and by the spring of 1972 jazz was still relatively uncharted territory to me. I didn't have a hip bigger brother or sister. None of my older mates were into jazz, not even the Zappa, Beefheart, Hendrix, West Coast-loving fraternity among them. No one ever lent me a stack of back issues of Downbeat and said: "Get stuck into these, pop kid, they're better than the rags you read." I had to find it all out for myself.

My initial engagement with jazz, as with so many aspects of my cultural life, came about through a series of chance encounters. It was ever thus. At 12 I'd bought a copy of Disc and Music Echo because I'd originally gone into the newsagents to buy a copy of the pin-up magazine Parade, but my Uncle Ken was behind the counter, working on what was supposed to be his day off. Rather in the manner of Vic Brown in Stan Barstow's *A Kind of Loving*, who goes into the chemist's to buy Durex but leaves with Lucozade, Uncle Ken's presence caused me to panic. I went in for a glamour mag and came out with the first thing I saw on the counter, a copy of Disc. At 13 I first read Record Mirror because there was one left in the back of the shop for a customer who had gone on holiday as I waited to be paid my paper-round money one Saturday morning. At 14 I started reading Melody Maker because I got kicked out of games in the gym one morning at school, and Dickie "Sick Note" Dangerfield was sitting in the changing room reading his and started taking the piss out of my NME. It seemed to be like this with so many things. There was little rhyme or reason but lots of happenstance. It was the same with jazz.

Although NME was now in its hip ascendancy, busy reinventing itself and its readership, Melody Maker was still the place to go for a broad range of music coverage. It carried erudite jazz writing from the likes of Max Jones, Richard Williams and Val Wilmer, and covered everything from 1930s trad revivalists to the outer reaches of the avant-garde. It also carried a small listings column called Radio Jazz. There, in boxed-off bold type at the bottom of the reviews page, would be a round-up of pan-European jazz programming on the BBC, RTF France, AFN Frankfurt, Radio Bremen, NDR Hamburg, Hilversum, Radio Sweden and many others. The information was invariably inaccurate and out of date, but it led me to some fascinating new discoveries.

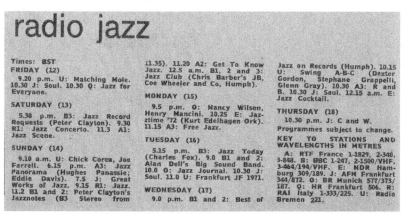

Melody Maker. May 13th 1972.

Being a compulsive dial-twiddler, I would tune in to the American Forces Network expecting to hear a Miles Davis concert, but they'd be running the NFL ball game from back home with full commentary. Or I might chance upon Radio Sweden through a blizzard of medium-wave interference and there would be some free-jazz ensemble in full flow. At the conclusion I'd grope monolingually through the presenter's often lengthy patter waiting for confirmation of what I'd just heard. "...Jerf skjiln doot Eric Dolphy wit..." Oh, right. Eric Dolphy. And on it went. Random encounter after random encounter with the signal drifting and fading and a world out there waiting to be discovered. I'd go wherever the jazz listings led me, mindful of Greenwich Mean Time adjustments and a growing suspicion that the column was only occasionally updated. Bill Evans. Fletcher Henderson. Oscar Peterson (always Oscar Peterson playing somewhere). Norma Winstone. The Tony Oxley Sextet. And here now in Red House Records, *Angle* by Howard Riley.

"Do you know the book?" asked the man behind the counter? "*Angle*?" "No. *Gormenghast*," he said, pointing to the title of Track Two, Side One. "What's that?" I asked. "It's *Lord of the Rings* for grown-ups," he replied. And he was right. It was. Another connection made. Another gateway opens. Another inner landscape to be absorbed. Lived in. Dreamed in. I found the first two volumes of Mervyn Peake's *Titus* trilogy in the County Library and they etched their Gothic mystery into the soft virgin clay of my brain like nothing I'd ever encountered before.

I'd read *Lord of the Rings* as a rite of passage, because other people read it and because someone told me that it was where Tyrannosaurus Rex took the title of their first album. I bought the same yellow-spine Allen and Unwin 1,000-pager that everyone had then, with its fold-up map of Middle Earth in the front. The topography fascinated me and I devoured the epic tale in a week. I finished reading it one squally showery morning sitting in a toilet cubicle in the sunken lavatories on Cambridge Market Square. The *Titus* trilogy was something else though. Somebody, it may have been the same guy in Red House Records, mentioned that if you can get past the dense prose style and the endless descriptions of castle outcrops, you're in. I was in from the off.

I marvelled at the character names: Barquentine. Rottcodd. Prunesquallor. Pentecost. Sepulchrave. Sourdust. I was entranced by the language. *Lord of the Rings* was all begetting and exposition. Eldror the Son of Crimdhras, born of the lofty hills and all that palaver. The plot raced along at a cracking pace and Tolkien wrote in undemanding prose, but the portentous saga-speak readily lent itself to gentle mockery, and I was never what you would call a dyed-in-the-wool convert. In contrast *Titus Groan* and *Gormenghast* seemed to be written in a style that had to be deciphered rune by rune as if it had been etched into the very stone of the castle itself. Words like polliniferous, presentiment, roseate and hierophants leapt from the page as if they had been frozen in marble halls all this time waiting for me to thaw them.

Steerpike is 17 when the first novel begins, as was I when I read it. Titus Groan is 17 when the second book reaches its terrifying climax. Gormenghast's labyrinthine corridors, alcoves and passageways expanded chapter by chapter. Peake's seemingly inexhaustible panorama stretched endlessly, defying human scale or perspective. The Cambridge that I wandered rapidly took on the aspect of Gormenghast's masonry and plaster. It was easy to imagine the narrow winding contours of St Edward's Passage or any of the bookshop-lined lanes mapped out as micro sections of Peake's cartography. I skirted the edifice of the ancient seats of learning much in the way that Gormenghast's artisans did as they awaited their entry into the Hall of the Bright Carvings. On days when Cambridge offered only a filthy Fenland sky and an unforgiving March wind, I huddled further into the book for comfort. The college cloisters, with their sun-denying tributaries of coarse stone, became inseparable from Gormenghast's imagined ones. Every architrave, balustrade, cornice or ivy-choked escarpment took on the characteristics of Peake's densely detailed otherworld. The Round Church on Bridge Street, the stone sundial in the Great Court at Trinity, and all the impedimenta of courtyards I not so much gatecrashed as gate-ghosted became indistinguishable from the crags, flagstones and rooftops of Mervyn Peake's story cycle.

The Titus trilogy began to shape my musical world too. *Moonchild* by King Crimson ceased to be a lengthy indulgence on their debut album and was newly populated by Peake's uniquely sculpted stage sets. Pete Sinfield's *Moonchild* could have been Fuchsia gazing out from the ivy-clad window of her secret attic, or absently dropping circle stones on a sundial as she walked and wondered. Robert Fripp's opening guitar cascade sounded like banners unfurling, a ceremonial for one of Titus Groan's baffling inductions.

Late in the year, around the time I was finishing the third book in the trilogy, *Titus Alone*, Charisma Records released the Bo Hansson album *Music Inspired by The Lord of the Rings*. I heard a few tracks on *Sounds of the Seventies* on Radio One and got Danny to play it in Kerry's. I mentally appropriated Hansson's Moog, guitar and keyboard sketches from Middle Earth and relocated them to Gormenghast, a setting to which they seemed eminently more suited. Hansson's LP honoured its literary inspiration with titles like *Flight to the Ford*, *The Battle of the Pelennor Fields* and *The Scouring of the Shire*. In my mind they transmogrified into *The Stone Lanes*, *A Field of Flagstones*, *By Gormenghast Lake*. I similarly reallocated *A Beard of Stars* by Tyrannosaurus Rex. That chainmail and Pixiphone sound suddenly seemed more comfortable in its new surroundings, as did numerous other records by the likes of High Tide, Curved Air, Egg and

Principal Edwards Magic Theatre. Anything that evoked a sense of the processional or suggested arcane ritual was cast anew in Peake World. *The Narrow Way* on Pink Floyd's *Umma Gumma* I reimagined entirely as choreography for some ancient Gormenghast ballet.

My Cambridge days were determined by whichever route I took into town. If my lift came in via the A428 I walked past Magdalene College, browsed in my favourite bookshop on Magdalene Street (called The Bookshop), then turned right at the Round Church and headed on down past St John's and Trinity into town. If I was brought in by the B roads via Bourn, Toft and Comberton, and the weather was agreeable, then more often than not I'd get my driver to drop me at Grantchester, walk past the thatched cottages in the high street and down to the Meadows. The churchyard and Old Rectory could have been any churchyard or Rectory and held no historical relevance to me. I wasn't yet acquainted with the poetry of Rupert Brooke and knew nothing of clocks stopped at ten to three and honey for tea. My destination though I was intimately familiar with. Thanks to Roger Waters' drowsy acoustic strum on *Umma Gumma* I inhabited Grantchester Meadows as mythical terrain well before I ever trod those lush riverside pastures.

In 1972 I started going there regularly, sometimes arriving early enough on spring mornings for the dew to still be glistening on the grass. It was a magical dream place. The languid Cam would glide silently through the low-banked meadows and the only sound came from the birdlife. By the end of the decade the M11 extension ran across the middle of the Meadows, and what I'm describing now is no longer possible to experience. There is always somewhere the distant rumble of traffic, but at that time Arcady was still unspoiled. One morning I sat self-consciously under a tree and read *Alice's Adventures in Wonderland* in its entirety, fully aware that I was sitting in Grantchester Meadows reading Lewis Carroll and playing the part of a me that now did that sort of thing. I hadn't read the Alice books as a child. I never read anything like that as a child and had only started taking serious books seriously when forced to by the onset of O Levels. Now at 17 I could suddenly see why *Alice* had been so readily adopted as a psychedelic text. To a seasoned tripper those erratic jump cuts, dream tumbles and nightmarish interludes made perfect sense.

The other integral Pink Floyd connection with the psychogeography of Cambridge was of course Syd Barrett. Syd's lingering presence cast a huge spectral shadow. Like many people at that time I still assumed he would make a third solo LP. He'd said as much in a Melody Maker interview with Michael Watts in 1971. "It should be 12 singles, and jolly good singles," he'd said, below that photo of him with short-cropped hair, a hesitant smile and expressive hand gestures. By the time I saw him at the Corn Exchange the hair had grown out and he'd acquired a straggly excuse of a beard. The eyes though told of a more invasive presence, a haunting. But I no more suspected that his recording career was already over than I could conceive that *Pink Moon* would be Nick Drake's final LP.

It was impossible to go about Cambridge without meeting someone who knew Syd, had seen him out and about, had been at school with him, or had taught him on his Foundation Course at Tech college. I ventured up Hills Road one day, tiptoed across the gravelled front yard of Number 183 and peered through what I assumed to be the front-room window. One of his paintings, a black-and-white abstract hung from the wall above an armchair. I took a leaf from the front hedge and kept it in a stylus box for years. I didn't know at that time whether he was still residing there or not. "I've been at home in Cambridge with my mother," he'd said in that Melody Maker interview. "I've been getting used to a family existence generally. Pretty unexciting." One evening I phoned the house from the call box at the bottom of my road – the number was in the local directory.

"He's in London doing his music," said Winifred, his mother.

Later that summer John Steele and Lawrence Himelfield started the Syd Barrett Appreciation Society. I was one of the earliest members: Number 15, it says on my membership card. At John Steele's invitation, and while the details were still fresh in my head, I wrote a short review of the Corn Exchange Stars gig, which was subsequently printed in Edition 2 of the SBAS magazine Terrapin. The review was a starry-eyed but faithful account of the occasion and contained an accurate recollection of the set list they played that night, details which have been repeated in many Barrett articles since (sometimes duly credited, mostly not). I feel like the W.C. Handy of Syd world. My one brief encounter with faded magic was endlessly regurgitated and mythologised as if it were the source of the Delta blues, when in fact it was just another gig at the time, one that I assumed would spawn a return to active creativity, not hasten a full-time retreat.

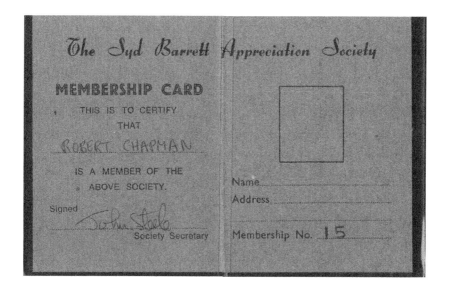

John Steele informed me there had been an interview with Syd printed in Rolling Stone magazine at the end of 1971. Learning of this I did what any obsessive would do. I hitchhiked up to London, walked into Rolling Stone's UK office on the second floor of a building in Newman Street off Oxford Street, and offered to buy a copy. Two beautifully aloof office girls looked at me with practiced disdain and directed me to a stack of back issues on the floor. "Which issue is it in?" one of them asked. "Do you know?" Flustered by their model good looks and their studied indifference I spluttered: "December 1972 I think." "Oh, next Christmas then?" one of them said dryly. I responded to this with the kind of cosmic repartee which had served me so well with Cindy the previous summer that she traded me in for a gas fitter. I said something along the lines of "I'm a year ahead of my time," or some such bollocks. Both looked at me with the pity and contempt my utterance deserved. I paid them my 20p and faded gratefully from their lives.

I became obsessed with that Rolling Stone interview, the last and in many ways the most poetic and perplexing that Syd ever gave. In the absence of a third LP with its jolly good singles, or news of gigs, or any kind of game plan at all, I inhabited that interview as if it were my own life. The feature carried no byline, and it was several years before I learned that Syd's guests that afternoon were Mick and Sheila Rock, and that it was Mick who conducted the interview. Every utterance seemed to trail off into the mist. "I'm disappearing. Treading the backward path." "I'm full of dust and guitars." He walks a lot. "Eight miles a day. It's bound to show but I don't know how." *The Madcap Laughs* was "like a painting as a big as the cellar".

There he was in all his diminishing glory, semi-detached, hiding his wings in a ghost tower, still being impossibly enigmatic. I started quoting the interview just for fun. It became a parlour game I played with myself, seeing how many of Syd's non-sequiturs and asides I could sneak into conversation, trailing off into mystery and ellipses for my own amusement, just to hear what the words sounded like tripping from my own lips. It always spoiled the fun when someone completed the sentence for me or took it as a cue for actual conversation. Like Syd I walked a lot each day. Not always eight miles but with all the hitchhiking and never having any money for bus fares my beat-up purple-and-white pumps soon became weather-beaten and mud-spattered. Like Syd I felt that I too was disappearing, treading the backward path. I was certainly becoming far more insular and introspective than might be expected of an otherwise garrulous and piss-taking 17-year-old. Every morning when I left my house I too, to all intents and purposes, vanished off the radar. I could have been anywhere, and in my head often was.

I'd lost touch with most of my schoolfriends the minute I walked out through the gates on the very last day of the final term. I bumped into a few at summer parties, where everyone was already acting out an impression of who they wanted to be next. At one such party that August, Brendan Brotherson, the public-school drop-out who had lent me his City Lights First Edition of Allen Ginsberg's *Howl*, greeted me like a long-lost stranger and shook my hand warmly. "This is what I do now. I shake your hand," he said. "We must never lose touch," he added mistily, as if we were all much older already and bonded in a different way now we were no longer schoolkids.

I wandered over to Sue Gillespie who I had shared a classroom with for five years and who was now sitting cross-legged, in rapt attentiveness as some older guy charmed her with the tried-and-trusted hippie ploy of not speaking while smiling meaningfully. I'd spotted Sue when I first arrived, either reading his palm or playing this little piggy. It was hard to tell. She affected not to notice me.
– Hi Sue.
She lazily lifts her head. The learning to look stoned look.
– Oh, I know you, don't I?

Yeah. I sat in the same classroom as you until a few weeks ago.

At that same party was Mickey Stephens, a kid in the year below me at school who had supplied me with my first joint, or rather me and a classmate had taxed him for one of the two joints we caught him rolling when we made a bogus trip to the sick bay a few weeks before the end of that last summer term. At the party he was full-on tripping, crashing in and out of rooms, keen to expound on his lysergic visions. A couple of us steered him into the garden just to give the furniture a rest. He proclaimed that the sky was a bag full of Bassetts, spelling out letters in liquorice allsorts shapes. We gazed up at the heavens but none of us could see what Mickey saw.

Lunky Lucas, one of the sixth-formers from school, went lunking by, cradling a small barrel of Watneys under his arm. We distracted Mickey from his alphabet sky sufficiently long enough to explain what a wanker Lucas was, indeed, what wankers all sixth-formers were. The antagonism and enmity already seemed anachronistic, residual concerns from long ago. "Plastic hippie," dribbled Mickey. "Big pseud." "Hype" we chorus. We told him that we fifth-formers always looked down on the Lower Sixth with their sewn-in flares and their pseudo-hippie headbands on hair that was barely long enough to sport the look. Mickey snapped out of his dream daze in an instant. "That's what we thought of you too," he said, meaning us fifth formers. The inalienable right of every micro-tribe to hate its predecessors. The generation gap that plays out within generations, not between them. Mickey tells us two of the fourth years had already taken heroin and were thinking of heading for an Indian ashram the minute they could leave school. "Which two?" we ask.
– Spooky Tooth.
– Spooky Tooth?
– Yeah, look. Spooky Tooth in the sky. Sitting on a sofa.

We couldn't see them but Mickey could.

That party was like the night of the teenage replicas. Everyone throwing shapes and shedding skins. All of us in transition. Shaking off vestiges. Wearing this season's new disguises. Trying to be someone better, someone new. Achingly self-conscious one minute, full of the exuberance of youth the next. I was no different to anybody else. We were all fumbling and stumbling towards our future selves. Later, sitting on the stairs with Dickie Dangerfield I said: "I need a crash pad for the night." I heard myself say it. I'd learned "crash pad" from the manual. Dickie already spoke fluent hippie and corrected me. "You don't have to say 'pad'. Just say 'I'm looking for somewhere to crash'." Yeah, that's deep. Some-Where-To-Crash. Cindy's friend Clare is suddenly there on the stairs. A little mouth with claws on. Well I despair. She tries to explain to me in simple tongue that it wasn't personal and that Cindy's going to marry her gas-fitter next year and you do understand don't you Rob?

All this disappears into memory mist. The playing-field of life levels out the minute you leave school. Suddenly all that teacher's pet, first prize on speech day, good at games, got his school colours shit doesn't mean a thing anymore. One or two of my former classmates came into Kerry's when Danny first worked there. Briefly it became a convenient meet-up spot as word got around. This one off to the oil rigs. That one working on building sites. None of them as far as I could see was enjoying the superior employment opportunities a Grammar-school education was supposed to bring to us working-class kids. Someone told me that our old classmate Chris Tozer was working at a garage in Shillington. Chris was the kid who had turned us all on to Monty Python, coming into school on Monday mornings acting out these surreal sketches from a show I'd never watched, having spotted it in the TV schedules and assuming it was about an actual circus.

Within three weeks of Chris going on about Arthur "Two Sheds" Jackson and Flying Sheep we were all watching it. I fancied seeing Chris again, so one fog-bound day in February I sacrificed the warmth of the County Library and the Fen-dampened Spires of Cambridge and walked eight miles from Sandy to Shillington. There was only one garage in the village and there was Chris in a blue boiler-suit putting nozzles into petrol tanks. He looked up from the car he was filling and peered at the bedraggled apparition in a blue duffel coat emerging from the late morning gloom. His face registered nothing and it took him a moment to recognise me. The conversation was brief. He said the least. Lindisfarne's *Fog on the Tyne* LP hadn't been out long and he'd bought it.

– Well you've got to, haven't you?

He kept saying that. And "Can't be bad." And "That's how it goes." The small talk got even smaller in the Bedfordshire mist until finally he said: "Well I've got to go for my dinner now." He stepped out of his boiler-suit, hopped on a pushbike and pedalled off home, leaving me standing there on a deserted lunchtime forecourt. I turned and walked eight miles back to civilisation. That's how it goes. And got.

Although Mick Rock's Rolling Stone interview with Syd appeared in the December 23rd issue, I always assumed it took place in the autumn. There is a reference to the day being warm, but the whole vibe of the piece seems imbued with the sadness of reflection, as if there is a post-summer chill in the air. Syd sounds hesitant, unfulfilled, seemingly aware that his life was on hold. I related to that aspect very much. The bit that intrigued me most of all though was when he shows Mick Rock a folder "with all his recorded songs to date. Neatly typed with no music". "I'll show you a book of all my songs before you go. I think it's so exciting," he says to Rock. That single paragraph inspired me to get my own writing organised. I owe the initial wellspring of my creativity entirely to that folder of Syd's. It wasn't even the writing down of words that appealed. It was putting them in a folder. I'd habitually been scribbling stuff down while on LSD trips, and then discarding it the moment the acid wore off. I wish I'd kept them all now, no matter how babbling and nonsensical they were. They would tell me something about myself at that age, my sensibility, my ability or otherwise to make words sing or dance. All of my subsequent songs, poems and sketches arise from that initial impulse to do what Syd was doing, to write enough words to fill a folder.

I still have that original folder. It's sitting here beside me as I type. A black A4 WH Smith's binder. It has a faded Flaming Star sticker on the front cover – John Steele's Stoke-based band. John was always offering to send me cassettes of their stuff, but I didn't have a cassette machine to play them on. I still have a letter from John, inviting me up to Stoke for a weekend. We never got around to it and John, to all intents and purposes, has disappeared off the face of the earth – untraceable even in this age of media surveillance. People do that. They do just disappear.

Syd Barrett managed it for the next several years. In the public eye he was gradually reduced to the sum total of our sightings, rumours and myths. "He's in London doing his music," said his Mum. If only. Syd became my invisible muse, absent from daily life, but instantly vibrant and alive on the records, describing his painting as big as the cellar. Wrapped in yellow towelling in that sparse Earls Court room with only a naked woman and a vase for company on the cover of the *Madcap Laughs* LP. A perfect depiction of the sparse intimacy of that album. Those two Barrett solo LPs didn't strike me as being weird at all. I absorbed the jump cuts and lyrical detours intuitively. They were the contours and crazy paving of acid itself. Their momentum choreographed many of my own early trips. They influenced all of my early writing.

As the weather got warmer and the cricket season got under way I used to wander across Parker's Piece and down Mill Road to Fenner's where I'd watch the cream of Cambridge University play what were invariably second-string sides from the County Championship. Fenner's had a splendidly ramshackle old wooden pavilion which was pulled down later that same summer. The crowds were thin to non-existent. I'd sit on the grass and watch play until lunch and then head back into town. My hair was shoulder-length by then and corkscrewed wildly in wet weather. One day, arriving at Fenner's before the start of play, I walked by the area set aside for net practice. A group of players were lazing languidly as only Cambridge undergraduates can. One of them wolf-whistled at me and emitted a shrill giggle, pleased with his scathingly satirical interjection. I turned to look at the gathering in their cricket whites. The perpetrator was club captain Majid Jahangir Khan, Emmanuel, Aitchison College, Lahore and Punjab University. He made his Test Match debut for his country the following year.

One morning my lift dropped me at the end of Madingley Road, and busting for a piss, I went into the small public lavatory on the corner of Northampton Street opposite the Chop House. There was an old guy lurking furtively by the two urinals so I went into the cubicle. When I came out he was still there and turned to greet me. He had a certain Julian Orchard look about him, or a Dick Emery comedy vicar perhaps. He smiled and uttered a tentative proposal. "Ten bob?" he said in a tremulous hopeful voice. I was being offered 50 new pence, presumably for services to be received or rendered, but we never got that far in negotiations. I was outraged. Ten Bob? TEN BOB, for my slender, supple, soap-scented, musk-dabbed young body? I went outside, sat on the roadside bench in the bright morning sunshine and pondered how I was going to spend my day. My would-be client emerged from the lavatory a few minutes later, got on an ancient bicycle and pedalled off in disappointment. As he passed he flashed a wolfish grin. In broad daylight more Cardew Robinson than Julian Orchard perhaps.

All I Want is Out of Here

Chapter 4

CURIOUS MUSICIANS WANTED FOR STRANGE BAND

It began with a Kellogg's Rice Crispies box in April 1964 and the chance to win one of 80 Burns Electric Guitars. All you had to do was fill in a spot-the-changes competition on the back of the box, send off your entry and wait. "Every entrant, win or lose, receives a signed photograph of that great new pop-music group The Ramblers," it said on the box. Despite the enticement of a signed photo of an unknown beat group, I doubt if I even entered the competition. The very thought of owning an electric guitar was beyond my comprehension. The allure however was immense.

All the groups I saw on TV played instruments that looked bright and shiny; even in monochrome they seemed to sparkle as they reflected the studio lights. Guitars were held high and almost everybody smiled. The drummer, unless he was called Dave Clark, sat at the back, elevated on a drum riser, and the rim casing on the kit sparkled too. The big bass drum usually bore the name of the band, and the camera would often catch the drummer mouthing the words of the song, keen to join in and not feel left out, being at the back like that. This was how groups presented themselves. TV smart and TV tidy. And TV was where I saw all my groups. I couldn't imagine how they lived or what they did when they weren't on the telly. Even later on when I saw photos of beat groups

goofing about or posing moodily for music-paper pics I couldn't imagine
them shopping, or standing on the terraces at a football match. I couldn't
ever envisage seeing a pop star in the street. Instead, they existed, as
Marshall McLuhan said of youth's engagement with the new electronic
media, "mythically and in depth".

It was probably because I engaged mythically and with as much depth as
I could summon, that I felt like there might be a place for me in this pop
life, a part of it I could join in with. Which is why at nine or ten I started
writing songs. I stopped again soon afterwards when the novelty wore
off. The songs weren't any good. Of course they weren't. I was at Junior
school, but I can still remember a few fragments and they remind me now
of where I was coming from then, this pop-mad kid who deliberately got
thrown out of Cubs just so he could run home and watch a programme
about Merseybeat on his telly. The first song I wrote was called *Over the
Ocean*. I think it had three verses, but I can only remember the opening
lines of the first one, which went:

Over the ocean
And over the sea
There, there is my love
For no one to see

It shows what I was capable of at that age, i.e. not very much. The first
two lines are tautological and reflect the ubiquity of sea shanties and
My Bonnie Lies over the Ocean. "There, there is my love" has the clumsy
scansion of a novice, although it's not significantly clumsier than some of
the sore-thumb lines in *Ferry Cross the Mersey* or *Don't Let the Sun Catch
You Crying*, both of which may well have influenced the song. That last
line "For no one to see" speaks volumes about a small boy's pre-natural
yearning for romantic love. One day I'll have a girlfriend, you'll see, and
she'll be out of reach to you. *Over the Ocean* disappeared into the dusty

recesses of memory for years, until one day in the eighties I heard Ricky Nelson's 1964 release *For You* on the radio and realised where I'd taken the melody line from, and possibly the lyrical inspiration too. The chorus of *For You* began "Over the highway and over the street", and there we have it. It seems that I was doing what all songwriters do when they start off, I was copying. The fact that my effort was callow and mediocre is irrelevant. I was doing it, that's the main thing.

With my second composition I opted for simplicity. Consciously aping the I-IV-V chord progression of surf music I wrote a song called *Twisting and a Rocking and a Shouting* and it went like this:

> Twisting and a rocking and a shouting all day
> And we'll keep that same big way
> Twisting and a rocking and a shouting all day
> And we'll keep that same big way
> Twisting and a rocking
> Rocking and a shouting
> And we'll keep that same big way

At this point there was an instrumental drum break identical to the one in The Ventures' *Walk Don't Run*, which was also a major influence on the tune and tempo. For the second and third verses of the song I simply repeated the lyrics of the first verse. Although economical with its sentiments the song did incorporate three of the major interests in my life at that age, namely twisting, rocking and shouting.

There was a bit of a gap before I came up with my next effort. Hugely influenced by Freddie and the Dreamers' 1966 cover of the Royal Teens' *Who Wears Short Shorts* and set to the tune of Frank Ifield's *Lovesick Blues*, the third song in my pre-teen trilogy was called *I Got the Belly Ache* and the lyric in its entirety went:

I got the belly elly elly elly aye aye ache

I sang this line endlessly, straining the patience of my mother and the endurance of several friendships to the limit. I sang it when I went to the corner shop. I sang it while trainspotting with my mates. I sang it as I played football and while aimlessly wandering the streets. I sang it with a hint of Frank Ifield's yodel in the inflection and with an increasingly hysterical cadence until older boys started hitting me. I always liked novelty records as a kid (all records were novel in a way), and there is no way I would wish to talk up a hip past for myself knowing full well that at ten I loved the Barron Knights as much as I loved any group.

During this period, me and the other kids in my street formed a band. In honour of the cul de sac in which we lived it was called The Spring Grove Trio. The fact that there were seven of us in the group leads me to suspect that none of us knew what the word "trio" meant. We played instruments so rudimentary and makeshift they made Skiffle sound hi-tech. Our armoury of sound comprised a couple of plastic Chad Valley guitars (permanently detuned) and an assortment of table-tennis bats with elastic bands attached. The drummer played a biscuit tin. I've no idea what our repertoire contained. I suspect we just did lots of shouting (an' a twisting' an' a rockin').

It was possibly the prominence of the biscuit tin that led to our demise when Mrs Lindley at Number 22 came out one morning, seized our prize asset and refused to hand it back. The band broke up after that and we returned to more primal musical impulses, like clapping our hands at the side of our heads while cocking a leg and singing *Little Red Rooster*, like the vocalist in the Barron Knights did. Flexing our puny torsos and singing the melody of *Wheels Cha-Cha* while imitating Mr Muscles off *Opportunity Knocks* was another huge favourite.

My song-writing went into limbo for several years once I left Junior school. Pop however continued to dominate my fantasy life. I dreamed far more about being in a band than I ever did of scoring the winning goal in the Cup Final or hitting a six in a Test Match. I loved sport as a kid and played and watched it all the time but it didn't spawn its own myth life – not like it did for some people. Nor was I much of one for "air guitar" (as it wasn't called then). I suppose I must have stood around at some point with a broom or a cricket bat and pretended I was Eric Clapton or Jeff Beck, but I have no lasting memory of the stance. My myth life took hold in other ways. I thought up imaginary bands with imaginary line-ups, drawn from existing groups of the day. I was far more inclined towards that kind of dream life than anything involving the phallic thrust of an imaginary guitar.

By the fourth year of Grammar School my song-writing had moved on to its next conceptual stage. I started to imagine the songs rather than write them. My magnum opus was the double A-sided single *Captain Fahrenheit/ Nova Scotia* which I conjured up in 1969. I imagined *Captain Fahrenheit* as a work of *Good Vibrations/Heroes and Villains* scope and complexity, with a back story involving numerous fragments painstakingly pieced together from a multitude of studio takes.

Nova Scotia was largely instrumental except for a brief choral interlude in the middle. Imagine a more abstract and extended version of The Beatles' *Flying*. In interviews with imaginary pop papers (conducted while simultaneously doing my paper round), I would elaborate at great length on my inspiration for both pieces. I'd tell the journalist that I'd recently spent several hours airborne, flying over Nova Scotia. I had no idea what Nova Scotia actually looked like. I'd never flown in a plane at that point either. I just liked the sound of the words. Nova Scotia also inspired an imaginary promotional film where the clouds changed colour with the aid of a filtered lens (again very *Magical Mystery Tour*, even though like most people I'd only ever seen the film in black and white). I would describe the processes behind the promotional film in great detail to an imaginary journalist from Melody Maker as he hung on to my every word while helping me deliver papers.

Apart from titles, the only other thing these unwritten songs had was timings. Timings were very important. *Captain Fahrenheit* was three minutes 54 seconds, *Nova Scotia* more in the region of five minutes 25 seconds with a long, slow fade. Timings gave the songs shape and structure. I could picture them all printed on the record sleeve. I would write lists of these songs in a rough book and admire the matrix.

For a thankfully brief period during the summer of 1968 I was heavily influenced by the flower-child aura of Donovan's *Gift from a Flower to a Garden* LP. Again, without having heard much of the record itself, I constructed an idea of what it sounded like from the titles alone. From this highly derivative period came an approximation of a song called *Jack and the Cows* (2.52). I devised that one while going for bored Sunday-evening walks. I'd wander through the wet willow meadows thinking drippy bucolic thoughts, pausing only to feed stringy weeds to the cows that came up to the fence to snort hot breath at me.

One imaginary song was called *Peculiar* (7.33). Another was called *We've Got an I on You* (4.20), which was heavily influenced by a Soft Machine song I'd heard on their 1967 John Peel session called *We Know What You Mean*. At 13, *We Know What You Mean* (*We Understand*) spoke to me of some weird new world I wanted to be involved in, to go where this group went, to understand what they understood. I heard *We Know What You Mean* again for only the second time in the autumn of 1971 when BYG put out those Rock Generation LPs with the earliest Softs recordings on them. By this time, *We Know You Mean* no longer sounded weird at all. It sounded like a nifty little pop tune. That's the difference between 13 and 17. At 13 my perception of weirdness was built around what I didn't know. By 17 I had a foothold in the terrain.

A lot of these songs came to me during the bored listless hours I spent alone. I'd think them up on my paper round. I'd think them up during detention at school, or while doing the numerous school holiday jobs I undertook to earn a little money. Sweltering in the relentless hot sun I dreamed up entire albums of make-believe songs while picking runner beans or carrots. During the school summer holiday of 1970, I sang an entire reggae arrangement of Billy J. Kramer's *Do You Want to Know a Secret* to myself complete with off-beat augmentation. It sounded utterly plausible and authentic and I'm still surprised that no one attempted a similar arrangement at the time, given that there were reggae versions of virtually everything else.

I did write an actual song during this period, although it was something of a one-off venture. Encouraged by those small ads in the back of the newspapers that invited you to send in your lyrics and have them set to music for a small fee, I composed a lovelorn ditty called *December Eyes*. I approached the task as if it were a school project, writing a song to see if I could actually write a song. I sent it in and received an immediate enthusiastic response. The reply, typed on company headed notepaper, stated that *December Eyes* would probably benefit from a country arrangement, and on receipt of my fee they would get down to the task immediately. I wrote back to inform them that in my opinion it suited a more bluesy ballad arrangement, something in the style of Fleetwood Mac's *Need Your Love So Bad* perhaps. Again, a response came back fairly rapidly stating that on reflection they agreed with my assessment and would adhere to my wishes promptly, providing I sent them some money.

By now I was growing less confident about the venture and it only took one brief conversation with Dad, where he explained the realities of vanity publishing and the dubious practices of fly-by-night operators, for me to quietly consign *December Eyes* and its country blues ballad possibilities to the bin.

My brief flirtation with blues arrangements also yielded a fragment of a song which I sang in my head to the tune of Chicken Shack's *I'd Rather Go Blind*. It went:
It would mean a lot to me/if you were to say to me/that you loved me.

It had a pleasing cadence and I envisaged it developing in triplet form. I sang it to my schoolmates while we were serving a detention period under the reception-hall stairs, clearing a small stockroom of outdated science books. "That's quite good," they pronounced and I promptly pursued the matter no further. It was an idea in search of a song, a mere impulse, but by my mid-teens these impulses, like nocturnal emissions, were becoming more regular.

By the time I reached 17, the era of the singer-songwriter was in full flow. Lyrics had to be about expressing yourself, chiefly your inner thoughts and feelings. This was problematic to me for several reasons. Uppermost among these was the fact that I didn't feel I had much of a self to express – or rather, among the multiplicity of selves I was trying on for size, I had no idea which of these might be most suited to further articulation. At school, Brendan Brotherson had filled copious notebooks with expressive scribblings about his feelings and what it was like to lay on your bed watching the car lights as they traced patterns on the ceiling. I gave that a go but it wasn't really me. All it did was emphasise how unexceptional my everyday observations were. Dickie Dangerfield lent me his copy of Al Stewart's *Love Chronicles* LP with its 18-minute title track about love's first stirrings and what it was like to get your end away. It went on for approximately a thousand verses and seemed self-regarding to a degree that I simply couldn't stomach. All I wanted to do at 17 was get out of myself, not further inside. I wanted to project otherness in a way that dissolved ego rather than reinforced it in a series of solipsistic lyrics about failed romantic encounters.

All those songs without words that I came up with in my mid-teens were essentially projections of a dream self, perhaps the only self I truly felt comfortable with at the time. By the time I started to write actual songs or approximation of songs, I still had little clear idea of what to do with whatever meagre talents I had at my disposal. What I did have frequently at my disposal was LSD, and that was the catalyst that got me writing. Those first meandering doodles on a scroll of paper at Danny's flat became a compulsion to get something down every time I tripped. At the time that was the only way I knew how articulate my sense of disengagement. Acid basically invented the writerly me. It helped me locate a voice, a lyrical other. Almost all the early stuff I wrote was written on acid. Much of it was drivel, but it would probably have been drivel anyway with or without the acid. Surprisingly, leafing through those early efforts now, the ones that I kept, I notice that an encouraging amount of it isn't drivel. It has momentum and drive. There are zig-zag detours and jump cuts but they all seem to make sense. There's a burgeoning lyricism there, a flow.

There is something very pure about those initial responses to LSD that you never quite find again once the inscape becomes more familiar. Without inhibitory filters or intellectual baggage, the stuff that poured out of me on those early trips was akin to a cleansing of the soul, an uncluttering. For some reason my thought-patterns on acid encouraged me to think in triplets rather than the tum-te-tum of quatrains. I fell easily into irregular metre, but the irregularity generally had a discipline to it. The songs galloped along with a pace and cadence influenced almost entirely by Syd Barrett. The words cascaded out of me on trips, they developed their own internal melodies and often came with dying falls and codas. I developed an instinctive understanding of assonance and internal rhyme (again entirely Syd's doing). I look at the best of these early efforts now and wonder why I didn't do more with them. That Rolling Stone interview was the inspiration behind me keeping the best of my efforts. I'd write them up neatly the day after my cosmic voyaging, hole-punch them and file them in that black folder.

It was a selection from this slim folder of songs and poetic fragments that I took to the Fisher House jam session shortly after I'd met Jack Monck and Jenny Spires, and it was those same neatly black or blue biro'd pages that I carried with me when I was invited out to their house in the village of Gravely in South Cambridgeshire, about 15 miles from where I lived. By then I'd also met a drummer called Dave, who like Jack had also seen my ad in Red House Records. Dave had been involved with a mixed-media theatre troupe called Welfare State down in the West Country, and had played with Mike Westbrook's band on a piece called *Earthrise*. By the time I met Dave he was domiciled in Bedfordshire with his girlfriend Jill. His drums were in storage in a huge cellar beneath the flat he and Jill shared in the village of Shefford. We met up several times at that flat, drinking endless cups of tea and passing dull drizzly afternoons playing records and talking about what we'd do once we'd got our band together. It took a bit of planning and a few false starts but one evening in early April we drove over to Jack and Jenny's. In my head Dave was going to replace Twink, we'd find a guitarist to replace Syd and we'd carry on as Stars. It didn't quite work out like that.

Jack and Jenny's cottage was bliss. As soon as I walked in the door I immediately incorporated its domestic ambience into my mythological communal idyll. Our rendezvous seemed predestined, full of portents and creative possibilities. I was momentarily convinced that this venture would be all that my Gong liaison could have been. There were herbs in storage jars in the kitchen including an ample vessel of home-grown grass. Jack and Jenny were accommodating hosts. "Tea and cakes arrived," as they did in Syd's Rolling Stone interview. Jack reached for an acoustic guitar. I got out my sheets of paper and it went downhill from there. Perhaps starting with a song full of irregular rhythms wasn't the best idea, but that's what I did. The song was called *Kissing Fish* at the time and was directly inspired by the slow-motion ellipsis of Syd's *Terrapin*. The same song has been through a few name-changes over the years. At one point it was called *Pisces*. At the moment it's called *At Swim Two Birds* and I've still never got around to doing anything with it. The words have been tweaked and improved upon over the years, but still remain largely faithful to the tempo and scansion of that first draft. The first verse goes (and went):

> Make a wish of this amiss is this/told bliss desist in tryst
> unmissed/ a splish of kissing fish persist/a spray of days delay/
> and scented anyway/ you say the things that come what may

Try arranging that when you haven't settled on a melody yet and you're equally uncertain how to tackle metric irregularity. Try singing it when you've never sung outside of a junior-school choir, never collaborated with professional musicians in intimate communal circumstances, don't have the faintest idea about the painstaking mechanics of constructing a song out of fragments, and haven't a clue as yet about how to make your inner voice your outer voice.

After a few lacklustre attempts from me, Jenny seized the initiative. She had a really good singing voice, effortlessly lilting and pure. A few of the tongue-twisting lyrical complexities were smoothed out as *Kissing Fish* eased into regular metre. I retired to the sofa and watched Jack and Jenny doing something I had never done before, i.e. explore the possibilities of raw material. They already knew something that hadn't yet occurred to me at all, that the lyrics were just a starting-point. Up until that moment I'd only seen them as static words on a page, set in stone almost. "What do you think?" asked someone. "It used to be my song," I said with a tad more self-pity than was necessary. It was the small inadequate voice of a novice, an absolute beginner way out of his depth.

Once the song was dispensed with, the main purpose of the evening subsided into small talk and pleasantries. The men had a smoke and the women went into the kitchen and talked about whatever women in their mid-20s talked about and 17-year-olds have no notion of. In the car going home Jill asked if we'd heard of someone called Kevin Ayers. She mentioned something about a daughter called Rachel, who had come up in conversation with Jenny. By this point I was so despondent about how the evening had gone that I didn't take the conversational bait and couldn't be bothered to pursue this tantalising titbit.

Yeah, I'd heard of Kevin Ayers. So had drummer Dave. In fact, I'd just lent him my copy of *Soft Machine I*. "You're going to have to learn to play an instrument, Rob," said Dave with some finality as the car pulled up at the A1 traffic lights in Sandy and I got out. That was pretty much the last I saw of Dave and Jill, apart from one final journey over to Shefford a few weeks later to retrieve my Soft Machine album. My pristine copy of *Soft Machine 1*, the one with the pin-wheel sleeve purchased from the newly opened Virgin Records in Oxford Street. In the interim period Dave had taken it down to Devon where it looked like the entire hippie population of the county had idiot-danced on it in hobnail boots. He returned it to me in a condition that record dealers would grade as "scratched to fuck".

I was going to have to learn to play an instrument. Those words utterly deflated me. How was I going to do that with the limited funds at my disposal? I'd been scouring the back pages of Melody Maker ever since I started reading it, window-shopping those display ads for instruments I'd never be able to afford. Here are some typical prices from the Melody Maker of May 13th 1972, the period when I was trying and failing to form a band: Second Hand Fender Stratocaster £145. Gibson SG Special £150 (HP terms available, £23 deposit). Gibson EB3 (immaculate, incredible action) £155 ono. New Fender Strats cost anywhere from £200 upwards. Even a decent Les Paul copy would set you back £70. Where was I going to find anything like that amount of money? Just to put that into perspective, a year earlier I was bringing home £1.25 a week in paper-round money. Now I had no visible income at all. My Dad, a skilled engineer, a toolmaker, was on £30 a week.

There was also the small matter of me being left-handed. As with so much else in life it was naturally assumed that most guitarists were right-handed. All the Melody Maker ads were for right-handed models "unless otherwise stated". There should have been a musical-instrument shop specifically geared towards left-handed people called Unless Otherwise Stated. Big posters of Paul McCartney and Jimi Hendrix in the window. Then there were all the accoutrements and accessories that went with buying the instrument: amp, effects pedal, guitar strings and the rest of it. There was also the not insignificant factor that to a beginner, musical-instrument shops in those days were fairly intimidating places.

On a day trip to London, me and Dickie Dangerfield headed for the Charing Cross Road and walked into one of the most prominent of those Melody Maker display-ad emporiums. "I see the schools have broken up for half-term," sneered the guy behind the counter as we gazed in wonder at the unaffordable bounty on display. His mate did a little scoff laugh and went on attending to a customer. As well as the alienating atmosphere, those painful few minutes in the shop were also memorable for the fact that a guy was actually hunched over an instrument picking out the first few bars of *Stairway to Heaven*. This has since become a guitar-shop cliché, but *Led Zeppelin IV* had only recently been released, and I like to feel that we were in at the birth of the phenomenon. As we departed the shop our humiliation and contempt for muso wankers was soothed considerably by the sight of an elegant woman, long of leg, dishevelled of deportment, clambering inelegantly out of the passenger seat of an E Type Jag while wearing no underwear.

Undeterred by the Charing Cross Road episode I was still intent on forming a band. The trouble was, I had a much clearer idea of what I was against, than what I was for. I had few tribal loyalties as such, merely a handful of useful prejudices, born out of adolescent recalcitrance and honed in the antagonistic milieu of a mediocre English Grammar school. Danny, Dickie and I set ourselves against everything the sixth-formers stood for. They were the personification of hype. I remember one of the few times I ever let one of them cross the threshold of my house. I used to walk the short walk home from the school bus dropping-off point with a guy called Nick who lived nearby. "Do you take Melody Maker?" he asked one evening, rather as one might say, "Do you take drugs?" (Although he never asked me that because he was far too straight.) I found the phrasing odd. "Do you take?" rather than "Do you read?" but yes I did "take" Melody Maker, so at least we bonded a little on that.

He came round to my house one evening after school to borrow an album. I can't remember which one. He saw my three Soft Machine albums, cupped a thumb and index finger to his pursed lips and went "Mmm, Soft Machine," much like any cultural pseud might do if they were appreciating a fine wine or the operas of Bizet. "Mmm, Soft Machine.

A delicate bouquet and an aftertaste of dribble." I reminded Dickie and Danny of this incident some months after we had left school. "Christ, they're everywhere, aren't they?" said Danny, and by that time they were. This much was indisputable. We often adopted the cupped fingers and pursed lips when we wanted to signify our contempt. This is how we defined ourselves at 17, through our litany of sneers and prejudices. It was much easier to articulate what you hated than what you loved. Adolescent boys are like that. It's different for girls.

At Tech college on Wednesday afternoons there was a wide range of clubs, societies and sporting activities to choose from. I opted for something called Music Appreciation, which sounded promising until I actually got there. A row of chairs was arranged in a semi-circle but the teacher hadn't arrived yet. Instead, two earnest sixth-form types were at the front of the room obsessively fiddling with the stereo equipment. Pink Floyd's *Meddle* LP had just been released and they were dropping the needle on the record, listening for a bit while adjusting the control knobs and then repeating the process with another track. It really annoyed me and I just wished they would let the assembled gathering listen to the record.

It took me a while to realise that it wasn't the music as such that appealed to them. What they really dug was twiddling knobs and playing with the hardware. Toys for boys. They were my introduction to a type that I'd encounter many more times over the years: the hi-fi bore, the woofers and tweeters brigade to whom the actual records were merely the means to an audio end. No less an authority than Clive Dunn had already identified the tendency in a classic edition of Melody Maker's *Blind Date* in 1971 where he responded to Emerson, Lake and Palmer's *The Barbarian* by suggesting it would be ideal music for a salesman to demonstrate hi-fi equipment with, much as you would use a sound-effects record to illustrate its stereophonic capabilities. I'd never met such a person at the time. I merely thought Dunn's review was a hoot, and it suited my prejudices about where progressive rock might be heading, but subsequently I met that salesman type many times.

When the Music Appreciation lecturer did arrive, he played us a piece of classical music and asked us to guess what it was. My understanding of the classical canon was very limited at the time. I suspected it was 20th century, but that was the limit of my knowledge. No one in the room guessed it correctly. It turned out to be the ballet *The Miraculous Mandarin,* and that was my introduction to Bela Bartok. The intensity of Bartok's music would provide me with far more sustenance over the years than watching a couple of guys twiddling with hi-fi knobs, but that was another cultural schism that would play out in many forms for some time to come. In the meantime, all I had was my youthful antipathy and a lot of unchanneled energy, a kind of lashing out to disguise my own vulnerability. Even my song-writing had a kind of bunker mentality. The songs were like little acid tapestries, static like friezes or woodcuts. They needed to come alive and be liberated from the page. Clearly none of this was going to bear fruit unless I could articulate in some way what I wanted to do, rather than what I didn't want to do.

With all this in mind I placed a "Musicians Wanted" ad in Melody Maker. It read: "Curious Musicians Wanted for Strange Band" – 7p a word plus 35p for a box number. Total cost 77 pence. The box number was necessary as we didn't have a phone at home and I couldn't afford to print my full address. The wording of the ad was, I suspect, an amalgam of Family's *Anyway* EP and a murmured comment made by John Peel halfway through the Gong side of the Glastonbury triple LP. "Curious band," he says as Gilli Smyth's space whisper softly leads the listener into the cosmic beyond. Danny had bought the Glastonbury Triple LP, complete with pyramid assemblage and assorted paraphernalia, as soon as it came out. I sat enraptured as we listened to it at his flat. The Gong side entitled *Glad Stoned Buried Fielding Flash and Fresh Fest Footprint in My Memory* remains in my mind the most accurate document of how powerful they sounded live at that time.

I sent off the necessary remittance to Melody Maker, little knowing what to expect in return. Within days a thick A5 envelope arrived containing a bundle of replies. One was from drummer Charles Hayward who had just left his band Quiet Sun. "The wording of your ad was very similar to what I would have put," he said. Another was from a guy in Oxfordshire, who decided to out-weird me by framing his reply in the style of a free-form poem, not dissimilar to the one Captain Beefheart wrote on the sleeve of *Lick My Decals Off, Baby.*

I was very taken with his response but did wonder about the practicalities of trying to form a band with someone 50 miles away in Oxfordshire. Or anywhere really, because once again I hadn't thought any of this through. I just wanted to be in a band. One guy drove up all the way up from Brighton to see me. He told me he'd been in a band called Louise, and seemed very keen to get started on a new venture. He lugged his guitar and practice amp into my front room. I showed him some of my lyrics and he nodded agreeably. In fact, he nodded agreeably at everything. He had that benign, placid outlook that was de rigueur at the time. Nothing seemed too much bother for him.

However, once he plugged his guitar into his powerful practice amp I got incredibly self-conscious about what Mum might be making of all this racket in the kitchen. The Louise guy just nodded agreeably when I suggested we go and find a mate of mine and maybe have a practice there. This involved a six-mile car ride, and when we reached our destination the mate (who in fact I hadn't seen since we left school and therefore barely qualified as a mate at all) wasn't in. My agreeable ad responder just nodded agreeably again. I wasted an entire afternoon of this sweet, gentle guy's life before finally giving up the ghost and conceding that there was nowhere suitable where we might sit and have a strum. At about 4.30 he dropped me back at my house, shrugged an "Oh well," shrug, got back in his car and drove all the way back to Brighton. He bore me no ill will, assured me it had been a nice afternoon, and gave every indication that it had been worth his while to drive all that way just to encounter someone who in almost every aspect seemed to personify the want-ad shorthand warning of "No timewasters".

Among the other respondents there was one guy who more than anyone seemed to offer hope. His tastes leaned towards jazz and the avant-garde. His letter mentioned tape loops and inasmuch as he thought a comparison might be helpful, he said that he played in a style reminiscent of Robert Fripp. His handwriting was neat and his prose style erudite. We exchanged two or three letters and I told him about my current home circumstances. I must have laid it on a bit thick about my somewhat fractious relationship with my parents because he referred to it in his third and final letter, which was bitter and heartfelt. He dashed my hopes of musical collaboration by explaining that he had just received a PRS cheque for about £27, which was he said the sum accumulation of three years' hard work.

He didn't specify what that hard work was, but concluded by telling me he was getting out of the music business because it was full of crooks and swindlers. He urged me to make things up with my parents and to think about pursuing a more lucrative and less painstaking career than working musician. I've often wondered since who he was and whether he acted on his own advice. Did he go into the theatre perhaps, or merchant banking? Did he, after a period of reflection, get his creative shit together and find a band full of kindred spirits? I'll never know. I can still remember the names of schoolmates I haven't seen in 50 years but I can't remember his. The main reason I remember Charles Haywood's name is because he had the same surname as one of my neighbours, and because only a few weeks after I received his letter I read about another ex-member of Quiet Sun, guitarist Phil Manzanera, who had just joined a band called Roxy Music.

The other significant thing I did around this time was sell my records. "Where should I take them?" I asked Danny and Dickie, meaning where should I offload them that wasn't the junk shop in Bedford High Street, a tiny premises that had a small uninspiring selection of second-hand stock, little of which was ever replenished and half of which seemed to be by the German band Savage Rose, a group that I still don't think I've heard to this day. David's Bookshop in Letchworth was suggested, and so Britain's first Garden City was added to my itinerary of hitchhiking destinations. Ten miles down the A1 to Baldock, and then either thumb or walk the remaining two miles into Letchworth. I sold the records in two impromptu visits, neither of which involved handing them over the counter in the shop itself. First, I got rid of my singles. A long-haired head gave me a lift, and as we pulled up outside the shop, curious as to what I was selling, he asked to have a look at my bag.

He probably couldn't believe his luck when he flicked through the collection, all my carefully and randomly accumulated 45s from the past three or four years. Singles nicked on shoplifting sprees. Spur-of-the-moment singles. Singles traded with mates for other singles. Singles treasured and cherished and coated in emotional resonance. Singles saved up for. Singles because I couldn't afford LPs. Singles made by Underground bands when underground bands still released singles. All gone in an instant for one generous lump sum from a grateful buyer.

Twenty years later I was trying to buy them all back again.

When I made the second journey to sell my LPs, the guy behind the counter told me that David himself wasn't in today, but I'd find him at the warehouse where all the surplus stock was stored and sorted. I followed his instructions down a weed-strewn pathway to a vacant lot at the edge of town where the man himself was sifting through a mountainous stack of LPs. Seeing thousands of records all strewn about like so much landfill does something to your perception of things. That moment has never left me, gazing at all that vinyl as if it was just debris. Stack upon teetering stack of it. All those matrix numbers. All creative endeavour reduced to this. A place where discarded albums came home to die.

At school I'd read that Bob Hite of Canned Heat had such a large collection of vintage blues LPs he kept them in a warehouse. Frank Zappa was said to boast an equally formidable collection of ex-jukebox doo-wop records. In our feverish fifth-form imaginations these accumulations took on the aspect of temple plunder, the bounty of ancient civilisations. Dickie, in particular, who fetishized the blues with the obsessive zeal of a post-war Delta revivalist, made these acquisitions come alive in my mind as he dropped his almost-permanent sardonic sneer to wax (literally) lyrical about Bo Hite's warehouse full of mythical treasures. Yet here I now was, standing in such a place and all I saw was creased and sun-faded cardboard, grinning images of hopeful hoofers and hopeless serenaders, end-of-the-pier turns and one-chance losers.

The famous and the familiar rubbed alongside the anonymous and the unknown. Beat groups and folk groups, mod groups and rocker groups, nubile young pin-ups and leathery nightclub crooners, cabaret acts and comedy acts, raucous rhythm-and-blues records, missed-the-last-ferry-boat Merseybeat records, bluebeat and blue-eyed soul records. Records by Irish show bands and Italian tenors. Records by groups who once looked pretty good together but were now just back-dated. Records by groups who were in permanent flux as they tried and failed to catch a trend.

LPs full of tunes written in smoke-filled offices in Denmark Street to client specifications, songs written in the back of diesel-choked transits while heading for a midnight fry-up at the Blue Boar café. Songs penned on Primrose Hill at dawn. Songs scribbled down with the studio clock ticking and the meter running. Songs written in damp attics and 12th-floor penthouses. Records that had been "picked to click" in the music papers. Discs deemed to be "for dancers only". Upbeat stormers "delivered with vigour and vitality". Tracks that had "a happy-go-lucky sparkle that was guaranteed to set your feet tapping". Records that had "a thumping beat", "a belting tune", "lusty vocals" or "intense blues stylings". Records that lacked "melodic content" or were "sung without conviction" by pedestrian, hackneyed, all-too-samey also-rans. The accumulation of a thousand reviews I'd read in my music mags. All of them once competing eagerly in the marketplace, only to end up here in this fusty-smelling big shed, consigned to the vinyl graveyard. I stepped over piles of cast-offs and handed David my own pile in exchange for a pittance.

The shedding of my LP collection was almost as savage as the culling of my singles, but at least I knew my 45s had gone to a good home, thanks to that long-hair who picked me up. There was no telling where my LPs would end up. All of my Tyrannosaurus Rex albums were viciously purged because Marc Bolan was public property now and no longer my private passion. Onto the teetering warehouse stack went *Nice Enough to Eat*, *Picnic*, *Bumpers* and *Fill Your Head with Rock*: those cheap compilation albums that had done so much to expand my tastes and outlook.

I still loved Caravan's *In the Land of Grey and Pink*, but it reminded me too much of Cindy and could therefore never be listened to again. I parted with The Blossom Toes' *We Are Ever So Clean*, bought during the last of my schooldays when Dickie Dangerfield told me that multiple copies were on sale for 20p in a small junk shop near Hitchin railway station. I bought one for me and one for Cindy. I sold albums that I'd chosen from my Mum's Grattan's catalogue and paid for in weekly instalments: Cream's *Wheels of Fire*, *Smash Hits* by The Jimi Hendrix Experience, Paul McCartney's first solo album, Santana's *Abraxas*, Leonard Cohen's *Songs of Love and Hate*. *Abbey Road* went, as did *Sgt. Pepper*, complete with inserts. I parted with my Edgar Broughton Band albums, Fleetwood Mac's *Mr Wonderful* and *Blues Jam at Chess*, even my beloved Lol Coxhill LP which I had refused to hand over when mugged. All of it tossed onto a pile behind David's makeshift desk with nary a backward glance from him or a murmur from me. I exited that sorry place a few pounds richer and much character-forming, life-shaping vinyl lighter.

I was consciously wiping my cultural slate clean when I did this. Purging myself of habit, much as the young narrator does in Colin MacInnes' *Absolute Beginners* when at the end of each year he commits his own pogrom, dispensing with all but a few treasured books and LPs. Like him I kept back just a few Holy Grail items. Pink Floyd. Syd Barrett. Soft Machine. Gong. Kevin Ayers. Nick Drake. The Velvet Underground. Everything else went.

The exercise was cathartic, and reflected the part of me that was resistant to habit. By 1972 I'd gone off a lot of the music that I'd loved only a year or two earlier. Bands that I'd worshipped during the 60s – The Kinks, Who, Small Faces, Pretty Things et al. – had either split up, mutated or developed questionable fashion sense. Musically, many of them had become bloated, stodgy and earnest – or had simply run out of steam.

They didn't owe me anything but then I hadn't signed a loyalty contract either. I was ruthless in this regard. Most of the bands on those Island and Harvest samplers only held my attention for two or three albums. By album three or four they had almost without exception slipped into familiar riffs and routines. Even the bands who continued to evolve, King Crimson for instance, no longer represented anything I wanted to pledge a habit-forming allegiance to. Most of all I no longer wished to be burdened by ownership. Subconsciously I was still preparing for the day when I would uproot myself, set off and find those creative soulmates that Daevid Allen said were out there somewhere. From now on I would travel light and leave no cultural footprint.

I went back on this pledge almost straightaway, of course. The 10p cheap singles at the front of the counter in Kerry's were frequently replenished, and proved just too much of a lure. I dipped in and helped myself whenever the boss wasn't at the counter, much as you would with Woolworth's Pick'n'Mix. One day I noticed a stack of *Magical Mystery Tour* EPs on the top shelf, remnants of a time when EMI didn't delete anything by the Beatles. "Do you want one?" said Danny, fetching a stool. I also started to notice more German bands in the Underground and Progressive Rock racks. That first newly credible issue of NME in February had carried an interview with Can, and during the following months there seemed to be a plethora of new music pouring out of Germany.

Later in the year Ian MacDonald wrote his definitive two-part primer for NME called "Germany Calling", which was invaluable in helping me separate the Grobschnitt from the Shinola. Krautrock turned out to be the genuinely progressive music I had been subconsciously yearning for since writers began applying the term to ELP and Yes. It was bands like Can, Faust and Kraftwerk that ultimately saved me from the pomp and grandiosity of progressive rock. I heard Can and Faust for the first time on John Peel's late-night radio show, but the first Krautrock LP I ever bought – months before the term was in common use – was by Cluster. I was in the newly opened Virgin Records branch in Notting Hill when my eye was drawn to a gatefold sleeve depicting crudely drawn yellow stars on a blue background. The pattern was similar to that of a popular hippie T shirt of the period, readily available by mail order from the back of Melody Maker. But it was what sat in the centrefold that thrilled me. There was no sign of any musicians or indeed of any human involvement at all, just a blue-tinted, bleak and austere photo of a bank of keyboards and trailing wires.

Suitably intrigued, I bought what turned out to be the second Cluster album. This was precisely what I wanted instead of virtuosity and ego. The machine music on that album wiped my aesthetic slate clean in ways that I couldn't have envisaged just a few months earlier. There were other electronic and experimental instrumental albums around at the time: me and Danny were both fans of the newly released *Zero Time* by Tonto's Expanding Head Band, but Cluster were coldly formidable in a way that actively challenged you to like them. When Messrs Moebius, Roedelius and Plank were making their stark industrial machine music, Kraftwerk were still putting flutes through echo units. Can sounded positively macrobiotic next to the factory-floor throb and diesel-engine drone of that Cluster record.

One day I found a few leftover shards of Rosalyn's window-pane acid in the bottom of an empty film canister. I'd had them for weeks – months possibly – and had forgotten all about them. The last lot we'd taken had done nothing at all, and I assumed that these would have gone off by now, assuming they'd ever been on in the first place. One sunny Saturday the family was out for the afternoon, so I sat warming myself against the south-facing side wall of our house and waited for something to happen.

As expected, nothing did happen, not even a tingle. In a spirit of "Waste not want not", I tipped the little canister up, necked the last tiny splinters of window-pane and went into the front room to listen to Cluster.

The buzz-saw oscillations of the opening track, *Plas*, surged up at about the same time as the first shimmery hint of acid kicked in. Within minutes my green and placid front room was a pulsating kinetic synthetic dynamo factory, and I was merely a cog in the machine room mechanism. The pores of my skin began to leak engine oil. Luminous automata rotated wildly from within the wallpaper pattern. The curtains caught fire. The music strafed my head with tracer lights and laser beams. Overwhelmed by the sheer sonic bombardment I hovered unsteadily over the stylus and with what seemed like artificial limbs and a Lightning Lad arm managed to take the record off the player. I replaced it with the becalmed churchy colour prisms of Pink Floyd's *A Saucerful of Secrets*. The room immediately became a more pleasant place, tranquil and meditative. The only trouble was that the mosaic carpet had now become sticky with primordial gas, and began undulating with sky-high sea waves of cosmic intensity. By now I had lost the use of my legs and there was no way that I was going to be able to negotiate this increasingly swampy terrain. I somehow managed to wade on withered stumps back to the becalming shores of the sofa from which safe haven equilibrium was at least partially restored.

It occurred to me later that had the family come back unexpectedly at that moment and found me crawling for dear life across a few square yards of carpet a degree of explaining would have been in order. That was the last time I ever took Rosalyn's window-pane acid, but by Christ some revelations manifested themselves that afternoon. The room was lit by gamma rays and several new stratospheres of reality became apparent. Each blinding insight was assimilated, absorbed or otherwise waved off down the cosmic highway with the promise that I would give it my fuller attention as and when circumstances permitted.

At one point the answer to life revealed itself to me while I was listening to *The Madcap Laughs*. As Syd's voice soared, molten energy surged up from the Earth's core. Buildings converged and concertina'ed. A beacon of red light radiated and flicker-flamed in synesthetic unison with Syd's lyric. At that moment I understood all the secrets of creation. I mentally filed away this micro-second of revelation, and resolved to return to my discovery at a less turbulent juncture. The insight flitted and fluttered through my mind throughout the afternoon, and on each occassion I duly resolved to return afresh later in the day and give it my full consideration. Alas, I was by then, as Storm Thorgerson once said of Syd himself, "orbiting very fast". As Arthur Koestler put it after taking psilocybin: "There's no wisdom there. I solved the secret of the universe last night but this morning I forgot what it was."

That was my experience too. Each time the planets took a twirl, the answer to life, as revealed on *The Madcap Laughs*, seemed to spiral a little further out of reach. Eventually my blinding revelation dwindled with the inevitability of a dying star until all that was left was a memory glimpse of a moment of illusory truth and some dust in vinyl grooves, magnified by the light but no longer yielding anything but static and crackle.

The following morning, washing my face in the bathroom sink I looked down at the bar of Shield soap in its dish. The sea-green stripes seemed to undulate. When I shifted my gaze a fraction to the right the undulations followed, making a smear splash of emerald on the white porcelain. The soap took on the aspect of fossilised rock, glistening in the morning sun. Late one night a few weeks later, I was the last one still up, all the family asleep upstairs. ("Don't forget to lock up." "Fill the kettle." All routine dutifully observed.) I let Rusty out for his nocturnal shagging and as he headed towards the open door the temperature in the kitchen suddenly dropped. This was not cold air from outside, but a more ominous chill, like a presence of some kind. I assumed that Rusty must have already slipped out into the darkness but when I looked down a sudden ginger glow shot past at high velocity. There was no whooshing sound – although the rocket speed warranted it – just the afterglow of a tom-cat trail, something spectral and unholy.

I'd been reading a lot about white magic, perhaps too much, and maybe reading too much into it too. I know what I saw though, the outline of something feline, hurtling out there into the midnight void. I've always been sceptical about acid flashbacks. From very early on they seemed to me the epitome of the bullshitting hippie trying to appear deeper than they actually were. I filed flashbacks away with people who told you they could see your aura. All part of the hokum and snake-oil paraphernalia of the period. But I was orbiting very fast during the late spring and early summer of 1972. At times I was only tangentially connected with reality, so who knows what was really happening to my pliable little brain? I would listen to Gong's *Camembert Electrique*, willing myself into that world, wishing that Daevid Allen had said: "Yes, come and join in with our cosmic games."

I'd inhale the vapour trails left in the wake of *Fohat Digs Holes in Space* and pirouette madly into the beyond. (If you want an aural representation of my head at that time it sounds exactly like the swirling space dust particles of *Fohat Digs Holes in Space*.) Late at night I would go outside and commune with Selene, spirit of the Moon. The town all asleep and quiet. Propelling myself away into the star-lit darkness, the words of another *Camembert Electrique* track resonating in my head. "And you tried so hard to get there/And you tried so hard to get there…" But I was still hopelessly rooted to earthbound circumstances, to my mundane life, to limitations.

Desperately wanting out. To be anywhere that wasn't here.

There was a row of cottages in Stratford Road, opposite the cemetery, I'd pass them on Sunday-evening walks up to the bird sanctuary or the Common. I'd gaze through windows and project my imagined commune life into those low-beamed, dimly lit rooms. I'd be in a band, me and my imagined mates, making communal music, growing our own vegetables in that plot over there by the railway line. Living a life that wasn't this one.

Chapter 5

ALTERNATIVE LONDON

I was standing outside Camden tube station gazing northwards up the High Street. The late afternoon clouds formed an ominous purple-grey arch of light. I didn't know Camden at all well. I'd never been to Implosion at the Roundhouse, nor any of those other gigs that looked so enticing in the back pages of Melody Maker. I'm not even sure what I was doing in Camden in the first place. I suppose it formed part of a vaguely homebound drift past the Kings Cross lock-ups and the coach station as I once again contemplated how I was going to teleport myself from this particular location to my dinner-table on time for tea.

I kept to the right-hand side of the street, and just before the canal bridge discovered a bookshop. Enticed by a narrow stairway at the back of the premises, I found myself in the poetry and literature section, the shelves of which were dotted with the rapidly expanding output of the alternative society. Theodore Roszak's recently published *The Making of a Counter Culture*, Richard Neville's *Playpower*, Timothy Leary's *The Politics of Ecstasy*, Jeff Nuttall's *Bomb Culture*, and all the other group manifestos and personal testimonies that were emerging from the Underground. It was within such a culture that I was trying to find some sense of purpose and place, and here were its route maps, all displayed in front of me in what I didn't know then was Compendium Books.

Pinned to the wall was a newspaper article, the gist of which was that you couldn't make a living out of writing poetry. The tone of the piece was brusque and unrepentant, a tough-love reminder to people like me that the craft of writing poetry, or writing anything for that matter, was not for idlers. At the time I was beginning to entertain some fanciful notion that there existed somewhere an outlet whereby I might be able to cobble together some kind of subsistence-level living out of reciting, perhaps even publishing, my trippy doggerel.

I was soon forcefully disabused of this notion. I suspect that the process began that very afternoon as I perused that newspaper clipping pinned to the wall. The article basically said: "Do not think for one minute that you are going to be the next Adrian Henri, Brian Patten or Roger McGough. Those positions are already filled and anyway the life of your average workaday poet does not resemble the lives of this select band of superstars." As if to provide further brutal evidence, a small box sat on the floor by the counter. It was full of loose-leaf folders, Banda sheets, handbills and Xeroxed booklets – self-published poetry and prose in all its myriad manifestations, good, bad, lucid and impenetrable. "Help yourself," said a sign, so I did.

I scooped up three or four booklets. *This View from Above* by Paul Green, it said on the cover of one of them. The author's name and the title were indented, white on white, like an inversion of the Beatles' name on the White Album. "Copyright 1970," it said on the inside back page. "An edition of 250 copies of which 26 lettered A to Z contain an additional holograph poem. Published by the Ferry Press 177 Green Lane London SE 9." My copy didn't contain the holograph poem, but I did get one of the several that had ended up dumped in a box a couple of years after its publication, thus giving added poignancy to the thrust of the article pinned to the wall.

I only gave *This View from Above* the briefest perusal in the shop, but I immersed myself in it when I got home. Initially I found Paul Green's poetry weird, like I found a lot of stuff weird when I was 17. I had been actively seeking out the weird for some time – weird music mostly, often projecting weirdness onto a whole range of stuff that wasn't actually weird at all when you got to the core of it. I'd worked my way through a lot of stodgy boogie rock in order to get to the good stuff, and was beginning to develop cultural antennae I could trust.

With literature though I was still a complete novice. In underground mags like Oz and Friends I was only slowly beginning to separate the cogent philosophy from the incoherent nonsense. For all the radical polemic and rigorous self-evaluation – Where is all this leading? Precisely what are we trying to build here? – there were endless pages of Dayglo drivel and some shockingly bad verse. Paul Green's poetry, however, was not shockingly bad. It was strangely beguiling, full of mazy irregularity and tangential thinking. At the time I didn't have the literary chops to be able to evaluate it convincingly, but one look at titles like "The Room Yes Square Long Beautiful and Loved" and "So Now It's the Cool and Diffident" alerted me to the fact that this clearly wasn't Alfred Lord Tennyson. One poem, "The Dedication", began:

> a cloud of rain is not the memory
> summer has gone curving past "cares"
> almost the blossom-shaded train
> you climb an enormous night

I was simultaneously bemused and intrigued by those speech marks around "cares". I immediately aspired to write like that. I wanted to have the measure of things with thoughts like those, to observe what Paul Green observed in his micro-universe of small-press poetry that you couldn't make a living out of and which ended up in a "Help yourself" box in front of a counter at the top of some stairs that led you further into the labyrinth of a new and exhilarating world.

I walked out of the shop into the late afternoon mizzle. Assuming invisibility, as I so often did when boarding a bus in London with barely enough for the fare in my pocket, I eventually found my way to my favoured hitchhiking spot north of Hendon. At the point where the M1 and the A1 diverted – the M1 curling left, the Barnet Way pointing straight ahead – I once again curved past "cares", stuck out my thumb, and continued to climb an enormous night.

****

London as a kid meant school trips to Regents Park Zoo, The Planetarium, Madame Tussaud's, Heathrow Airport. London in my early teens was football matches, railway terminals and engine sheds. By the time I reached my mid-teens it was gigs and a growing sense that this was where the alternative action was. I was allowed to go off and wander about in the big city from quite an early age. Mostly my parents assumed I was trainspotting or at the match with a group of mates, but often I wasn't. I was exploring record shops and bookshops and seeking new pleasures. By 1972 the ripped innards of the city were revealing a whole new reality to me.

I pondered the Blakean graffiti "The Tygers of Wrath Are Wiser than the Horses of Instruction" emblazoned on the wall outside Euston Fire Station. (Blake was words on a wall to me long before he was words on a page.) Here was Lol Coxhill busking on the Hungerford walkway between Waterloo and Charing Cross stations. There was Bob Downes and his band Open Music running an open-air workshop in whatever area of green space they could find. There were the Hyde Park Free concerts for the growing multitudes of hippies and heads. There were impromptu gigs on the waste ground at the top of Portobello Road in what wasn't yet called Meanwhile Gardens. There were gigs at the Quakers' Friends' House and St Pancras Library, two-shilling lunchtime gigs at the Lyceum. Accommodating spaces in the most unlikely places were opening up everywhere.

One Thursday afternoon in deepest dark December I'd accompanied Danny and Clifford up to the Smoke. We took the coach from Bedford bus station and headed for the Record and Tape Exchange in Goldhawk Road where Clifford traded in a few pre-release promos for cash. I handed over Melanie's *Candles in the Rain* and a couple of other unwanted albums, receiving in exchange just about enough to cover my fare. Somewhere between the record shop and the coach station I managed to lose my ticket which meant that the money I'd gained on my discarded LPs went towards having to buy another ticket for the journey home. I made a net loss on the day but a cultural gain overall, because that trip to the top end of Portobello Road, even on a day when the rain-spattered market barrows were empty and the streets were all but deserted, was the magnet that drew me back time and time again. Increasingly I began to take daylight refuge in that W10 and W11 enclave where the denizens of the Underground went about their business.

On an earlier visit Danny had accompanied Clifford to a conference of record-company bosses and small-business executives in Ladbroke Grove. Danny told me he was one of the few white people in a room populated by reggae and soul men, managers and agents, label bosses and record pluggers, artists and musicians, plus a smattering of Black (and White) Panthers and other ideologically interested parties, as the Afro-Caribbean community collectively attempted to organise viable alternatives to the machinery of the mainstream. The liberated zone of Vietgrove was the fulcrum point of all such activity, and whenever I stuck out a thumb on the A1 and headed for London it was invariably to the top end of Portobello that I gravitated.

What I discovered almost immediately was that whatever it was that the Underground press still paid lip-service to in its harking back and its hankering, that era was over and many of the alternative society's most committed participants had long since fled to the ashrams and Welsh cottages, to the Scottish crofts and remote communes. There were still plenty of lingering reminders of old ideals gone to seed, but what had replaced the shimmering mirage of hippie Nirvana was a much scuzzier, hand-to-mouth reality.

The Notting Hill Gate end of Portobello Road was all pretty pastel-coloured terraces with quaint cottage gardens. The antique shops were owned by languid old queens in cravats, blazers and nautical caps who stood in their shop doorways watching the passing trade. Once you hit the Westway overpass, however, you were in another world. The side streets, crescents and squares were lined with shabby buildings in various states of disrepair. There was a preponderance of off-white architecture, flaking paint and plaster. Gardens were litter-strewn and overgrown with weeds. Porticos listed. Windows, when you could see in at all, were draped with makeshift Indian-print curtains. More often than not, shutters or blinds were permanently closed. Walking through one of those neighbourhoods one blustery spring morning I saw Steve Took, the actual Steve Peregrin Took, leave a house and sway up the road a few yards in front of me.

Freakishly thin, he wore a long black trench coat which seemed to emphasise the elongated distortion of his aspect ratio. He looked like the wind might blow him over. For those few moments as I followed in his wake, I tried to breathe in whatever musky scent he might be exuding. In many ways that's what I was attempting to do full stop, up at the top end of Portobello. Imbibe the essence of an alternative world, a world that like the exotically perfumed spectre of Steve Peregrin Took was still lingering among the ruins and the slum-clearance rubble.

By 1972 the Beautiful People had long since vacated the cosmic playground. London was now newly populated by the drifters, the cast-offs and left-behinds. Despite increasing evidence to the contrary, I still thought the answer might lie in crash pads and communes. I clung tenaciously to the idea that if I could establish a base in London everything else would fall into place. I went to the offices of BIT, the alternative information service on the top floor of an empty building on Westbourne Park Road, hoping they might be able to offer me emergency accommodation. All I found when I climbed the uncarpeted stairs was a room overflowing with flotsam, dream-seeking refugees, people just like me. There was nowhere to sit, so I stood around in that large airless room for a few minutes, listening to the voice of a harassed women behind a wooden partition shouting into a phone. The ambience of the place was one of nothing happening quietly, interspersed with sporadic outbursts of agitated noise from behind the partition. People stood or sat waiting, their impassive faces staring at an unoccupied counter. After about 20 minutes I slunk away down the stairs and headed back towards Notting Hill Gate and the welcoming retail comfort of Virgin Records.

Virgin had recently branched out from its mail-order business and opened two record shops: a small branch above a shoe shop in Oxford Street and a more expansive premises in Notting Hill Gate just along from WH

Smith, virtually opposite the Gate cinema. The huge bean-bags in the window of the Notting Hill branch were a novelty I'd never encountered before in a record shop, and I took to sprawling there when too footsore or uninspired to venture any further for the day. Every trawl and traipse up and down Holland Park Road or Ladbroke Grove seemed to involve at some point a stop-off at Virgin to become part of their human window display of the prone and the stoned with their headphones on.

It was there I first listened to the machine throb of the second Cluster album, administering the culture shock of Krautrock while others dived deep into their West Coast or progressive rock. Virgin used to leave the records in the sleeves in the early days, a practice that was rapidly curtailed when stock started disappearing. More than once I saw a long-hair surreptitiously conceal an album under his Afghan and make for the plate-glass exit door. On the counter was a dish full of small change, an emergency fund for those desperately in need. It probably wasn't meant for 17-year-old Awayday wastrels like myself, but there were times when my pockets were nearly empty when I scooped up just enough coins to ensure I could afford a bus back to my Hendon hitching point on the A1. Richard Branson saved my sorry ass on more than one cash-strapped occasion.

My search also took me to Gentle Ghost, the self-styled non-profit-making employment agency in Holland Park. Their box ads in IT and OZ pledged to find work for a wide range of alternative voices. These included everything from astrologers, artists, decorators and designers to alternative removal men, alternative jewellers, alternative secretaries, publishers and proof readers. The ad also mentioned poets, so I took my chances and wandered in. The article on the Compendium wall was correct. There was nothing down for beginners like me with their trippy scrawls and their ill-formed ideals. I pointed to a poster on the wall in vain. "It says poets on there." The Ghost guy mumbled something vaguely discouraging and went back to his mountain of paperwork. I had my best cynical head on that day and gave off a less than benign vibe. None of the Gentle Ghost set-up seemed very alternative to me. It just seemed to be a job agency for hippies. I would probably have expressed these sentiments more forcefully if the guy hadn't got up and walked me to a side door and back up the steps to the street.

I also went to Release in Elgin Avenue to see if they could help, even though their sole remit was to give legal aid and advice to people who had been busted. "Try BIT," said a disembodied tired voice when I pressed the buzzer. I waited for the signal to push the door open but it never came. By this time the BIT small ads in the Underground mags were desperately pleading for crash pads. "We're having to turn people away," they said. "We also need Green Shield stamps, cigarette coupons, spare change." Any lingering hopes I had that New Jerusalem could be financed by Green Shield stamps and spare change were conclusively dispelled the day I walked into the Free Shop at the top end of Portobello Road.

The Free Shop was a regular fixture of Notting Hill throughout the 1970s. During the punk period it could be found directly under the Westway, but in the spring of 1972 it was at 353 Portobello Road, about 100 yards up from the Frendz Magazine office, in a row of commercial premises just before the Spanish school. At this point it was known as the Free Exchange Store, and had been incorporated into The Soul Garden Shoppe which sold all the usual head-shop accessories. The free section asked for unwanted books, records and clothes. Their Underground mag ads promised: "If you've got no bread and nothing to bring, feel equally free to come and take what you need." The day I walked in there, one guy did exactly that.

Stereotypically dubious with his slit eyes and Bandito moustache, he dropped off three or four packets of incense at the counter and helped himself to a fur coat. I looked at the shop assistant and waited for a reaction but none was forthcoming. When the Bandito guy had left I said something really earnest to him, something along the lines of "If everyone does that there soon won't be a free shop to take freely from". My comment was met with a benign shrug of liberal tolerance. Back in Bedford, Danny and I treated that whole "Hey man don't get hung up on details" vibe with derision. Standing in the Free Shop that dull and overcast day I simply didn't have the verbal ammo or enthusiasm to come back at this gentle guy behind the counter with his simpering "Be nice to freeloaders" smile and his apparent indifference to contradiction.

Broadly speaking, the boundaries of my terrain were Maida Vale to the north, Shepherd's Bush to the west, Holland Park and Hyde Park to the South. Oxford Street and Soho were about as far as I ventured into central London, and then only rarely. Mostly I stuck to Notting Hill and Ladbroke Grove. Vast tracts of the East End and South and South East London remained uncharted territory. On one occasion, misjudging the optimum moment to bail out from a lorry lift, I ended up in New Cross. I might as well have been in Dover. Unable to bluff my way through the barriers and onto the tube station I was forced to spend what little spare change I had just getting back to somewhere that was recognisably London. I winged it every time I stuck out my thumb on the southbound A1. Heading into Bedford or Cambridge for the day with 30p in my pocket was one thing. Getting dropped off in Archway or Hampstead or Billingsgate Market was another. I turned fare-dodging on the buses into an art form. I never sat in cafés. I hardly ate or drank a thing from when I left home at around half eight or nine in the morning until I returned home, often dehydrated and light-headed with hunger, in time for my tea.

When I wasn't earnestly seeking out the last vestiges of the alternative society, I just wandered about, browsing in bookshops, head shops, record shops. My journey up to Release in Elgin Avenue took me beyond the drab, shabby terraces of the Goldhawk Road and Shepherds Bush, where the totters could still be seen on their daily rounds, and into the wide tree-lined avenues and mansion-block vistas of Maida Vale and St Johns Wood. I chanced upon a little wooden shack on a footbridge over the Canal in Little Venice that sold records and would sometimes while away an hour or so browsing there. The shack was tiny, with barely enough room inside for a couple of customers. Most of the stock was stacked up on the footbridge pavement. One day I turned up there and the shack had just disappeared. All that remained were a few square feet of bleached paving stone as a reminder of what had once been.

Marc Bolan had lived in Little Venice for a while and his shimmering aura permeated my musings as I ghosted about the place. I stood in Blenheim Crescent on more than one occasion gazing up at the rooms that Marc and his wife June had rented during the Tyrannosaurus Rex days. Now that he was in his pop-star pomp I did my begrudging best to ignore him, but the lure of his charisma was still formidable. One day I lingered outside Lord's Cricket Ground for a while before conceding that the home of cricket would be considerably more difficult to gatecrash than Fenner's. The gateman gave me the kind of glare that said: "I know your game."

Giving up and moving on I passed a news vendor's hut just along from the ground and saw Marc Bolan's unmistakeable visage on the cover of the newly colourised IT magazine. "Bolan. Who Needs Him?" it said in bold yellow beneath a photo of Marc in his glittery satin pop-star jacket. Parting with my 15p I decided to see what the denizens of the underground press had to say about him these days. The answer was nothing. The joke was on me. I'd been sucker-punched by a stunt I would have been proud of pulling myself. There was no T Rex feature. Just the usual Furry Freak Brothers cartoon, ads for water beds and sheepskin coats, personal ads

("Aquarian guy seeks groovy chick"), and BIT desperately seeking cash and Green Shield Stamps. There were blurry black-and-white pics of the recent rain-drenched Bickershaw festival, there was a block ad for the newly released Glastonbury triple album, reviews of forthcoming LPs by Curved Air, Hot Tuna and Jim Capaldi, and updates on the latest atrocities in Vietnam. But no Bolan.

My essential tour guide for these journeys into the heart of the Hiptropolis was Nicholas Saunders' survival manual *Alternative London*. It was initially published as a slim volume in 1970, but I had the massively expanded 350-page third edition that came out in 1972. *Alternative London* covered everything from the fundamentals to the fringe. There was practical advice on finding somewhere affordable to live, and practical suggestions about how to furnish and maintain your home. More esoteric fare was covered under headings such as Food Cults, Herbalism, Ecology, Mystical, Other Cures, Drugs and Communes. The book frequently blurred the fine lines between blagging, scamming and begging.

On the one hand it offered handy hints on the locations of subsided canteens where you might be able to walk in off the street and find a cheap meal (the BBC, certain Fleet Street newspapers, Selfridges, most Civil Service buildings). On the other hand, its tips on how to scavenge vegetables from gutters and barrows at the end of market day, or the bins at the back of restaurants, made me acutely away of what happens when the Welfare State safety net isn't there and you find yourself adopting the time-honoured methods of the vagrant.

Alternative London simultaneously suggested a city it might be possible to inhabit and one that you could just as easily be ground down by. The allure of the bright lights I'd been drawn to as a boy was frequently tempered by awareness of the harsher realities that Ian Anderson gave vent to in Jethro Tull's autumn of 1971 single *Life Is a Long Song*. One morning very early on in my quest, I stood on the platform of an outlying tube station on the Metropolitan line, Harrow on the Hill it might have been. It was lightly snowing, and there was a poster ad on the wall for the newly released M*A*S*H film. I remember that. I watched, semi-detached from it all, as a red tube train came in and filled up with commuters. It was as if the doors were jaws and the train was swallowing them whole. I thought of that line in *Life Is a Long Song* where the everyday routine of catching the Baker Street train "grinds you under its wheels".

That ambivalence about London never left me. It always seemed a place that could make or break you. In Nicholas Saunders' compendium I discovered codes I could potentially live by, and others that prohibited my participation purely through lack of money. The "You are what you eat" advice in the Food Cults section was refreshingly explicit about how expensive and impractical it was to maintain a healthy vegetarian diet. This was something I thought about every time I pressed my nose to the window of the newly opened Ceres in Portobello Road and realised that I couldn't afford even the most basic of their snacks. Despite this, it was *Alternative London* that provided me with my beginner's guide on how to become a vegetarian. Aligned to my growing interest in Eastern religion was a growing belief that my body was my temple and that I should try treating it as such. For a boy who would have happily taken chocolate-spread sandwiches into school for his lunch for five years, and frequently did, this was a radical leap of faith. More recently, my liking for unhealthy foodstuffs had been sorely tested by the café next to Tech college that all the day-release students used to pile into at lunchtime. My infrequent visits were enough to put me off pre-packed sandwiches for life, and I vowed to never again purchase anything that sat under a plastic container on a counter, and which looked and tasted like it had been there for days.

The first direct advice I garnered from *Alternative London* was in the section on Macrobiotics. I read up on yin and yang and undertook the ten-day brown-rice diet. This was accompanied by a period of systematic fasting in order to secrete the poison (mental and biological) from my body. By now I was virtually fasting by default anyway. Abstinence I found easy. I never ate breakfast and unless I grabbed a piece of fruit before I set off in the morning for my day at Mirage Tech I rarely ate again till teatime. In my mid-teens I shed any lingering adolescent puppy fat. By the time I was 17 I was probably borderline anorexic. Mum now looked on with a mixture of bemusement and concern as I foreswore regular evening meals in order to pursue the ten-day rice regime.

Things didn't get off to a promising start. Not having a clue about rice, I walked hopefully into an Italian deli in Bedford and bought what turned out to be pudding rice. I cooked up this thick stodge in the same way me and Nick Tate had stirred that calcified glue while tripping in his Cambridge flat. I forced down the entire soggy bowlful before reluctantly conceding that I hadn't so much cleansed my body as Araldited it. Having never once cooked a meal for myself, and having no other culinary guides than Mum's Be-Ro book, and Fanny Craddock and the Galloping Gourmet on the telly, I was to all intents and purposes a nutritional neophyte. When it came to transitioning from meat and two veg to balancing the yin-yang ratios of grains, cereals and pulses according to strict macrobiotic principles I was at a total loss. There were no hippie food co-operatives then, and it was virtually impossible to find vegetarian options on the High Street.

Eventually I found a small health-food shop in Bromham Road in Bedford. I'd walked past the shop many times on the way to Brendan Brotherson's house, but had barely glanced at its unenticing window display of protein pills and vitamin supplements. Now, with no alternatives available to me, it became my unlikely source of vegetarian food. The shop had that vaguely antiseptic potpourri and lily-of-the-valley smell that non-hippie health food stores had then, but they did sell brown rice. I bought enough to see me through my ten-day diet, which I stuck to rigorously. After about four days I experienced a natural high, a feeling of light-headedness and a sensation that my brain was breathing in and out. At the end of the ten days I began adding a few lightly fried vegetables to the meal, and discovered almost inadvertently that there wasn't that much to the basics of cooking. Mum meanwhile, thought I'd gone off my rocker. She didn't think much of me undermining her role as house chef either. My youngest brother, who was eight at the time, gleefully pointed out the Arsenal footballer Pat Rice on the Sunday Soccer round-up, and taunted me as only an eight-year-old can for bringing alien foodstuffs into a house where coffee was called Camp and spaghetti came in tins.

I continued to play catch-up with my reading. Filling knowledge gaps in the pre-history of the counterculture. Jeff Nuttall's *Bomb Culture* described an artistic milieu that on first encounter seemed old and grey, even though the book was summarising events that had occurred barely five or ten years earlier. This was the world of Alexander Trocchi, Better Books, and legendary names like Miles and Hoppy. The pages resounded to the sloganeering clamour of the English Beats, Ban the Bomb, and trad jazz played on the back of floats during CND marches. Five or ten years ago is just a blink of an eye to me now. It was ancient history at the time. The House Unamerican Activities Committee or Aldermaston might as well have been Pompeii. Richard Neville's *Playpower* introduced me to Danny the Red, the Amsterdam Provos, and the events of May 1968. In free-and-easy prose Neville essayed the inner workings of the Underground press, the overland trail to India, and his penchant for schoolgirls. The final chapter was a hedonist's manifesto, a clarion call for less work and more play. The Appendix reprinted lengthy extracts from *Project London*, a booklet distributed among the Underground in 1969, which was basically a manual on how to find free stuff in the big city. Neville presented it as a historical document, and while it contained much useful information on how to survive, many of those skills, as in *Alternative London*, simply seemed to revolve around scamming and creative illegality.

When I first started hanging out in Kerry's, Clifford lent me his copy of Jerry Rubin's *Do It*. Like Richard Neville's tome, much of it advocated a libertarian free-for-all. In 1970 I'd witnessed Rubin's memorable disruption of Saturday night peak-time TV when he and the Yippies took over *The David Frost Show*. It was front-page news the next day, and utterly enthralling to a 16-year-old who barely a week or two later was watching the feminists hurl flour bombs at the Albert Hall Miss World contestants, while Bob Hope (a comedian from the Dark Ages as far as I was concerned) uttered his immortal line about anyone who would disrupt an event like this "must be on some kind of dope". I fervently wished at that time to be on some kind of dope myself and was fascinated by the way that the radical fringes of the underground, be they Women's Libbers or Yippies, were subverting mainstream media in this way. Rubin's book blew giant raspberries at the straight-laced, buttoned-up Western world. Its main purpose however was to promote the self-serving Rubin himself.

Do It also contained instructions along the lines of: "Hey man if you just want to take a shit in the street just take a shit in the street." I wasn't sure how public defecation was going to aid the revolution in any constructive way and neither was Clifford, who had similar misgivings about the book, pointing out that it was likely to be a black person doing menial labour who would be cleaning that shit up.

While *Playpower* and *Do It* came with huge cautionary caveats, the one person I loathed and distrusted instinctively was Timothy Leary. I tried reading *The Politics of Ecstasy* while tripping on acid and while not tripping on acid, and on both occasions saw through the bullshit dogma with equal lucidity. Had I been psychedelically active just a few years earlier I've no doubt that philosophically I would have been on that Prankster bus with Ken Kesey and the gang. I distrusted Leary on every level. From his spurious academic credentials to his messianic preaching, everything about the man screamed fake. There was one underground press photo of him in Golden Gate Park that particularly stuck in my mind. It was the famous occasion where he preached "Turn on, tune in, drop out" to the adoring faithful. The photo was taken not from out front where he tended to look like the new lysergic Messiah, but from the side of the stage while he was listening to other speakers. I noticed the way his brown shoes were arranged neatly by his side as he sat there cross-legged in his stockinged feet. He always seemed to possess that quality to me, no matter how native he went, a man who always had his brown shoes on standby. In my countercultural education I still had a long way to go and a lot to learn, but taking against Leary was one of the boldest instinctive moves I ever made. Everything I subsequently learned about the man justified that initial teenage impulse.

The Penguin Modern Poets pocket volumes had introduced me to Adrian Henri, Roger McGough and Brian Patten. Number five in the series introduced me to Lawrence Ferlinghetti and Gregory Corso. (Ginsberg I already knew.) Volume Nine alerted me to Denise Levertov, Kenneth Rexroth and William Carlos Williams. The book I warmed to most was the 400-page Penguin anthology *The Children of Albion: Poetry of the 'Underground' in Britain*. It was here that I discovered Pete Brown had a life outside of writing lyrics for Cream and singing with The Battered Ornaments and Piblokto!. *The Children of Albion* also featured Spike Hawkins, whose singularly oblique perspective remains an influence on me to this day. Trocchi and Adrian Mitchell were in there, as well as Tom

Raworth, Anna Lovell, Bernard Kops, Tom Pickard, Ted Milton and all the others who wrote like that and who made me want to write like that.

There used to be a small bookshop near the top end of Kensington Church Street that carried a selection of Chinese and Japanese poetry. From there I bought *Poems of Solitude*, a hardback anthology of works from the T'ang Dynasty, and a Penguin Classics paperback, *Poems of the Late T'ang*. My route into oriental literature had been a typically circuitous and untutored one. I'd been initially drawn to Chinese poetry after reading Ezra Pound's *Cantos* in Bedford Library. I knew nothing of Pound's relationship with T.S. Eliot at the time or of his crucial role in the development of literary modernism, or indeed his support for Mussolini. One day the page opened on verses containing Chinese graphics, and intrigued by all those emperors and ancient dynasties and names I couldn't pronounce, I dived in. In my ignorance I initially grouped Pound with the Beat poets I had read: Gary Snyder, say, or Ginsberg in chanting mode. I knew nothing of the literary context of the *Cantos* or of the difficulties of translating Chinese poetry accurately into English. I was blissfully ignorant of ideograms and idiolect. All I had to go on was the deceptive simplicity of the language and that wondrous imagery, all that thunder in heaven, all those silken cords of sunlight.

That same Kensington Church Street shop also sold me *The Penguin Book of Japanese Verse*, which introduced me to the 5-7-5 syllable form of Haiku. As with Chinese poetry I was initially taken with the exoticism of the imagery: cherry blossom, lotus flowers, the moon reflected on still midnight lakes. The language was familiar, sparse and uncomplicated, but the relationship between the images was complex. Haiku seemed to pack a lot of jump cuts and intriguing juxtaposition into its three-line form and I readily fell into that kind of thinking. A depiction of nature. A concise emotion. An enigmatic question. A touch of Zen.

All this reading matter was relatively cheap and readily available. Paladin published Neville's *Playpower*, Nuttall's *Bomb Culture* and Leary's *The Politics of Ecstasy*. An earlier generation of imprints – Everyman's Library, Jonathan Cape's Travellers' Library, Martin Secker's New Adelphi Library – had made modernism and the avant-garde affordable to a mainstream audience. Now Panther and Corgi published Burroughs and the Beats in slim paperbacks for 40p or less, along with James Baldwin, Philip Roth and an abundance of science fiction. I bought Bob Dylan's *Tarantula*, published by Panther in 1972, for 35p. Compliant liberal librarians played their part too, stocking many of these titles. The first *Whole Earth Catalog*, radical works on fringe theatre and the anti-psychiatry movement. From Joseph Berke to R.D. Laing and Mary Barnes, I found them all in Bedford County Library.

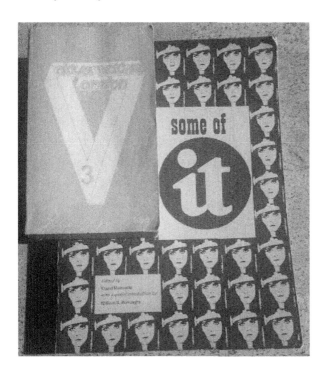

Foundation Texts. Essential reading.

The acquisition I treasured more than any other was *Some of IT*, an anthology of writings from the early days of International Times, first published in January 1969. I found mine in Compendium, and it alerted me to a whole new cast of characters. *Some of IT* constituted a syllabus in its own right. It extended my knowledge of Burroughs (and his co-conspirator Brion Gysin) beyond that initial trio of cut-up novels. The anthology also contained interviews with Morton Feldman, Claes Oldenberg, Buckminster Fuller, Charles Marowitz, the Living Theatre and Julian Beck. It had features on Antonin Artaud and Sartre. It introduced me to the Bradley Martin alias of John "Hoppy" Hopkins, and the poetry of Tuli Kupferberg and John Esam. It carried the original version of Kevin Ayers' cautionary and sceptical *Song for Insane Times*, still called *Song for International Times* at that point. It also featured Daevid Allen's lengthy cosmic travelogue *Letter from Banana Moon Observatory*, written in Deya, Majorca, in 1968 and etched in the familiar multi-coloured felt-tip script he used when he wrote to me four years later. The piece contained the first mention of Gong, which Allen described as "a kind of electric tidal music".

In an editorial in Issue 9, Tom McGrath asked: "What are you doing to those walls when you project hallucinations onto them? Why not go out and paint a mural instead?" That bold provocation from McGrath fed into my own increasing awareness that there was a philosophical and political dimension to all this outsider activity that transcended hedonism and playpower. The piece did more to fuel my own internal debate than any amount of Leary grandstanding or News of the World scare-mongering ever could. McGrath's message was coming directly from the heart of the Underground, not from a false prophet or a bunch of booze-soaked hacks in Fleet Street. I found plenty to take issue with in what McGrath said – my reasoning being that at least the hallucination belongs to you, the mural belongs to the council – and his assertion didn't stop me wanting to take acid, but it did prick my conscience sufficiently enough to further evaluate the purpose of it all. Was all this chemical bombardment putting me on the path to Nirvana or was it just a pleasant Away Day?

****

I was sitting in Sunny Hill Park in Barnet on yet another overcast morning in a dreary year. My southbound lift had only taken me as far as the outskirts of London and it was one of those days when the city seemed foreboding and out of reach, as if there was an invisible force field between me and the capital. Dick Whittington in reverse. Don't go there. Turn back. As I deliberated on whether to cross the A1 and hitchhike home I sat on the parkland grass and flicked through the BIT *Directory of Communes* guide I'd bought in Compendium. The communes were listed by region: the majority seemed to be in Wales, the West Country or remote parts of Scotland. Several were illustrated with a hand-drawn sketch of the location – the homesteads all looked attractively rustic and ivy-clad. In contrast many of the descriptions sounded a salutary warning about what truth seekers should expect from the communal life. "Communes are not crash pads," warned one. "Don't come if you just want to take drugs," said another. "We need people with practical skills." These skills prioritised manual labour: hedging, felling and trenching; digging ditches for the purposes of pipe-laying and the irrigation of water; renovating out-houses; and ploughing barren or overgrown fields for the growing of crops.

A mere handful emphasised the spiritual aspect of communal living: the yoga, the meditation, the potential for personal growth. One of the few situated in London gave a Clapham address and mentioned Buddhism. I sat in Sunny Hill Park and thought about what Daevid Allen had said to me in his letters: "There's lotsa communes which unlike ole Gong can welcome with uncomplicated conscience and mutual benefit creative gents like yourself." I flicked on through the guide, looking at all those remote, off-the-beaten-track places with their crofter ideals and their harsh edicts, but I kept coming back to the one in Marney Road, Clapham, thinking "What if what if what if".

In the Compendium free box I'd also found a self-published anthology of writing. I sat reading that too as the A1 traffic roared by. One earnest tweedy piece of prose had a pejorative side-swipe at a character, describing him as "approaching 40 and still not published". How old and embittered that sounded to me. Imagine getting to that age and you still haven't had anything published. I didn't have a clue how hard the road ahead might be. I just thought about being old, really old – 40 no less – and not having seen your name in print. Later, when Elkie Brooks, the former lead vocalist with Vinegar Joe, started having solo hits, the pop papers mentioned that she was in her early 30s. I'd seen her singing with Vinegar Joe at Bedford Teachers' Training College when she was still being an English Janis Joplin. Imagine having to wait till you were 32 to have a hit. Age was still a complete abstraction to me then. At 17 I couldn't imagine being 22, let alone 32. In a deserted Sunny Hill Park on an unsunny morning I sat reading literature plucked from a help-yourself box about people who couldn't get published. The clouds grew darker and threatened rain. I huddled into my jacket and ate the sandwich that was in my plastic bag. I turned again to that Marney Road page in my Communes guide, got up and hitched penniless once more into the centre of London.

The house was on the north side of Clapham Common. Barry and Eve, it said in the Commune Guide. Barry opened the door. Not tall, as I recall. Longish hair. The gentle disposition of someone versed in

Eastern religion. It specified in the Directory that you were supposed to write or phone first, but without fuss Barry invited me into a spacious upstairs room at the front of the house. Two large windows looked out onto the road. There was a low table with an effigy of Buddha placed in the centre. Incense was burning. Barry made me my first-ever cup of tea taken without milk – a mint infusion – and asked me what I knew about Buddhism. I knew very little. Only a few months earlier the sum total of my knowledge had been gleaned from the covers and track titles of Danny's Quintessence albums. The Eastern theology I'd immersed myself in at the Bedford County Library ashram had mostly centred on Hinduism and Hindu deities.

I was honest and told Barry that my knowledge was scant but that I was keen to learn, and wanted to be on a path that lead to somewhere more fulfilling than my present circumstances would allow. The atmosphere in that upstairs room was calm and cordial, just Barry enquiring softly between sips of mint tea and making no demands of me. Everything I wanted seemed to be in that room. The simplicity and centeredness, the lack of clutter. Once I relaxed into the ambience I spotted Eastern adornments I hadn't noticed before. A figurine or two. A pattern on a blind. An empty vase. The traffic noise on the South Circular a distant hum. If Barry had said "Move in today", I would have headed straight back home, collected a bundle of clothes, renounced all my worldly goods (i.e. a few albums and a stack of old music papers) and devoted myself to a monastic life in that terraced house on the north side of Clapham Common. I was probably there for less than an hour but when Barry showed me to the door I thought I had found my retreat. I walked straight to the Library in Clapham Old Town, flicked through the Evening Standard and started looking for jobs.

There was one at Oakshott's Supermarket just up the road, shelf-stacking and serving at the till, it said in the ad. I just walked in off the street and a supervisor gave me little more than a cursory once over and said I could start tomorrow. "Just bring your National Insurance card with you." Never having worked full-time for a living I didn't have a National Insurance card. I wasn't even sure what one was, so stalled a bit and said I had a few things I'd need to attend to. "No problem," he said. "You can start Monday then if you like. Eight o'clock. Janice here will sort you out some overalls, won't you Janice?" It was that easy. Within an hour of stepping out of that house in Marney Road I'd already found a job. Barry hadn't even said I could move in. Nor had I considered that there might be other people to see. He hadn't said yes but then neither had he said no. Without so much as a hint of a promise I started to imagine myself in my new life. No need to bother with the Oakshott's job. There would surely be plenty of others.

Instead of hitching up to London once or twice a week I started going up almost every weekday. A plan of action quickly fell into place. I'd get a job, somehow, so I could afford to live, somehow, or at least exist in alternative London. I started getting the morning edition of the Evening Standard as soon as it came out and looking through the Sits Vac pages. With barely three O Levels to rub together l went through a brief desperate phase of considering any dreggy employment I could find.

One morning I found myself in a tiny cramped annexe room at the top of the Cumberland Hotel off Oxford Street, filling out a form with a blunt pencil, along with about 20 or 30 other desperate applicants, all male, mostly foreign. One portly German lad insisted very loudly and very inaccurately that this was the very hotel where Jimi Hendrix had died barely 18 months earlier. Every five minutes or so one of us would be called into a tiny room for an interview. I didn't have the energy or enthusiasm to correct the Hendrix fan as he sat there pontificating animatedly about the location where his idol may or may not have choked on his vomit. After five minutes of form-filling and hanging about in that airless room I kind of lost the will to live. I reasoned that however bleak my prospects might seem, my life hadn't been leading up to being a kitchen porter or laundry-room skivvy in a London hotel. I left the migrant unskilled labour of London to their hopes and dreams, and was back out on Oxford Street within minutes.

"Make good money on commission. Excellent presentation skills required," it said in the ad. It gave a Stockwell address ("just behind the Tube Station") and an 11 am interview time. I sat on a low wall next to a newly built row of shops and waited for the clock to tick round. Twenty or 30 other hopefuls were gathered there, all ages. Young secretarial types in midi coats and knee-high boots, smartly turned out, dressed for the office. Blokes in their twenties, thirties and forties, furtively smoking, some smart, some scruffy. This young guy with jet-black hair came over and stood beside me. "What do you reckon, paintings or encyclopaedias?" he asked. "It's bound to be one or the other, isn't it?" I didn't have a clue what it was. Like everyone else I was lured by "Make good money". I hadn't given a thought to what the job might entail. I wasn't even sure why he'd said encyclopaedias. "Door-to-door selling," the young guy explained, and sat down beside me to wait.

The doors opened a little after 11, and we all filed up a narrow staircase into a small makeshift conference room. Five rows of chairs had been laid out for those lucky applicants who could soon be on the verge of making good money on commission. A thickset South African guy bustled into the room and went straight into his spiel. It was encyclopaedias. "We don't sell to peasants," he said bullishly. "We avoid the housing estates." He indicated the gilt-edged piles of books on the table beside him. Told us how crammed with knowledge they were and how we might learn a lot from this quality product, just like what he had. "Gazing around the room I can already see just from looking that some of you will make excellent sales staff," he said. I'm sure he was looking in our direction when he added: "And I can also see how some of you won't be suitable."

There then followed a short break while we were given time to reflect on our suitability before the formal presentation began. "Come on, let's go," said the young guy with jet-black hair who introduced himself as Pete. We laughed at the oiliness of our host as we headed back down the stairs to the street. Pete said he lived nearby and invited me back to his flat in Brixton. I told him about Buddhism and Barry and the Marney Road communal house. I also told him I was trying to form a band and had put an advert in Melody Maker which hadn't really come to anything as yet, but I was still hopeful. "I'm a drummer," said Pete.

He told me he'd been in a group called Black Velvet. "The group who did a single called *African Velvet*," I said. The very same. I remembered *African Velvet* getting played on the radio when it came out. "I was also in a group called Heaven," said Pete. "The band who made that double album on CBS?" I said. The very same also. I remembered the gatefold sleeve and the lavish display ads in the music papers. "Yeah, it had a big promotional budget but it didn't sell," he said. Pete told me he was looking for a new band. I repeated what Dave the drummer had told me, that I needed to learn an instrument. "Not necessarily," said Pete. His flat turned out to be a small cramped place he shared with his Dad. Pete's room was just like mine at home except that he didn't have to share his with two younger brothers. He had a teetering stack of old Melody Makers beside his bed just like I did. LP records lined the wall next to a record player. Clothes were strewn everywhere. Pete went out to make a cup of tea and I heard him arguing with his bad-tempered Dad. Get a job and don't bring people back here seemed to be the gist of it.

It was just another of life's chance encounters. An hour or so spent in a stranger's bedroom, talking about music, creativity, hopes and dreams. I said I'd be into getting a band together when I moved to London. Pete gave me his phone number and said I should definitely give him a call when I did. We both agreed that we wouldn't be selling encyclopaedias any time soon. I left that small Brixton flat full of renewed energy and didn't encounter Pete again for quite a while. By the time I did our circumstances had changed immeasurably.

This being the early 1970s the Underground was filtering through into television in all kinds of novel and unexpected ways. Rock bands showed up in the most unlikely places: schools programmes, religious slots, Saturday morning kids' shows. And on weekday afternoons, at around the time I'd be arriving home from my daily adventures, Anglia TV began transmitting Richard Hittleman's 30-minute *Yoga for Health*. I'd expressed an interest in yoga to Barry at the Clapham Common retreat, but when he asked me which branch I was following – Hatha, Bhakti, Kundalini etc – I was too ashamed to answer "The one that Richard Hittleman demonstrates at four o'clock in the afternoon on Anglia TV" (which turned out to be Hatha, had I known at the time). *Yoga for Health* opened with a multi-layering of triangles from which formed into a spiralling mandala. Superimposed images of lithe assistant Lyn Marshall flickered across the screen before Hittleman himself, in half-lotus position, levitated into view in the bottom-right-hand corner just below the titles. The opening image of the programme was always the same: Californian Hittleman and one of his demonstrators, Cheryl or Lyn, sitting on yoga mats, cross-legged, meditating.

Hittleman would then slowly open his eyes and with a curiously tight-lipped smile deliver an introductory homily. I tried to ensure that I was home whenever *Yoga for Health* was on. I would join in with the exercises and then in that quiet late afternoon window of opportunity before my younger siblings got home from school I'd practice the moves again in the front room, breathing and flexing my third eye until the house erupted with the clatter and chaos of children. As with the rice diet, I felt immediate benefits from Hittleman's structured 28-day exercise plan. I observed the principles of slow graceful movement and of working within the parameters of one's own physical limitation. I stretched to release energy and felt a warm surge shoot up my spine. I emptied my head of unnecessary clutter and learned for the first time how to meditate.

I tugged my long hair "rhythmically and not too quickly, 25 times without pause" in accordance with the scalp exercise. I adopted the breathing exercises. I assumed the lion posture to firm the muscles of my face and neck. I tried the head twist, the locust, the rishi and the cobra, all the time focussing on the area being exercised and trying not to let my mind wander. I was never supple enough to assume the full lotus with the soles of the feet pointed upwards (but then neither I noticed was Hittleman). Some of the more contortionist postures remained beyond me too, but I was grateful to *Yoga for Health* for beaming Eastern practices into my living room on a regular basis. The regime galvanised me and polished up my body temple a treat. Meanwhile my earthly circumstances hadn't advanced one iota.

My London visits became increasingly tinged with desperation. I phoned Barry at Marney Road a couple of times but got no reply. I stood in a succession of piss-stained call-boxes feeding 2p pieces into the slot while waiting for Pete to pick up and say: "Yes, I'll form a band with you." One day I finally got through and his Dad answered. No, Pete's not here. No, he didn't know what time he would be back. In the end I think I must have bothered him one time too many because he grew angry with me, shouting furiously down the line. "Look I don't where he is or when he'll be back. Stop phoning this number." By now it was late June and I was getting nowhere. On a whim I decided to write to my London Uncle and Aunt, asking if there was any chance I could stay at their house until I got my shit together with a band or a job or a poetry gig or a combination of all three. They had a large house in Islington, two old houses in fact, that my uncle, a builder by trade, knocked into one when houses in that part of London could be bought for a song, back in the bombsite days of the 1950s. While I waited to hear from my relatives I continued to plug away at trying to find a London job that didn't merely involve keeping my head above water.

I was in a phone box in a crowded street in Fulham when Barry's voice finally came on the other end of the line. He was amiable enough, although a little distant. "Well, we still have a few people to see," he said cordially. Despite his reasonable tone I knew there and then I was receiving the brush-off. There was no chance I was ever going to live in that house of tranquillity with the exotic wall hangings and the incense burning and the Buddhist wisdom on the bookshelves. Perhaps there never had been any chance. Maybe this was all mere delusion on my part and had been all along. Many are the faces of Maya. I walked out of that phone box in the full glare of a sunny June afternoon, and once again assumed invisibility, as I so often did when I boarded a bus with barely enough for the fare in my pocket. Eventually I found my way to my favoured hitchhiking spot north of Hendon, and at the point where the M1 and the A1 diverted – the M1 curling left, the Barnet Way pointing straight ahead – I once again curved past "cares", stuck out my thumb, and continued to climb an enormous night.

Chapter 6

FREE RIDE

"Have you ever seen two blokes sucking each other off?"

They never get straight to the point when you're hitchhiking. There's always the preamble and preliminary enquiries. This one had started off with: "I was in Grantchester Meadows the other day and I saw a couple, a man and a woman, having oral sex. Have you ever seen a couple having oral sex?"

I'd gone to my regular spot on Huntingdon Road in Cambridge to hitch back home to Sandy. Past the playing-field railings of the college to a convenient little pull-in bay by the bus stop. Perfect location. Never anybody there. Not too close to the corner of the road. Nobody likes to adjust their driving speed to accommodate a hitchhiker when they've just turned a corner and gone up a gear. Fifty yards up the road gives them plenty of time to see you and decide whether they want a passenger. I must have mentioned to the guy who picked me up – mid to late 30s, scowly – that I'd been to Grantchester Meadows and he took this as his cue. From a man and a woman in the meadows – al fresco naturally – we quickly progressed to two men and then after a thoughtful pause, "Would you like to..." I declined his offer and asked to be dropped off at the roundabout at Caxton Gibbet. I still had some way to go on my journey but I didn't much care for his menacing vibe. No sooner had I got out of the car by the site of the old Ermine Street Gallows than my driver just turned around and headed back towards Cambridge looking for fresh young meat.

There were many similar predatory encounters. Getting into a stranger's car often involved covert and unconscious negotiation – compliance might be assumed by the merest detectable shift in body language. "Runaway are you?" asked one creepy old guy (old to me anyway, probably in his late 40s/early 50s), giving me the inquisitive once over the moment I got comfortable. I was hitching into Bedford. This was soon after I'd first decided to go on the lam and pretend I was still attending college. It's almost as if he could sniff out some nascent vulnerability in me, uncanny in a way but a telling indicator of how people like that operate. Relaxation or a friendly demeanour were frequently misread. "Show us your cock," said a lorry driver as he pulled into the transport café car park about a mile from where I lived. "Go on," he smiled, staring hard at my groin. It was a sunny afternoon. He was affable and unthreatening but I was glad there were several feet of spacious cab and engine casing between us. "How big is it?" he enquired. "Four inches? Six inches?" He was pretty insistent, so in the end I showed him. He seemed happy enough with the display and pursued the matter no further. We jumped out of the cab and went our separate ways.

Not all encounters were as friendly. "Are you IRA?" barked one of the two young commandos in the front seat of the car that had stopped at my regular not-off-to-college hitchhiking spot. They were twitchy, muscular and testosterone'd to the max. "Because if you are you can fucking get out of the car right now." This was not long after Bloody Sunday, at a time when most people on the UK mainland barely knew what the Irish

Republican Army was. Having convinced them that I was not the tool of a terrorist organisation they eased off on the interrogation, but it was a long eight miles to Bedford that morning and I was glad to get out of their vehicle. Another time, another pair of squaddies had equally menacing intent. These two talked quietly about keeping me in the car and not letting me out at Baldock as I'd asked. I sat in the back and pretended I couldn't hear their every whisper. They must have decided that sodomising me and bundling me into a ditch wasn't worth the aggro because they let me out at my specified destination.

I came of age during the golden age of hitchhiking, at a time of great expansion in the motorway and dual carriageway network but before crippling third-party insurance and tachometers put paid to 90% of the hitchhiker's regular stoppers: lorry drivers and commercial travellers. Hitchhiking was probably my dominant mode of transport throughout the 1970s. It was free (only once do I ever remember being asked for a contribution towards the petrol), regular and dependable. I was an intuitive lift-thumber, even when other options were available. I first hitchhiked when I was 13. Some trainspotting mates told me there were a dozen or so steam engines lining up to be scrapped at Cohen's Yard just outside Kettering. It was the school holidays, spring 1968, and I was obliged to look after my younger brother Chris, who was 10. "I'll say I'm 16 and you say you're 14," I told him as we began the long walk from the railway station to the scrapyard. An elderly couple picked us up and did indeed ask how old we were. They looked doubtful when I told them but they still dropped us at Cohen's Yard. Avoiding the main entrance and the guard dog as instructed we scrambled down an embankment to a siding, and walked among the rusty weather-beaten old engines that were awaiting the cutter's flame. We walked all the way back to Kettering town centre. It seemed to take forever.

On June 23rd 1971, just after my O Levels had ended, I took an early evening train up to London and went to see Kevin Ayers and The Whole World at City University. The Pakistan Civil War was on and it was a benefit for the Kastur Relief fund. Also on the bill were The Edgar Broughton Band and Hackensack who played in a small bar downstairs, and Bridget St. John who opened on the main stage for Kevin. Who was late. Very late. Bridget played a couple of extra songs at the end of her set and apologised for Kevin's absence. There was another lull. An announcer made a further apology and asked us all to put our hands in our pockets for the relief-fund buckets that were passed around.

I got talking to a couple of students who were also into Kevin Ayers. Three weeks earlier I'd had a letter printed in Melody Maker's *Any Questions* column, asking among other things when Kevin and Bridget were going to make the album of children's songs they had both mentioned in interviews. The printed answer promised that the album was in the pipeline, but it never did come to fruition. I mentioned my letter to the guys I was sitting with. They both remembered reading it. "Fame at last," one of them said and we went back to waiting for Kevin's appearance, also still in the pipeline. When he did eventually shamble on, to relieved applause, he sat on a chair at the left side of the stage, almost in the wings. Hunched over a semi-acoustic guitar he said, "This song's called *A Funny Thing Happened to Me on the Way to City University*," and launched into a new song about not serving strangers in blue suede shoes.

Realising that I wasn't going to make the last train out of Kings Cross, I asked the students I had befriended if I could stay at theirs. They said this wasn't possible but did suggest I go up to the PA guy at the end and maybe he would make an announcement. As I walked towards him with the crowd already filing out, he launched into another plea on behalf of the relief fund. Realising that my problems were small beer compared with the upheavals in Pakistan, I chickened out. A year later I had little hesitation in going up to total strangers in Cambridge while tripping and asking them if I might cadge a bed for the night, but as a kid not yet out of school I lacked the confidence.

As a result, I found myself in Northampton Square in Islington at two o'clock in the morning without a clue how I was going to get home. Someone pointed vaguely northwards and suggested I try flagging down one of the newspaper delivery vans as they made their way out of Fleet Street with the 2 am editions. There were indeed a lot of these vans about, and lorries too, but they all seemed to be leaving Fleet Street in an unbroken flow and I couldn't see any practical way of getting one to stop. I headed hopefully up a long street dotted with all-night cafés and taxi drivers. It was a warm night and on the other side of the road a Middle Eastern-looking guy in an open shirt stood in his café doorway surveying this lone inhabitant of the nocturnal world as he wandered past. He beckoned me over. Fearful as I was of the hours of walking ahead of me, I hoped that he was going to offer me a spare bed. He made vague conversation in broken English and didn't seem that interested in where I had been or how good Kevin Ayers was. The small talk dwindled to nothing. I looked forlornly up his side passage-stairs to where a comfortable bed might be, then carried on walking.

Looking back, I realise that I often put my life in danger like that. I was 16 at the time. A kid out on the streets of London at 2 am, lost and reeking of desperation. What if the café owner had been of a certain mind? What if he had said, "Yes, there is a bed up there, do you want to come up?"

I still have no idea where I was in London that night or the route I took to get home. I do remember that I was in Muswell Hill at one point. I also remember, as the traffic dwindled to nothing, running up to a stationary car at a red traffic light and frantically asking for a lift. The driver obliged, and somehow after a further lucky lift or two I found myself with the dawn light glowing in the East, getting out of a lorry that was traversing the A1 at Hatfield. I've never forgotten that sense of euphoric relief as I walked across the road to the grass verge of the roundabout that would get me home in one more ride. I had beaten the night. It was a beautiful Midsummer's dawn. I could feel the warmth on my face. I'd seen Kevin Ayers perform *Stranger in Blue Suede Shoes* for the first time. Some months later I wrote a short poem about it all.

> Dawn walkers
> Leave trails of night behind
> Concealed in daring air.

It's a trifling fragment, like pretty much anything else you write at that age, but it encapsulates that O Level summer perfectly.

On Friday March 3rd 1972, a week after Syd Barrett's Stars had played Cambridge Corn Exchange, the band had been expected to perform again at Essex University, supporting Kevin Ayers and Nektar. I set off for Colchester in the late afternoon and soon found myself on the outskirts of Cambridge in the unfamiliar terrain of a large housing estate. The Cambridge United graffiti didn't exactly have the menace of "MUFC" or "Firm", but this sure wasn't the willow-lined riverbanks of the Backs, or the cow-grazing pastures of Fen Causeway. I was only vaguely familiar with the demarcation of Town and Gown back then, but as the daylight began to fade I was glad when a man of the cloth stopped to pick me up. The conversation was pleasant enough. He didn't seem to mind having a long-hair in his car, and he exuded that benign air of benevolence common to happy-clappy vicars at the time.

When he enquired politely as to my faith, I said that I was becoming increasingly interested in Buddhism. "Yes," he said, giving an ecumenical sigh. "Young people today seem very taken with Eastern religion. I suspect that it's just a passing fad." While this wasn't exactly the Borstal Governor's explosion in *Scum* when Godber announces that he feels himself "increasingly drawn towards Mecca", the tone of condescension was audible. When he dropped me off near to Essex University my kindly Rev handed me a little booklet and sent me on my way.

No 223

for SHELTER and FRIENDS OF THE EARTH

KEVIN AYERS
DICK HECKSTALL-SMITH
NEKTAR

In the Dance Hall, University of Essex, Friday, 3rd March
8.30 - 3.00 a.m.   Bar till 1.00   50p

Essex was a brand-new campus, less than ten years old that first time I visited. The gig was absolutely packed and the bar was rammed. People sat blocking entire stairwells. The mere act of wandering around became a physical ordeal. And to compound it all an announcement was made on stage that Syd Barrett's Stars would not be appearing. There was a general groan in the hall but I didn't get the impression that many were there to see Syd Barrett anyway. This what they did every week, their regular Friday-night student piss-up. I sat on the stairs for a while, tired and hot, people-watching. A guy stood at the top of the stairwell surveying the scene. "Weird scenes inside the goldmine," he intoned meaningfully to his friend, who nodded sagely. I couldn't wait to relay that prime piece of pseudery to Danny. I read the pamphlet that the kindly vicar had given me. It was full of homilies about helping the poor and doing missionary work, which I suppose is what my godly driver had been doing by picking me up.

Kevin Ayers, having disbanded The Whole World, played one of his first duo gigs with Archie Leggett. German band Nektar were the headline act, and I should have had the sense to leave while they were on. They churned out the kind of turgid boogie rock that everyone seemed to play then. It had little in common with Cluster or Can, or any of the other German groups I was becoming increasingly fascinated with. Against my better judgement I stuck it out to the end and drifted out into the cold night air with what seemed like the entirety of Colchester's student population. As in London the previous summer I didn't have a clue where I was or how I would get home.

Someone pointed me in the direction of the dual carriageway and I walked a long campus road to what turned out to be the A12. I clambered down an embankment in hope of a London-bound lift and it was only at this point that I realised how late it was. This wasn't London at 2 am. This was the Essex countryside at 2 am. There was nothing on the road. Not a single vehicle going in either direction. The silence was all-encompassing. After what seemed like an age I picked out the distant rumble and headlights of an approaching lorry. I was so desperate for a lift that when he got closer I jumped up and down, frantically waving my arms, as if trying to flag down a rescue helicopter from a remote hill-top. About an hour later my kindly driver prodded me awake as I lay sleeping soundly on the engine pillow of his warm cab and dropped me on the North Circular. Again, I found my way as if by homing device to the familiar roundabouts and lay-bys of the A1 and from here negotiated another nocturnal journey back to my warm bed.

In those first weeks of post-college liberation, before I ventured further afield than Bedfordshire, I sometimes broke up the routine of sitting in the County Library all day by hitching a three-mile ride down the A1 to Biggleswade. On dull grey mornings I'd sit in the nondescript town library – no William Burroughs or *Necromancy* on those shelves – and just watch people going by. Then I'd wander from shop window to shop window in the High Street for a bit. Not so much creative dérive as abject boredom, my only purpose being to get through another day. On Mondays I took to carrying my transistor radio with me, just so I could listen to Vivian Stanshall or Kenny Everett guesting on Radio Four's *Start the Week*, presented by Richard Baker. At that point Everett's career was in limbo, the DJ having been exiled from Radio One in July 1970 for a harmless comment about the Minister of Transports' wife passing her advanced driving test by bribing the instructor. Radio Four always kept a door open for him though, as it did for Vivian Stanshall, Ivor Cutler and all those other idiosyncratic spirits who drifted effortlessly from John Peel's *Top Gear* to the former Home Service.

It was on one such Biggleswade Monday morning, my radio cradled against the gusting wind, that a frail elderly lady approached me in a side street, dressed only in a dressing gown, carpet slippers and floral nightie. "I haven't been out of my house for 20 years," she said vacantly, pausing on the pavement as if awaiting any instruction I might have for her. When none was forthcoming she floated feather-lightly back towards her garden gate, a shaky apparition as tiny as a sparrow. The encounter was no weirder than several others I experienced in that period when my own life, like Kenny Everett's, was in limbo and I too was exiled from any meaningful sense of purpose or motivation.

When I wasn't wandering aimlessly around Biggleswade I ricocheted aimlessly between Baldock and Letchworth. In *On the Road* (which I still hadn't read at that point), Jack Kerouac and Neil Cassady rode from coast to coast. My less expansive horizons were mapped out by the B656 as I walked from a town dotted with Russian spies to a garden village with no pubs. During the tit-for-tat machinations of the Cold War, Alec Douglas Home, Foreign Secretary in Edward Heath's Conservative Government, had only recently expelled an entire Baldock street full of Soviet attachés. I used to wander those same nondescript streets imagining scenes from *Callan* being played out behind the respectable net curtains.

I would then head for Letchworth, where I killed time in David's Bookshop and the small library on the Broadway. I frequently walked the entire route between the two towns and it always seemed to be raining. I was sticking out a forlorn thumb on one such squally morning when Mrs Crutchface passed me in her car and shot me a look of withering contempt. Mrs Crutchface was the wife of Mr Davies, a foreign-languages teacher at my old school, christened Crutchface by the fifth-formers on account of his Jonathan King/Geoffrey Boycott wobbly gob. Crutchface initiated methods of intimidation that made all the other head-slappers and parade-ground bullies among the teaching staff look tame. Even by 1960s psycho standards, Crutchface was in an idiosyncratic league of his own. His favourite trick was to pull a boy's hair and then yank him backwards until he fell over, with Crutchface's hand still tightly grasped to the back of his skull. It was a frequent sight in the corridors. You would walk out of a classroom at the end of a lesson and there would be Crutchface bending over some poor unfortunate, shouting like an army sergeant, while the boy squirmed to be let go. I was the recipient of his bullying on more than one occasion. I even told my Mum about it, something I rarely did. You didn't grass or squeal or complain or go running home to your parents. On encountering the fearsome Crutchface, I did.

"Oh, he does, does he?" she said when I told her about his preferred methods of child abuse. The next morning there was a note ready to give him should he ever bully me again. Inevitably he did bully me again, the very next day I think, and as my hand hovered over my pocket ready to give him the note, he screamed "TAKE YOUR HANDS OUT OF YOUR POCKETS BOY!" with such ferocity that I immediately withdrew my hand. I never did give him that note.

One morning I walked out of class to see him dragging Bobby Taylor along the ground like a rag doll. Freckled, speccy, mild-mannered Bobby Taylor, a hole-in-the-heart kid whose condition was known to all, perhaps even to Crutchface. As we schoolboys looked on aghast I noticed a group of sixth-formers gathered at the end of the corridor, also looking on, impassively I assumed at the time, but not so impassively as it turned out.

One afternoon, about a year later, my classmates and I gathered against our will on the muddy playing fields to watch the annual staff versus pupils Rugby match. It was just a few months before I left school and the day was windswept and drizzly. When the first kick went in I barely noticed. Crutchface got up, dusted himself down and ran enthusiastically once more into the fray. The second ruck was a bit more obvious. Two or three sixth-formers piled on top of him and there was a bit of afters, a noticeable scuffle, another injudicious boot or two went in. On the third occasion he went down in a scrum and was given a proper kicking. The referee, geography teacher Mr Raines, waded in – after a decent pause I thought – and broke up the melée. He issued a half-hearted warning to the boys responsible, Crutchface wiped his bloodied nose, and there were no further incidents. I have rerun this scene many times in my head and it always goes on for a bit longer than it actually did. I like to imagine that the retribution lasted for the rest of the game, but I know that in reality it amounted to little more than those two or three brief scuffles. Even so, it was one of the happiest days of my school life.

Mrs Crutchface taught history to the A stream, so she never taught me. And here she was now on the B656 driving between Baldock and Letchworth and giving me a vinegary look. Most of my school reports suggested that I would never amount to anything and here I was, footsore and bedraggled, walking along a grass verge in the rain and still not amounting to anything. She glared at me with such disdain that I felt compelled to flick her a good old-fashioned V sign. A mile or so later the rain came on harder, so I headed off the road, climbed a wire fence and retreated into a sparse copse for shelter. Here I discovered a veritable trove of weather-soaked, jizz-stained porn mags, presumably discarded by lone lorry drivers and sales reps after their desultory roadside wank, and now returning to pulp and mulch in the heavy rain.

Hitchhiking was not for the impatient or easily agitated. Sometimes a car would slow the moment I stuck out a thumb. On other occasions I was rooted to the same spot for what seemed like half a day. I spent many an idle hour stranded on some country B-road as the post-lunchtime lull in traffic dwindled to silence and I listened and watched in vain for an approaching vehicle. In such moments you develop an intimate relationship with your surroundings. Landscape and location leave an indelible mental imprint. A litter-strewn layby, a grassy verge, the gentle undulations of a distant hillock. You learn by experience that if five or six lorries are closely bunched in a convoy, not one of them will have the opportunity to stop for you.

You develop a similar instinct regarding who might stop and who will definitely not. You make eye contact with every driver who passes. Not too hopeful, not too despairing. The relationship between driver and pick-up is a microcosm of life: temporary, existential. Conversation rarely rises above the banal, an introductory "How far you going/been waiting there long?" followed by the sporadic exchange of pleasantries. Arguments are uncommon, but not unheard of. I learned to keep a diplomatic silence whenever someone advocated bringing back the birch, or expounded on how they would solve the immigrant problem. One guy, Australian, taking me into Cambridge one day, spelled out his racial theory in paranoid detail. "They got the genetic advantage you see," he drawled. "A black guy and a white chick will always have a black baby. And vice versa. Soon we'll be overrun. You'll see."

I encountered the full gamut of human life. There was the genial young army officer who picked me up on the A1 and spoke in pure Monty Python banter. "Gordon's the name, driving's the game," he said with the clipped breeziness of the amiable crackpot as he offered a firm handshake and I struggled to keep a straight face. He explained that he was getting off "the main drag" at Hatfield because he was heading over to St Albans. He had "previously pranged two charabancs" while on active duty and was the first person I ever heard refer to Buckingham Palace as "Buck House". "London?" said another of life's south-bound lorry drivers as I climbed gratefully into his cab. "Yeah," I said. "Where are you going?" "Switzerland," he replied. I had never been south of New Cross at the time. He talked of an Alpine world exotic and utterly out of reach to me. We had the same initial exchange when I got into his cab a few months later, having failed to recognise him. All lorry rides blur into one after a while, differentiated only by the comfort of the seating and the smoothness of the suspension.

More than one person gave me a lift regularly. During the period when I was returning home after a day spent trying to find my alternative London, I could set my watch by the young guy in a white transit van who picked me up at Apex Corner in Mill Hill and dropped me at the turn-off to Welwyn Garden City. We rapidly developed the relaxed familiarity of kindred spirits. He had been a roadie for Hawkwind and was still close to the band. I should qualify this by stating that this was a period when approximately half the long-hairs I met claimed to have been a roadie for Hawkwind at some point, so initially I was wary. But everything he said had a plausible ring to it, and several of the stories he came out with later bore fruit in the music papers. I soon twigged that he was bona fide. He told me that the band had just recorded a single version of *Silver Machine* and reckoned that it could well put them in the Top 20. We laughed at the sheer unlikeliness of this but agreed that, well, you never know. On one of the last occasions he picked me up he told me that DikMik was leaving the band. "DikMik is always threatening to leave the band," he said. "But this time he's really going." When I read in the NME a few months later that DikMik had indeed finally left Hawkwind I allowed myself a quiet smile.

The Conservative MP Sir Gerald Nabarro owned a fleet of Daimlers with personalised number plates, NAB 1, NAB 2, etc. One of those passed me as I stood at an A1 roundabout one day. Given Nabarro's well-known loathing for immigrants, the permissive society and long-haired layabouts, it's perhaps unsurprising that he declined to offer me a lift. One early evening in March, with the darkness encroaching and foul weather brewing, I enjoyed what remains to this day my only ride in a Rolls Royce. My driver explained that he had chauffeured them all – you name it, Mohammed Ali, Frank Sinatra. The Rolls, he told me, was a gift from an oil sheik. "He said to me 'Look after the car until I return'. I asked him when that would be. 'Oh, perhaps next year,' he replied. That was six years ago." I sat in the back and listened to the engine purr. I had never been in a car that purred. It felt so positively decadent that I slipped off my shoes and felt the plush carpeted floor beneath my feet. He was only going 20 or 30 miles up the road, but for that short time I drowned in luxury.

In sharp contrast I sat in many a diesel-drenched Foden cab or in cars that were kippered with cigarette smoke. I was once given a lift into Bedford on the back of a tractor trailer. As I sat there, sprawled uncomfortably on an itchy seat of burlap sacking, I had the dubious pleasure of watching a tailback of resentful drivers build up behind us. At one point I reasoned it might just be quicker to jump off and walk. To compound the ignominy, it started to rain. Another time on the A1 I was offered a lift in a motor-cycle sidecar by a young biker couple. They drove fast, and the sidecar had no protective front shield. I could barely breathe, and had to sit with my face down and mouth closed to protect myself from the G Force and the insects. Late one afternoon coming back from Bedford, as we passed the turn-off to the village of Cople my driver quietly crossed himself. He saw me glance at him. "My son was killed there," he said quietly.

I hitchhiked so often that I grew bored with the niceties of small talk. Occasionally I resorted to making stuff up just to pass the time. This usually involved inventing a life for myself similar to the one I aspired to. I told one apparently unsuspecting old couple that I had recently had a book of poetry published by Penguin called *The Subway to Sunset*. "Oh, Penguin," they said. "Very impressive." Sometimes the fantasies were trivial and low-key, told merely to amuse myself. On other occasions they were implausibly outlandish. I told one guy that I had been instrumental in setting up Granta Magazine. I said this because I had just learned the other definition of instrumental that didn't mean a piece of music without words. I had also just discovered the literary journal Granta. "How did you help set up Granta?" my driver asked sceptically. Sensing his doubt, I panicked. "Oh, I lent them some money," I said. I could tell he was looking at this 17-year-old long-hair, dressed in a blue duffel coat and scruffy pumps, thinking: "Oh, I've picked up a right little bull-shitter here." When I failed to recognise the same old couple who had picked me up a few months earlier they caught me off-guard by asking about the

Subway to Sunset anthology. They had looked out for it in WH Smith, they told me. Thrown off guard, I explained that its publication been held up for a few months. Again, the air of scepticism in the vehicle was tangible.

Sometimes the bullshit and lies came to me. One old guy who gave me a lift into Bedford told me that he was the father of Ronnie Bond of The Troggs, and that Ronnie had written *Wild Thing*. The fact that I knew *Wild Thing* was written by Chip Taylor and that Ronnie Bond was from Wiltshire, while my driver appeared to have a broad Bedfordshire accent didn't deter him one bit from his ever-spiralling fantasies. For that brief 25-minute ride my driver's mythical other life seemed no more fanciful or delusional than my own.

The front doorbell rang one Sunday morning and it was London Uncle come to pay a visit. London Auntie wasn't with him. She'd popped round to see other relatives, and anyway it wouldn't take long, he said. I'd forgotten all about the spur-of-the-moment letter I'd sent them asking if I could come and stay at their house till I found a job, or a commune, or a spiritual retreat, or a band. I hadn't bothered telling Dad either, and he looked bemused as London Uncle, with evident discomfort, paced around the living room and explained why he felt compelled to visit. You'd have thought I'd asked permission for his daughter's hand in incest and not just asked if I could stay at his Islington terrace for a bit.

"Frankly, this has been a great embarrassment to me," he huffed, brandishing my offending letter. Dad continued to look bemused. This comedy of awkward manners eventually reached its dénouement with me saying that although I still intended to become a writer or a singer or a Zen scholar, I promised that I wouldn't burden London Uncle with further letters like this one. Mum, who didn't care much for London Uncle or London Auntie, and dreaded their Christmas half-hour stately visits, where they talked unceasingly about the achievements of their children and asked little about hers, stayed in the kitchen until the episode was concluded.

Dad came from a large family and consequently I had many uncles, aunties and cousins. Despite this, there was little of the bustle, bonhomie or chaotic intimacy of, say, a large Jewish or Irish clan. Mass gatherings were few and far between. An air of polite modesty prevailed. There were relatives whose houses I never visited, despite living only a few streets away, and others where strict permission and advance notice were always required before you so much as knocked on their door. Much of this I put down to the family's spectacular lack of geographical mobility over the previous 800 years. The exodus of the Chapman tribe is one of England's less remarkable diasporas. The first documented bearer of the surname, according to our Norman filing-clerk forefathers, appears to be a Geoffrey Chapman, located in Huntingdonshire in the 12th century. I suspect there is a direct bloodline link between those Huntingdonshire Chapmans and the ones who had fetched up 15 miles further south by the 1800s. That's barely two miles a century. Farm by farm, feudal lord by lord, field by fallow field, acre by acre, they edged slowly towards the midday sun until they settled in Tetworth, a triple boundary-bordering parish so administratively inconvenient that for centuries neither Bedfordshire, Cambridgeshire or Huntingdonshire could agree who it belonged to, so they split the indifference.

Dad was the second youngest of eight kids. His younger brother, Francis, was known as "Bay", so-called because as a boy Dad couldn't pronounce "baby". Francis died of TB aged three. On his headstone, where he lies buried next to his own father, he is referred to as Francis ("Bay"). Dad was the youngest survivor of the pack, the runt of the litter, with five older brothers and two older sisters, a couple of whom weren't strictly blood relatives at all, but siblings "taken in" as a result of out-of-wedlock indiscretions. Some families took in washing. Mine, it seems, charitably took in unwedded waifs and their offspring. Such affairs were not up for discussion, and remained strictly off limits and unspoken. All the respective parties are dead now, and if it hadn't been for the heart-to-heart chat I had with Dad on my bed that Christmas when I returned home like the unprodigal son, they would all have gone to their graves with me being none the wiser. Mum's the word. Or in this case, Auntie. And Uncle.

A couple of weeks after London Uncle's visit I was in the back garden, having just watched Billie Jean King beat reigning champion Evonne Goolagong in the Ladies' Final at Wimbledon. The women's final was played on a Friday in those days, and I made no pretence at attending college. I just wanted to see if the amazing young Goolagong could retain her title. Grummar had popped round to see her daughter. "Finished college for the day?" she asked. There was an awkward pause as I dredged a redundant memory bank for plausible excuses. "He's going to be a writer. Aren't you boy?" said Mum. It had such a hollow ring to it that I felt instant remorse for all the days I was wasting like this. At the same time there was a tone of defiance in her voice. "We'll show fancy London Uncle with his lardy da ways, won't we?" "Yes," I felt compelled to reply. "Yes. I'm going to be a writer."

Despite London Uncle's admonishment, I was still determined to find an outlet for my creativity. In that same copy of IT that had carried the bogus Bolan cover there was a small box ad for a collective known as New Dwarf Groups. Next to a silhouette of a tall, lean flute-player were addresses in Plymouth, Godalming, Oxford, Hampstead and Aberdeen. Oxford seemed feasible in a way that trendy Hampstead didn't, so one drizzly morning I set off for a city I'd never been to in the hope of finding a communal workshop atmosphere in which I might still flourish. I seriously underestimated how long it would take to hitch 60 miles across country with no direct routes or dual carriageways. By 11 am I was sitting in the porch of a village pub somewhere in the middle of God-knows-where-shire watching the ceaseless rain roll across lush green acres of countryside. "No," said the landlord, "We don't sell tea, only coffee." He was happy to let me sit and shelter for a bit, but he and his one customer kept a wary eye on me as I waited for the rain to ease off.

By the time I reached Oxford, the day had brightened a little and the sun was making a half-hearted effort to shine. I had assumed that Dwarf Group HQ would be a community centre/youth club-type affair, but the premises turned out to be an old wood-built warehouse set back off the road in a puddle-cratered yard. It was a ramshackle looking place. No number on a gate, no Dwarf Group nameplate etched in a groovy font, no silhouetted Pied Piper man, no indication from the outside that the building was occupied or in use at all. I couldn't find an entrance, front or back. I climbed a rickety fire escape to what looked like a door, but it was either locked or stuck fast. I couldn't even really tell if it was a door. It might just have been a blocked-up loading bay. Eventually, by dangling precariously off the stair rail, in clear view of the street, I managed to look through a tiny knothole in the wood. The place was unoccupied, but there was evidence of recent use. A stack of handbills on a workbench. Paint pots on the floor. A bicycle propped against a wall. I stared through the crack in the wood for a few seconds until the wind blew grit into my eye and made it water. I walked disconsolately back down the fire escape and headed for home. I had been in Oxford for barely an hour but was soon trudging along the A24 sticking out a thumb. It started to rain heavily again.

By late afternoon I was standing outside Irthlingborough Diamonds football ground on the A6 in Northamptonshire and it was pissing down. Nobody wants a drenched passenger in their car. They would no sooner pick up a hitchhiker in the pouring rain than invite a stray soaking-wet dog into the passenger seat. I stood there rooted to the same spot for so long on that prematurely dark Midsummer's evening that the illuminated Double D sign on the side of Irthlingborough Diamonds' social club began to glow bright orange. I arrived home dishevelled, damp and despondent at around nine o'clock, having spent 12 hours on the road in yet another fruitless search for a place to be.

Veronica turned up unexpectedly at the house the following Sunday. It was a rare hot day and we went for a long rambling walk round the wet willow meadows and up the sand hills. She said everyone in Bedford was missing me and wondered where I was. It had been weeks since anyone had seen or heard from me. She was checking just to see if I was OK. It hadn't occurred to me that I had "gone missing", but I was so far out to sea by that point that I barely had a grasp on anything. I rambled feyly about my spiritual search while Veronica offered the occasional side-on smile at my windblown utterances. I worked dialogue from the Syd Barrett Rolling Stone interview into the conversation wherever I could. "I walk a lot," I said. "About eight miles a day. It's bound to show but I don't know how." "Well, you lose weight for a start," said Veronica, as if it was the most stupidly obvious thing I'd ever uttered. At one point we stood on a footbridge over the river and watched the tidal flotsam go gliding by. I asked Veronica if she knew that song *River Man* by Nick Drake – she didn't. I said that I imagined some river sprite further upstream sprinkling petals into the water. She must have told Danny that, because when I next saw him he reminded me with unconcealed mirth and a "What the fuck is happening to you man?" expression. I walked Veronica back to the bus stop and said I was glad she'd been to see me. "Don't be so anti-social," she said. I vowed not to be so anti-social.

My lift on another rare sunny day was an elderly gentleman with liver spots, pale blue eyes, thin silvery hair and fang-like teeth. As if guided by some unspoken impulse he turned off the main road barely a mile out of Bedford and headed down a narrow gravel driveway towards Cardington Lock. When we reached a clump of bulrushes that hid us from view he turned off the engine and talked about Buddhism. Unlike my staunchly Anglican driver that night in Cambridge, he didn't hand me a pamphlet. Instead he spoke of how he'd been some sort of diplomat or cultural attaché in Tibet in the 1950s, and had travelled in remote regions where Westerners never trod. He told me he'd helped monks retrieve the treasures and sacred texts from their temples before the Chinese invaders could ransack them. I told him about the house in Marney Road, Clapham, about Barry and Eve, and how I was still hoping against hope that they'd find a place for me. I told him about my macrobiotic rice diet and he told me about the yak dung the Tibetans burnt so they could cook their food. "They didn't know where they were, some of them," he said, alluding to his role in the evacuation of pilgrims and monks following the Chinese invasion. "They were not of this world." And then he began stroking my long hair. "You're a loner like me," he said. I wasn't aware that I was a loner. I still wasn't that self-aware about anything much at all, but in my rapt attentiveness I must have suggested a certain availability, I suppose.

At that moment a couple of anglers came crunching up the gravel path, off for an evening's fishing. Although they were about 30 yards in front of where we parked, their sudden presence seemed to panic my driver. He hastily withdrew his hand from my hair, started the engine and drove me home. He suggested we should meet again and perhaps go to some woods near Henlow that he knew about. He thought that a Sunday might be ideal. His motivation was clear and while I wasn't fully complicit I didn't say no either. Bi-curious is the word they use now, isn't it?

A week or so later he picked me up again. It was starting to rain and I was glad of a lift, any lift. We didn't turn off the road at Cardington Lock this time. Instead he drove all the way to Sandy, mentioned the woods again, and when he pulled up we chatted for a while before I got out of the car. He talked more about mysticism and magic and offered to lend me books. He mentioned *The Way of the White Clouds* by Lama Anagarika Govinda, which I'd already read, and Christmas Humphreys – a name I'd seen but whose work I'd not as yet explored. He talked way beyond my understanding about the Tibetan Wheel of Existence. I mentioned the books on witchcraft I'd read and he talked about Purgatoric ghosts and devils and long-lost sorcery sects. I talked about the *Yoga for ealth programme I was watching and Health* programmes I was watching on TV, and he mentioned obscure forms of Tibetan yoga that I was unfamiliar with and which Barry had certainly never mentioned.

"I have seen monks meditating naked on mountain ledges in freezing temperatures. They get their warmth from here," he said, tapping the space between his eyes. He mentioned once again the Chinese invasion of Tibet and the suppression of the guerrilla resistance – the first time I'd heard the term guerrilla that wasn't in the context of the Vietnam war. He began to elaborate on his involvement with the campaign to help holy men find safe passage out of their own country, but misted up after a while and the sentences trailed off. I asked him about immolation, and about the monks I'd seen setting fire to themselves on the TV news in protest at the Vietnam war. I'd been both horrified and transfixed by the images of those monks sitting cross-legged outside the Pentagon and at American embassies around the world, rigid, immobile, seemingly beyond pain. I felt sure they must already have left their bodies and entered some higher spiritual realm. My kindly old attaché talked to me about the trance-like state which slows down the metabolism until the body is completely cataleptic. I continued to ply him with questions about the great lost civilization that stood at the roof of the world and he answered every earnest enquiry with patience and good grace, although he frequently used terms and concepts that were way beyond my comprehension.

We watched the rain on the windscreen for a bit. He suggested in vague halting terms that he might be going back to the Far East soon, and what with me being a loner I might want to come with him and be his secretary or houseboy or something. He still thought a visit to Henlow Woods might be in order first though. In fact, he seemed even more keen on this than he was the first time he'd picked me up. I said I'd meet him next Sunday, as he asked. The following Sunday was bright and sunny, and at the appointed hour I took my youngest brother up the Rec to watch our local cricket team instead. The old man passed me on the road a few weeks later but didn't stop to pick me up. He just looked on straight ahead with the fixed expression common to many drivers who didn't pick up hitchhikers, although there's always the possibility that he might not have recognised me, as I'd had my hair cut really short by then.

"You look like a bloody Martian," said Dickie Dangerfield as I walked into Kerry's for the first time in ages, displaying my newly shorn locks. The hair thing had been troubling me for a while, although not half as much as it bothered some of those who offered me a lift. "Are you a boy or a girl?" asked one old farm hand as I hitched from B Road to B Road towards Cambridge one morning. I thought he was joking but he persisted. "What are you then?" he exclaimed in broad yokel as I grew increasingly uncomfortable and embarrassed. Another time on the A1 a smartly dressed businessman – Far Eastern, Malaysian or Korean perhaps – gave me a stern lecture on how I'd probably get far more lifts if I had my hair cut. When I suggested, fairly politely, that I was quite happy with my appearance as it was, he pulled over onto the hard shoulder and ordered me out of the car. Now that I looked like a bloody Martian there was no longer any danger of such disagreements.

June 1972. Scoop neck top. Purple velvet tunic. Mixed messages.

It had been over two years since I'd had a haircut, May 1970 in fact. On the very same day that four students were shot dead in Ohio, I had a suedehead. By the time I had it cut again it hung well past my shoulders. In 1970 I'd been inspired by John Lennon's new look on *Top of the Pops* when he performed *Instant Karma*, by the prison cuts of the Manson Family girls, and by Julie Driscoll. What I had now owed a little to the look Syd Barrett sported when he was interviewed by Michael Watts in Melody Maker in 1971. The other major influence – not so much on the style, more on the gesture of renewal – was David Bowie. In January 1972 Bowie gave his infamous "I'm gay" interview again, to Michael Watts of Melody Maker, and was featured on the front cover sporting that immaculate mod coiffure. It caused a frisson, shall we say? It didn't immediately inspire me to go out and get my own locks cut off, and I didn't go much on the chequered jumpsuit and boots combo he was wearing either, but something latent undeniably stirred within me. I think that the attraction had as much to do with my LSD intake as it did the Ziggy look per se, but the confluence of the two, zap pow hallucinogens and the bi-boy space-age mod persona shifted my inclinations seismically.

LSD had already had a profound effect on my creativity and my growing sense of spirituality, now it kerblammo'd my sexuality too. Resistance to such drastic chemical realignment was futile. Fundamentally LSD suggested that existence, the way we all went about our daily lives, was essentially illusory – a game, a masque-play in which we adopted persona appropriate to our circumstances. I began to see the falsity in things, particularly bloke things, the ways guys strut and shrug and hold their ciggie in a man way and quaff their beer like that. Adopted masculinity was all part of the charade, a repertoire of social conditioning and learned responses. Acid began to methodically strip away my layers of illusory self. It was as if I was hovering above myself and looking down at this character who was acting the part of me. Somewhere in amongst all those tangled layers of self, lurked a less masculinized me, someone who couldn't be doing with all the superficial palaver and sheer hard work of being a regular heterosexual bloke.

Which is partly why I felt that same manhood-shredding shiver so many young males experienced when Bowie put his arm round Mick Ronson on *Top of the Pops* when he was singing *Starman*. That simple act of transgressive affection permitted me both androgyny and the refurbished psychological wardrobe that went with it. It allowed me to toy with the fluidity of identity in ways that I hadn't considered before. After all, Ziggy Stardust was a persona too. When the album came out I immediately embraced it as sci-fi acid rock. The concept I thought a tad flimsy, the narrative didn't really hang together, and the costumes didn't quite match the ambition. I tired as quickly of Ziggy as I did a lot of things, as quickly as Bowie did actually, but I did play the album a lot on acid. I saw tracer fire strafing the night sky, and laser beams being shot out of ray-gun guitars.

Bowie's entire career up until that point had been a series of restless identity shifts. In early 1972 he was still that one-hit wonder who had sung *Space Oddity* on *Top of the Pops*, played the San Remo pop festival and then disappeared into the Underground again. I loved The *Prettiest Star* and *Holy Holy*, fully expecting either of them to be the follow-up hit that never came. Bowie talked in interviews of his meeting with Chime Rinpoche, a genuine Tibetan lama, and about retiring to a monastery. That intrigued me too. When *Hunky Dory* sold well but didn't set the world alight, I had him down as another Underground artist who was never going to be famous. And then came that Melody Maker front cover. Wham Bam!

I'd been wearing androgynous clothes for some time, granny cardigans, scoop neck t shirts with flared sleeves. I tried in vain to find girls' ballet shoes like the ones Marc Bolan wore, but I did buy a perfect purple velvet tunic jacket from Kensington Market which I wore all the time once the warmer weather came and I shed the drab blue duffel coat I'd gone around in all winter. I also started slipping out in the evening having applied a little of Mum's lipstick and face powder. Then the people who gave me lifts really did start to stare. If those squaddies had picked me up then I almost certainly would have wound up bum-raped and dumped in that ditch. I chanced my luck every time I went out. One evening, Danny, Dickie and I sat in the Wimpy Bar. I was in full-on camping it mode and remarked on the lipstick trace I'd left on my coffee glass. Dickie looked at me with something approaching revulsion and told me to stop embarrassing myself in public. Danny later told me that he thought I must have balls of steel to have stepped out on a Bedford evening looking like that. Dickie though was repelled and in evident discomfort. Dickie Dangerfield with his long curly hair and his thick luscious lips. Dickie who I'd never seen in close proximity to a girl, let alone going out with one.

Not long after that, the pair of us were walking down Bedford High Street on a sunny July afternoon. *School's Out* by Alice Cooper came blasting out of a shop and we were discussing how great it would have been if the record had been released the previous summer when we left school. It still sounded great now but it didn't sound like ours somehow. We didn't own it in the way that the kids in the year below us at school could claim it. It would be their anthem, their joyous confirmation of liberation as they poured out of the school gates, let free for the summer, forever, completely. *School's Out* was also a reminder of how utterly disembodied I had become from workaday structures and from the routines of term time and holiday time. I was suddenly jolted into the realisation that I couldn't see myself going into another college year in September still pretending that I was attending classes. I decided I would tell my parents that I had left Tech. I figured that I could always bum around on the dole for a bit and see what came along. In that final chart week of July, *School's Out* by Alice Cooper, *Silver Machine* by Hawkwind and *Starman* by David Bowie all entered the Top 20. The Underground went overground. In retrospect it's clear to me now that was the week when the pop 1970s really claimed its own identity and kick-started the decade. That was the week the pop 70s stopped sounding like the rock 60s.

****

It's the double-take I remember most. It must have been a Saturday rather than a weekday because there is something unhurried about the memory, and a clear recollection that the traffic was lighter, fewer long-haul articulated lorries, no rush-hour dash for home. I can't remember why I would have been in London at the weekend. Perhaps it was one of those waste-ground gigs I'd been to on the patch of W11 land that wasn't yet called Meanwhile Gardens. I was at my favourite hitching spot, the bus stop on the A1 between Hendon and Mill Hill, when a young guy in a car pulled over. I got in, glanced briefly at my driver and immediately did a double-take because he looked like Nick Drake. I'd only seen Drake on album covers but the likeness was remarkable: unshaven, the hair maybe a little darker than it looked on the LP sleeves, but the same full lips shaped for a ready pout. We drove a little way and I launched into the obligatory pleasantries. "Nice evening," I must have said. Or, "Going far?"

His reaction was immediate. He seemed to stiffen. Hands gripped the steering wheel tighter while his face set itself into an expression of resentment. The body language was obvious, and the barriers came down so quickly that I resisted any urge to talk further. I must have clambered into a hundred or more cars that year but no invite rescinded itself as swiftly as his did that pleasant summer's evening. The journey passed in agreeable silence. There wasn't much on the road, the sun in its fullness was sinking in the west. As we approached my home town I gauged that my driver was going too fast to slow down unless I gave him fair warning. "This is where I want to get out. Sandy," I said as we approached a suitable pull-in point. "Sandy. Nice name," he said as the car slowed to a halt. The only words he spoke for the entire journey. I got out and off he drove, towards the setting Saturday sun and the northern sky.

The episode disappeared into the mists of memory. I barely thought of it again for more than two decades, until February 1997 in fact, when I was reading a Mojo article by Patrick Humphries to publicise his forthcoming Nick Drake book. By now the myths surrounding Drake had blossomed. He had become a phantom, an aura. I still knew little about his personal life and the likelihood of him having a car – or even being capable of driving one – suddenly seemed absurd to me. Wasn't he supposed to be near-catatonic in those final years? Then I got to the bit in the feature where Humphries talked about how Nick used to take off all over England in his car and I was suddenly hurtled back into that moment.

I told the rock writer Ian MacDonald about the encounter. Sandy was the clincher for him. He told me about Sandy Grey, the singer who had been close to Nick for a short while, or as close as anyone could be. I also brought it up with Cally Callomon at Island when I reviewed the CD reissues of Nick's three albums for Mojo. Cally told me that Nick had often hitchhiked in his youth and had little doubt that he would have picked up a fellow long-hair not that much younger than him. Me, I'll never know. I'm happy to believe that it wasn't him, just some taciturn guy heading for Stamford or Peterborough, who regretted pulling over the minute his passenger tried getting chatty. The chance meeting stands now as a symbol of my year of estrangement, adrift from things, a young life measured out in days spent by roadsides. It's my ghostly liaison at the crossroads moment. My parallel-earth collision at the intersection of myth and reality, where parallel destinies briefly intertwine. This seemingly insignificant episode has left its intrigue trailing down the years, illuminated by the glowing embers of legend, magnified by the tantalising remnants of fragmentary recollection.

All I Want is Out of Here

Chapter 7

THE GLITTER FACTORY

I stood at the entrance to the Granada TV warehouse on Ampthill Road in Bedford watching muscular men loading huge heavy boxes into the backs of delivery vans. Inside the huge heavy boxes were huge heavy television sets of a kind that have long since been consigned to antiquity. The warehouse foreman saw me standing there and asked who I was. I said I had been sent. He took one look at my scrawny frame, smiled indulgently, gestured towards the big strapping lads and sent me on my way, but not before he had obligingly filled in my form stating that I was physically unsuited to the form of work required.

The next job they sent me for was a Laboratory Assistant post (general duties) at Shuttleworth Agricultural College at Old Warden. I hitchhiked three miles up the A1 from Sandy and was dropped at the roundabout at Biggleswade. From there I walked four miles or more down a country lane to the college. It was a sultry summer's day. The cow parsley was high, and red and pink poppies dotted the roadside verges. I pondered, not for the first time, which poppies contained opium and how I might distil their derivatives for dream-like purposes. I walked through tree-shaded wrought-iron gates and wandered down a windy path that led me into the expansive grounds of the Old Warden estate.

In the distance was a mansion house, but immediately on my left, about 200 yards from the entrance, was a building that housed the lecture theatres and laboratories of the teaching establishment. I looked through a window where students were hard at work, paused a moment, then turned on my heels and walked straight back out again. I thought of the elderly, sour-faced lab technician at my old school, who used to trundle chemical-laden trolleys from room to room and offer admonishment for which he had no jurisdiction to those of us who happened to be lounging about in the corridors during lunchbreak. I thought of all those "Young Farmers Do It in Wellies" stickers in the backs of cars and the tales I'd heard about the oafish lunks who frequented Young Farmers' discos. Oh, man, look at those cavemen go. I thought of my CSE Grade Four in General Science, a grade that could be achieved simply by spelling your name correctly on the exam paper. I thought about all this and realised that my life was not leading up to this moment.

I'd been running on empty for some time and it was a relief to sign on the dole. With little or no money at my disposal there had never been an inexhaustible supply of options open to me, and well before the end of college term I had spent days just mooching about, killing time in bus shelters, recreation grounds and graveyards. My grasp on reality by this point was somewhat tenuous. While this illusory state of mind persisted, I remained convinced that there would be an inexhaustible supply of ways of avoiding work for the foreseeable future. "I couldn't find the place," was the excuse I presented to my parents and to the dole office when they asked me about the Agricultural College job. I assumed that "I couldn't find the place" would be good enough to convince both parties and buy me more time. I was wrong.

"Your Dad said it's a good job he could find the place when he went looking for work," Mum commented the following morning. Her words, although delivered casually, carried the unmistakeable weight of parental disappointment. Deluding them into thinking I was still at college was one thing. Being perceived as a work-shy shirker was another.

There was a young guy who lived over the back of us called Patrick. His dad was the local window cleaner and was out with his bucket and ladder come rain or shine. Patrick, a couple of years older than me, hung about his backyard most days doing little or nothing. His reason was a bad back, the excuse cited by many full-time work dodgers in those days, safe in the knowledge that it was easy to fake and difficult to diagnose. Mum let her feelings be known whenever she saw Patrick ambling about the yard. She expressed similarly strong sentiments about Colin Cowdrey the English cricket captain who had been excused National Service on account of his flat feet. This condition didn't appear to stop him running about the field in Test Matches, as Mum was happy to remind us whenever she saw Cowdrey on the TV cricket coverage. Mum was of that generation who grew up in the 1930s and saw many people, including her own father, more often out of work than in. These things lingered long in the memory. Meanwhile, her eldest son, for whom she had cut plenty of slack as he went about his dysfunctional business, now appeared to be turning into Patrick over the back.

Unemployment had recently hit a million for the first time since the 1930s, but our area had been spared the worst of it. There was still plenty of light industry to go round and a fair amount of the heavy stuff too. While I avoided gainful employment, Dad drove a round trip of 60 miles each day to Vauxhall Motors in Luton. Bedford had a Vauxhall plant too, as well as two fully functioning steel works. Eight miles to the south of Bedford was Stewartby brick works, at that time still the largest in Europe. The Bedford League for amateur football boasted five divisions full of works teams. Most firms had enough players to field a reserve side too.

The ranks of the unemployed may have recently swelled to six figures, but in Bedford, the fact that you hadn't secured a job within weeks of signing on was a cause for suspicion.

The dole office called me in after three weeks. Upon being summoned for inspection I received a grilling from a very inquisitive and persistent benefits officer. Why hadn't I found gainful employment yet? Where had I been looking? Caught cold by his aggressive line of questioning I back-pedalled unconvincingly. Clutching at straws I mentioned that I was probably going to be living in a commune in London soon, even though I knew that any hope of that had all but disappeared. The benefits officer asked me precisely what was meant by "soon". I said I'd have to phone the commune. He indicated the open door of an office, pointed to a phone and invited me to call them now. I waffled something about not being able to remember the number and there in that airless room on a warm afternoon my bluff was called, my feeble ploy was rumbled and I realised the game was up.

A small cluster of factories and warehouses had grown up on the edge of the London overspill estate in Sandy, light industry mostly. I walked into the first of these warehouses I came to and was immediately offered a job. I trudged home with the reluctant steps of a man who could and would be expected to start tomorrow. Yuletide Industries Ltd made and distributed Christmas goods: tinsel, glitter, decorative baubles, ribbons, bows, artificial Christmas trees, Christmas-tree lights, name-tags for presents, you name it. If you got it out of the attic and decorated your living room with it at Christmas, they made it.

At the front of the building, the boss's office and two smaller admin rooms were divided by a narrow corridor that looked onto the factory itself. Half of the factory floor was taken up by large rectangular benches where women (and it was all women) sat packing glitter into tiny tubes or folding little boxes for the various seasonal goods. Five long machines were given over to the manufacture of tinsel, which I learned for the first time was spun like cotton, but on an extended metal shaft not a wheel. Girls I recognised from the year below me at Junior school who had failed the 11+ and gone on to the Secondary Modern spent their hours setting the brightly coloured tinsel machines into motion, then walking alongside the shaft as it extended the material to about 15 feet in length. They then gathered up the spun material at the other end and plunged it into a rotating hot metal tub, like the ones used to make candy floss at the fairground. The clockwork routine of the girls, walking up and down all day winding and scooping was the most visible manifestation of physical labour in the place. Most other work was done from a sedentary bench position by women young and old, often mothers and daughters.

The very first task I was set gave me an immediate insight into the soul-crushing mundanity of unskilled labour. A small pressing machine with a conveyor belt attached sat in open floor-space in front of the works canteen. I had to place a piece of cardboard on the conveyor belt, press a button to activate the machine and then walk round to the other side where the cardboard would arrive having had a perfect two-foot-by-two-foot square punched into it. These pieces were used to line the bottom of boxes of goods as extra packaging. I would discard the excess trimming, place the cardboard square in a pile, insert another piece, press the conveyor belt activator at the other end, walk round the machine and repeat the process all over again. I did this for several hours a day, back and forth, back and forth.

Because the machine was set apart from the general bustle of the factory I was the focus of idle attention for anyone who looked up from their work. As the only male labourer on the factory floor, I developed a crippling self-consciousness as I went about my drudgery. Dressed in a scoop-necked lilac T shirt with flared sleeves, this pouty ambi-boy with short-cropped hair didn't know where the fuck he had landed. Only a month or so earlier I had been focussing on meditation and yoga, and the possibility of assuming the missionary position in the Far East. I had attempted to treat my body as a temple and to adhere as closely as I could in 1972 to a macrobiotic diet. Now in the staff canteen I was staring in puzzlement at the oxidised-copper coloured gunk at the bottom of a disposable plastic cup before realising it was the remains of the machine tea that someone had discarded a day or two earlier. This was the stuff that I was expected to drink at break time.

Another major factor in my reluctance to ingest food and drink on the premises was the arrest and well-publicised trial and conviction of the mass poisoner Graham Young. Newspaper reports of the trial had gripped the nation. Like everybody else I devoured the details of the court proceedings on a daily basis, and was both fascinated and horrified by this chemistry freak, who – since childhood it emerged – had been treating family and subsequently workmates as guinea pigs and research material for his macabre experiments. He'd finally been caught (for the second time we all later learned) while selectively spiking the canteen tea with thallium at a laboratory in Hemel Hempstead, barely 35 miles from where I lived.

Proximity is everything when you come from a small town. When I was 11, I had been similarly gripped by the whereabouts of the cop killer Harry Roberts, who had gone on the run after murdering three police officers in Shepherds Bush. Stories were spread by older boys to us younger more gullible children that Roberts might be lying low in our neighbourhood, using his survival skills to come out at night and hunt for food – and possibly kill children. Part of me knew this was unlikely, but it wasn't the part of me that shivered and hurried on past churchyards and woodland spinneys when the sun was going down in the evening. Roberts was eventually caught near Bishop's Stortford, only 35 miles from Hemel Hempstead, after a massive manhunt and three months on the run. At his subsequent trial it emerged that he had built secret night camps all over Bedfordshire and Hertfordshire. "See, we told you," said the older, gloating boys.

The other murderer of local notoriety was James Hanratty, who in April 1962 was hanged for the shooting and murder of 36-year-old scientist, Michael Gregsten, and the rape and attempted murder of Gregsten's mistress Valerie Store, as they sat in a car in a layby on the A6 at the appropriately named Deadman's Hill at Clophill 12 miles from where I lived. The case was controversial at the time and there was little clear evidence for a conviction. Both Ludovic Kennedy and Paul Foot ran campaigns to have Hanratty's sentence overturned – the latter attracted the support of several high-profile names in the late 1960s, most notably John Lennon. In 1997 a police inquiry into the reopened case concluded that Hanratty was innocent. DNA evidence in 2002, however, proved otherwise. At the time of the murder in 1961, loyalties were divided. In my own household Mum thought he did it, Dad thought he didn't. Or was it the other way around? I can't remember now.

I frequently used to pass that notorious A6 layby on the way back from local football matches. It wasn't just a small roadside pull-over off spot. It was quite a lengthy layby, hidden from passing traffic, set well back off the road and running through the edge of Maulden Wood. When I used to go and watch Luton play with Shillington schoolmate Chris Tozer (he of *Fog on the Tyne* fame and gainful garage employment), his Dad would sometimes give us a lift home. Passing the layby on dark winter's evenings he would pitilessly play on our fears and make jocular references about murderers that might still be lurking there. I would shrivel down in my seat until we had passed the macabre location.

Hanratty was a London-based car thief and housebreaker who was hanged by the neck for his most notorious crime. Harry Roberts was a high-profile psychotic who had worked alone and was the subject of a massive media-publicised manhunt. Graham Young, however, had walked innocuously among us, going about his deadly business while calmly writing down observations about his victims as they went into convulsions before his very eyes. I saw no reason not to suspect that a copycat poisoner might be carrying out similar experiments at my place of work. With this in mind I stopped drinking the machine tea and started taking a flask in instead. I only ventured into the canteen to swill the flask out and throw my empty sandwich wrapper into the bin. I would cast a wary eye around the room to see which of my fellow workers might be our own factory's Graham Young. Meanwhile my colleagues, placid and inoffensive women and girls who packed production-line Christmas goods and had no access to poisonous substances, sat innocently sipping their machine tea and talking of local matters. None of this assuaged my fears. After a couple of weeks, I started cycling home for my dinner, taking 15 minutes or more out of my precious lunch break to eat an oven-warmed meal with dried-up gravy that Mum had prepared an hour earlier for my youngest brother when he came home from Junior school.

It was weeks before I spoke to anyone at work unless spoken to first. I just clocked on at eight, awaited my boss's instructions and watched the minute hands tick round until I could stamp my punch card and go home. Endless hours were measured out by the Radio Two news jingle. "Don't clock-watch. It only makes the time go more slowly," said Linda, one of the young girls at the packing counters, and the first to regard me as anything other than an oddly dressed curiosity. She was right but

I could do nothing to cure my habit of glancing at the clock every five minutes. Time had never dragged so slowly in my life as it did in those first few weeks in the glitter factory. More than once I experienced that weird sensation where time appeared to stand still or even go backwards. I would look at the clock at 2.45 and vow not to look at it again until I heard the three o'clock news jingle. I would disappear into my thoughts and what little imagination I could muster, summoning sexual fantasies and dream scenarios of communal life or being in a band. I would hum entire pop tunes in my head. Finally, unable to resist the temptation any longer I would look up at the clock and it would be 2.48.

The overhead radio speakers droned away in all their disembodied blandness. David Hamilton on Radio One. Tony Brandon, then John Dunn on Radio Two. The volume low enough for the factory noise to drown out the disc-jockey patter but too loud for me to be able to block out the torture of the daily playlist. My arrival at Yuletide Industries Ltd coincided with some of the most awful chart records ever inflicted upon a captive audience. *Rock'n'Roll Part 2* by Gary Glitter. *Ooh Wakka Doo Wakka Day* by Gilbert O'Sullivan. *Seaside Shuffle* by Terry Dactyl and The Dinosaurs. Records devised seemingly to convince me that Graham Young was the DJ, the lunch buffet was laced, and the last thing I would ever hear on this Earth before dying an agonising death would be the Neanderthal gruntings of the artist formerly known as Paul Gadd as he loomed over me laughing.

I hated it when Gary Glitter gained critical cachet from people who ought to have known better. I always thought there was something deeply fraudulent about his entire shtick. Too sinisterly sleazy to be a novelty, too corpulent to be a presentable Jackie Magazine pin-up, his music too lumberingly hamfisted to be affectionate pastiche, he never conned me for a minute. I watched in horror as this product of some managerial office Frankenstein experiment was welcomed unconditionally into our pop lives and his records soared up the charts. I felt that a little bit of rock'n'roll's Holy Grail was desecrated whenever they hit the Top 10. I used to walk around that factory hearing those tinny handclaps and that crappy primeval chant of "Rock and Ro-wo-whoah, Rock and Roll" and would feel my legs grow leaden, as if I was being dragged through quicksand down, down into the very bowels of hell.

I got home from work at night too brain-dead to do anything other than eat my tea, watch telly and retire to bed exhausted. I no longer had the energy to read anything of substance, or meditate, or think about *Yoga for Health* or any of those other activities that had given my young life validity and purpose. My dad did this every fucking day of his working life. I could barely hack it from week to week. The one thing an unskilled labouring job did give me though was money. For the first time in my life I had the novelty of a weekly pay packet. Since getting kicked out of college I'd had no income of any kind. I was used to going about my escapades with little more than small change in my pocket. Now I brought home something resembling a living wage. I gave Mum £3 or £4 for "house-keeping" and the rest was mine to spend. I didn't drink or smoke. I'd stopped going to the pictures and to gigs. I hadn't had a girlfriend for months. I quickly accumulated disposable income with little to dispose it on.

Every Saturday morning among the display ads in the back of the Daily Mirror for surgical trusses, incontinence pants and garden sheds was a promotion for the VEF 204 Russian radio, with a shop address in Shepherds Bush Green, London. Mail-order delivery or over-the-counter purchase, it said. The world at your fingertips for £14.99 plus P&P. Six short-wave bands. Medium Wave and Long Wave. On a grey overcast Saturday morning in September I headed for Kings Cross. On a train. With a return ticket that I'd paid for rather than chance my thumb to get me there. When I got to London I bought a Red Rover ticket, something I hadn't done since I'd stopped visiting the capital's football stadiums or engine sheds with my schoolmates.

It seemed strange to be riding around London on public transport without assuming invisibility in the hope that no fare collector would notice me. It seemed odd too not to be pressing my nose up against the sweet-shop window of Alternative London in the hope that someone would notice me and invite me in to share the wares. I walked into a shop in Shepherds Bush, with purpose rather than the simple aim of passing time. I handed over hard-earned money for goods, and then went and sat in a café with a new-found short-wave world at my fingertips, packaged up in a cardboard box. I bought an Underground mag for old time's sakes – IT or OZ probably – then headed home. Previously I would have wandered round Holland Park or Ladbroke Grove for several fruitless hours before finding my way to Hendon or Mill Hill to hitchhike. Now I rode the tube back to Kings Cross and tried not to think about work on Monday.

Linda the friendly girl asked me where I was from. Australia, I said, channelling the spirit of Daevid Allan and Banana Moon. Later in the day she wandered over and told me that one of the women at the packing benches had said I was talking soft and that I was Mavis Chapman's eldest. Another time I mentioned to her that I was in a band, and again she must have put the word around as one of the girls from the tinsel machine told me she was having an 18th birthday party soon and could she hire my group. "Do you play stuff from the Top 20?" she asked. No, I mumbled. "We only do original material." Even my imaginary band was getting hassled to do the wrong kind of gig. Eventually the boss, Mr Bechstein, a genial man, sent me to work in the warehouse at the back of the factory where I excelled on my first day by writing in marker pen the incorrect address of a company in Portugal on four hundred boxes full of Christmas goods. Also out the back, I noticed for the first time, was the outsource section where women on what was known as piecework brought in huge bags of decorative seasonal goods they had assembled at home, and were paid a pittance for their efforts.

Ron the warehouse supervisor took what seemed to me an unhealthy interest in my (lack of) sex life and was keen, often at break time, to tell me about his. Ron was in his thirties, married without kids, and would describe to me in great detail his favourite positions, sometimes demonstrating them with the help of a chair. "I sit like this," he would say as I sipped my tea, "and my wife sits astride me like this. Have you ever done it like that?" One day, catching me dream-boating my day away as I attempted not to mislabel more boxes, he asked if I had a girlfriend. No, I replied. "Oh, I'm surprised," he said. "You're a good-looking lad."

I often suspected that we were just an anecdote away from "Have you ever seen two men sucking each other off?" and an invitation to explore the less accessible recesses of the warehouse. Later I learned that Ron was having an affair with the woman who oversaw the out-work payments, so he was clearly generous with his wanderlust. I imagined the pair of them in that chair, doing what he had described so graphically to me.

Apart from Ron the warehouseman, Mr Bechstein the boss and occasionally Mr Bechstein's less-genial brother, the only other male on the premises was Bill the maintenance man. Bill operated at a sedate pace, affecting deafness when it suited, and generally went about his business in his own time. He was given the task of instructing me how to operate a hugely complex-looking machine in a wire cage, which made decorative bows. The machine – one part Marcel Duchamp *Large Glass*, one part Heath Robinson – whirred and clanked and juddered away and frequently broke down.

"This machine operates on the principle that..." Bill began hopefully. "On the principle that..." This was clearly as much as he had learned from the manual or as much as he could be bothered to impart because he quickly abandoned the sentence and showed me how you fed a ribbon spool into the machine and where you placed the box to collect the completed bow on the other side. He also made it clear that "the fucker is always breaking down" and that I was to take my time in coming to find him when it did, thus ensuring me some quality skiving time. The machine was hidden away in an alcove corner behind the tinsel machines, next to a paint-spraying facility that no one ever seemed to use. I could sit on a chair reading the paper or my new improved NME without being bothered by anyone. Bill was right, the fucker did break down frequently. I would watch the ribbon snag in one of the numerous cogs and wheels and wait for it to wrap itself tightly around the mechanism before casting a hopeful eye around the building as if I was genuinely trying to locate Bill's whereabouts. Bill would eventually amble over, fag in mouth, give me his best-prepared "The fucking fucker's fucked" speech and I'd be taken off the job until it was repaired. I used to hear the percussive clank of that machine in my sleep.

Eventually another work table was installed in the space between the ribbon cage and the tinsel machines, but instead of the group of women I expected to be migrated across the factory floor, they stuck me and Linda on high chairs to sit and assemble boxes full of gaudy crap. Linda was chirpy and amenable and asked me all about myself. She said she was saving up to get married, although she never once mentioned a boyfriend. She'd been to the local Secondary Modern and told me she left school without getting any qualifications except in Homecraft. I told her I'd been to the Grammar school and had three O Levels. "Oh, a brainbox eh?" she said clearly impressed with this massive haul of certificates. After that she started calling me Brainbox instead of Rob.

Long before I was familiar with the name Marshall McLuhan or the concept of the global village, I knew that the medium was the message and that all the best messages came from the radio. I still trawled the ether for jazz courtesy of the Melody Maker listings, but now I also had Radio Peking and Radio Moscow and numerous other foreign broadcasts at my disposal. Russian announcers spoke in American or British-tinged accents, depending on where they had been taught. The official Pravda party line was churned out in news bulletins, which meant a constant supply of stories which mentioned the British proletariat and the ruling class. From somewhere in the Far East a strident voice battled through the crackle and static to tell me about VD rates among American troops in Vietnam.

The short-wave bands were frequently punctuated by the abrasive atonal sound of a jamming signal, a noise I had been familiar with since the summer of 1970 when successive Labour and Tory administrations attempted to block the medium wave output of the pop pirate Radio Northsea International. The most mysterious interlopers on short wave however were The Numbers, the coded transmissions I first chanced upon late one night when I heard a flat, monotonous East European voice read out a series of seemingly random digits. It was only later that I learned these clandestine transmissions were being broadcast by government agencies and were intended for espionage operatives behind enemy lines during the height of the Cold War. Such chance encounters alerted me to the fact that the electromagnetic spectrum carried some very strange cargo. Tuning purposefully to a specific location on the waveband was only ever half the fun. It was what you found between the stations, that's where the action was.

Radio and TV were notoriously leaky systems, prone to transmission breaks and interference, and there was a lot of leakage about in the analogue 1970s. Atmospherics obeyed laws that didn't recognise national or regional boundaries. In its earliest days, Radio One was on 247 metres Medium Wave, a wavelength it shared with Radio Tirana. On October and November afternoons with the dusk light fading, I used to wait for the Tirana call sign to come floating in like the mythical Albanian spirit the Avullushe. It would appear faintly at first, like a star slowly becoming visible in the evening sky, but gradually a mournful eight-note trumpet refrain would increase in volume until it was audible enough to provide eerie counterpoint to whatever pop hit was playing on the BBC.

This spectral intervention marked out a time of year for me, a haunting presence in the ether, as dependable as the first cuckoo of spring. The medium wave was full of ether ghosts in those days, a disembodied cacophony of heterodyne whistles, megacycle harmonics, Cold War codes, astral chatter. External interference could come from anywhere: a motorbike going by without a noise suppressor, the one o'clock hooter from the nearby garment factory. When our next-door neighbour turned on their TV in the late afternoon it would interfere with the signal from our radiogram on the other side of the wall. Because of all this, I became instinctively attuned to the unique properties of the electromagnetic spectrum. I visualised the curvature of a wavelength, its contours of invisibility, the ionospheric ceiling, the ocean bounce.

In the modern digital age, TV pictures pixelate, freeze, fragment. In the olden analogue days, images multi-layered, fluttered and flickered. There was an organic quality to the interference. If the horizontal hold went on the blink, the broadcast images spun like the fruits on a one-armed bandit. The blandest of newsreader faces could be transformed into a Vorticist Pope scream. On sultry summer afternoons the telly played up a treat, and continental interference frequently superimposed itself upon the home transmissions. French voices babelised *Blue Peter* or *Secret Squirrel* into obliteration. Random fragments collaged. Photo negatives of foreign newsreader faces and newsreel images would flicker across the screen until eventually a caption appeared apologising for the interruption to normal programming.

Watching tv with the expectancy that things could and would go wrong became the natural order of things. Subconsciously I willed it to be thus and lived for those moments. Such instances permeated my dreams, partitions and fourth walls came crashing down. The world wandered off script. One Sunday morning on Anglia, I watched Marc Bolan in his pop star prime performing two songs and being interviewed by Humphrey Burton for an ITV show called *Music In The Round*. The programme was meant to run for half an hour but at about three minutes to twelve things ground to an inclusive halt. No credits rolled. Instead Burton, off camera as I recall, asked if there was time for one more number. Instructions were issued to the floor crew, a boom mic was lowered and a make-up girl came on and fluffed up Marc's pretty little face. I soon realised that what I was watching was an unedited version, inadvertently broadcast. At midday, the transmission suddenly cut out without explanation. The whole thing had the unreal air of one of my dreams. It typifies that year for me. Unrehearsed. Unreal. Only notionally grounded in reality. A 'did I imagine that?' quality to it all.

One Saturday afternoon I was at the kitchen sink filling a kettle when Mum's sister Joan came hurrying past the window towards the back door. I went out to greet her. "Mum's up the shops," I started to say. "It's your Grummar," she explained. "She's been taken to hospital." When Mum got back she immediately took off on her bike again and when she returned two hours later she was inconsolable. "She's goona die!" she wailed. Dad couldn't placate her any. "Oh, I know it, she's goona die," she repeated, dismissing his comforting words. But Grummar didn't die. Not that time. She'd had a stroke which left her partly paralysed down one side and she walked, a little unsteadily, with the aid of a stick for the rest of her life, but she was a tough old bird my Nan, and she'd grown up in tougher times.

In contrast to the polite formality and standoffishness of some of the Chapman clan, Mum's parents were hospitable by nature. From the moment they got up in the early morning until they went to bed at night, the back door of their house remained unlocked. You never had to knock before you walked in, and they were always welcoming. There would be a glass of pop in your hand before you'd had chance to sit down, and sixpence thrust into your pocket when you left. Resistance to this charitable gesture was futile, a refusal genuinely did offend. One of my earliest memories of Grummar is of her emptying the bottom of her purse to give me her soon-to-be-obsolete farthings. Mum's maiden name was Payne, and more than once when I was in full adolescent chatterbox flow Grummar would look at me knowingly and say: "You're a Payne you are." With minimal adjustment to the spelling, many would have agreed with that assessment over the years. But Grummar wasn't offering a play on words. She recognised some other inheritance.

"Your Grandad was a bit of a firebrand in his younger days," she would say with a look that spoke volumes – as indeed it had to, because that's all she would ever tell me. The truth I only ever gained in increments. I eventually learned that there was a time in the years after the Great War when Grandad was blacklisted by almost every farm in Bedfordshire, the chief reason being that he was unwilling to barter for a living wage. He was a proud and principled man and wouldn't work for less than he had been promised. He wasn't given to forelock-touching or doffing his cap to the gaffer. He told me tales of lining up in the town market square in the early morning, like a 17th century dockside slave minus the shackles, waiting for the arrival of a farm owner, or one of his representatives, who would duly inform the attended gathering if there was any work to be had for the day. He would go "you, you, you and you", picking out those who looked the most able to do a hard day's graft in the fields.

An all-too common scenario during the Depression was that an agricultural labourer would be hired at an agreed day rate. Invariably someone else, equally desperate, would turn up and offer to work for less. At this point the gaffer would pay the first worker off and put the cheaper man to work. The dismissed worker would down tools, rue his luck and slope off to seek employment elsewhere. Not my Grandad. Backing down was not an option and he would pick a fight instead, sometimes with the man who was offering to undercut him, sometimes with the gaffer himself. As a result, he was shunned by almost every farmer who knew him, or knew of his reputation. In the 1920s the only man who would give him work was a landowner called Fred Tear, who farmed a few acres in the neighbouring village of Potton. It was while working for the good Mr Tear that Grandad met Grummar, who was working "in service" for the family at the time. Employment at Tear's, as with all land work, then and now, was temporary, seasonal and unreliable – and whenever Grandad was forced to try his luck elsewhere it usually ended up in a fight or an offer to fight.

Like the Chapmans, like most families, the Paynes had their secrets. Mum's older sister was born just six months after Grummar and Grandad married. Such was the nature of small-town disapprobation and gossip that when they reached their Golden Wedding anniversary in March 1976 my maternal grandparents didn't announce or publically celebrate the fact, still fearing – Grummar in particular – that even after all that time someone would do the calculations and notice that their eldest daughter had turned 50 just a few months later. The fear of wagging tongues put paid to any commemoration they might have been considering – which is deplorable to contemplate, given that they remained happily in love, for richer or poorer, till the end of their days.

They had married in great adversity during the year of the General Strike: he 23 and virtually unemployable, she 18 and carrying his child. Neither set of parents attended the Registry Office wedding. Grummar's mother disowned her, and the name of her father is not recorded on the Marriage Certificate. The witnesses were Grandad's brother and her brother. As was the norm in those days, they had to get a county court order to marry without parental permission. They bonded in the kind of adversity that few ever need contemplate.

Grummar was 62 when she had that stroke. Just a few months earlier she had been fit and active, working in the beaning fields, doing the kind of seasonal land work she did all her life. Grandad collected his pension

in 1968 after twenty contented post-war years with the Water Board –
dredging river beds, tidying banks and maintaining sluice gates at a much
kinder pace than he had been used to in his firebrand days. After retirement
he worked as a cleaner at the local Secondary Modern school. Along with
several other elderly citizens, he had a nice little earner going on there – a
gig that was only curtailed in the mid-1970s when an inspector, concerned
about health and safety factors, found the oldest of the cleaners to be
92. Now that Grummar was housebound and convalescing, Mum took
on the task of looking after her during the day. In addition to cooking a
midday meal for me and my youngest brother she also prepared one for
her recovering Mum, cycled up to her house with the food wrapped safely
in a tea towel in the bike basket, and served it while it was still warm. She
did this for the entire time Grummar was dependent. Instead of going
home for my dinner I took to joining them at my grandparents' house for
an hour's respite from packing Christmas goods.

A few weeks after I started working at the glitter factory, a personal ad
appeared in the back pages of Melody Maker. Something along the lines
of "Female, 18, seeks soulmate and adventures. Ready to take off and find
more. Maybe a commune or something." Had I been the kind of person
who would place adverts like that, those were the kind of sentiments I
too might have expressed. Desperate to escape the clutches of unskilled
factory work and still hoping to find some kind of spiritual retreat I
sent off a letter in reply. A few weeks later, by which time my horizons
had shrunk to the size of a cardboard-cutting machine, a reply arrived.
"Your letter was delivered to the wrong box number," it explained. "We
are a small spiritual community in... (Kent? Surrey? South London?
The location escapes me now). I can't recall the exact details, but they
sounded like one of the more clannish and devotional Eastern sects that
were beginning to spring up at that time. I was invited to come down and
participate in one of their group meetings "where a questing spirit of your

kind would be most welcomed". There was a great deal more of this in a hand-written reply that ran for a full page. The letter ended. "We cannot help feeling that the mix-up of letters was more than a coincidence and that your communication was destined to reach us."

For once my wariness far outweighed my curiosity, and I instinctively thought no. I've never been a natural team player or joiner, and neither the sentiments expressed or the specifics of the set-up appealed to me. From the moment I contrived to get myself kicked out of the Cubs when I was eight, just so I could get home on time to see that programme about Merseybeat, I had an aversion to clubs and enforced participation. When the first youth club opened in Sandy, I preferred the company of my older mates who lounged malcontentedly at various locations around town, rather than going into a purpose-built facility on warm summer evenings just for the dubious pleasure of playing ping-pong.

Similarly, when a boxing club was mooted, I was the only Grammar school boy from my town who elected not to get in a ring and try to punch someone's lights out. Not even the inducement of local boy made good Joe Bugner, who presided over the opening of the venue, could convince me that donning boxing gloves was a good idea. Should I be required to fight at all, and I occasionally was, I preferred to brawl on an impromptu basis. It was the same with organised religion. My parents weren't churchgoers and I was never the Sunday-school type. Living with a small group of Buddhist scholars just off Clapham Common in circumstances conducive to learning and growth would have been just fine. Sunday afternoon meets sounded a happy-clappy commitment too far for my liking, so I declined the cult's invitation and threw the letter away.

Something about the correspondence gnawed away under the surface and bothered me for weeks. That explanation that there had been a box number mix-up didn't convince me one bit. I had thrown out the Melody Maker that contained the original ad so I couldn't check, but I was an obsessive music-mag reader and I couldn't ever recall clocking a personal ad which invited readers to a religious meeting. The letter made me aware that there might be more duplicitous forces at work here. During the 1970s several new sects sprang up in the UK, each with their own guru or divine providence. Many suggested that converts donate all their worldly possessions to the greater good and surrender to the divine will of the godhead, especially the one with the fleet of cars and private jets. It made me very cynical about certain spiritual impulses at large in the counterculture, and the type of person they hoped to attract.

My own spiritual instincts leaned more towards little Zen lightning-bolts of clarity, seasoned with the reasonable doubt of agnosticism. I was far more willing to embrace the "Look at the sky/look at the river" pantheism of Syd Barrett than the dubious reincarnation credentials of some chubby little be-robed fakir based in California. I was, when it came down to it, unwilling to surrender my bullshit detector. By the autumn of 1972 I decided I'd dropped my guard quite enough for one year, and I'd seen how far that had got me.

The charts continued to fill up with shit records: Donny Osmond, more Gary Glitter, Jonathan King in varying incarnations of dreadfulness. The radio played them all. *Mouldy Old Dough* by Lieutenant Pigeon was number one for the whole of October. I didn't mind the novelty of it at first. The record's relentless bounce and that faintly unsettling title chant were no more irritating than a lot of chart fodder at that time. I'd liked the band in the late sixties when they were called Stavely Makepiece and put psychedelic phasing on their records. One day the girls on the production line downed tinsel and did a little formation dance to *Mouldy Old Dough* in the narrow aisle between their machines. They formed a line, held hands and executed a sort of joyless side skipping jig. It was both wondrous and bizarre to behold. And for some reason it made me sad. I don't know why. Perhaps it was because they looked a little bit sad too, jogging there in their restricted space. It was an impromptu unrehearsed moment of temporary respite from the drudgery of labour. A thing done just to pass some time. The moment the song finished they just resumed their work as if nothing had happened.

It had a been a few months since I'd chanced an acid trip at home, so one misty autumn Saturday afternoon I dropped a tab. Dad was out. Mum was round at her Mum's and I assumed the presence of my younger brothers and sister would be no obstacle to having an interstellar time. If they got too bothersome I could always retire to my bedroom to read my music mags or listen to the radio. I had pen and paper ready just in case the lysergic muse paid a visit, and was gazing serenely at the shiny emerald gradations on the front-room curtains when I noticed a car with a trailer attached driving very slowly up the road. Inside the car were Dad and two other occupants. On the back of the trailer was a piano. It was only at that moment I remembered that Dad had offered to take the surplus-to-requirements piano from a local pub that was being renovated.

The vehicle pulled up outside the house. Two burly men and Dad got out of the car and began offloading the piano from the trailer. I opened the front door in anticipation and felt obliged to help them manoeuvre the old Joanna through the narrow front door. In my already tripped-out state this assistance consisted of me cupping three fingers under the keyboard and hoping that somehow the instrument would levitate itself. "Someone's not pulling their weight," huffed one of the burly men suspiciously as the piano proved difficult to negotiate through the narrow door arch. Eventually after much struggle and little evidence of levitation the instrument was man-handled into the front room and the burly men went on their way. My eager brothers and sister gathered around the thing and I retired upstairs to resume my holy communion. After a while I heard a heavenly chorale of percussive tinkling coming from downstairs. The noise was so joyously persuasive that I felt compelled to investigate further. My youngest brother, Geoff, was pounding out an atonal rhythmic cluster of notes that to me in my altered state sounded transcendental. "We have a new Mozart in our midst," I shouted, convinced in this moment of rapture that Geoff would go on to become an acclaimed concert pianist while the rest of the family could retire on his riches. Reconciled to the new reality I retired upstairs once more to the warm tingly embrace of my trip.

Later in the afternoon, having plateau'd pleasingly on my microdot, I noticed that the pounding chiming church tones had ceased and that things were quiet downstairs. Mum, on returning home, had declared the piano both an eyesore and an earsore and was now involved in an earnest and somewhat one-sided discussion with Dad about its instant removal from the front room. One thing Dad hadn't considered when he offered to take the instrument off the pub's hands was that a piano which has sat in the stale and stuffy confines of a bar for several years will reek of the seasoned accumulation of cigarette smoke and spilt beer. As a result, the front room now carried the unmistakeable odour of The Rose and Crown at closing time.

"It's stinking the room out," was Mum's appalled assessment, one which Dad reluctantly agreed with as he retired philosophically to the teleprinter and his pools coupon. The piano, having been in our house for no more than three or four hours, was hauled unceremoniously outside to the garden with far greater ease than it had been hauled in, and there in the late afternoon light of a misty Autumn Saturday was chopped up and set ablaze.

Just hours after I'd washed down a microdot hoping for a quiet beatific afternoon in, followed perhaps by a contemplative come-down stroll to the recreation ground or the riverbank, I was standing astride the piano, Keith Emerson style, still tripping my face off, frenziedly smashing the instrument to splinters with a large axe. With the structure fiercely ablaze, I seized upon this moment as an opportunity to divest myself of a multitude of past lives. Fetching my old radio, my now redundant battery-less Fidelity Rad 11, from my bedroom, I announced theatrically that I was going to toss it onto the burning pyre as a gesture that would stand as a symbol for the renouncing of my youth. I would build myself anew from the flames and ashes of adolescence, a kind of cultural immolation and rebirth. This ceremony of the blazes would serve as a ritualistic cleansing of old habits and former selves which even as I spoke were crackling away like Buddhist protesters among the yellowed ivory and the charred soundboard. I made to throw the radio in the fire. "No, you don't," commanded Mum. "You're to give that radio to your brother. It's still perfectly usable."

It was my 18th birthday on November 10. I think I might have mentioned it to Linda but I had little cause to celebrate and thought no more about the non-event when I walked into work that Friday. I was sitting at the benches, spooning glitter into tiny tubes, when I became aware of the low hum of distant singing from across the factory floor, barely audible above the tinsel machines, the rattling bow cage and the radio. I only realised shortly before the plaintive verse ended that the girls were singing "Happy Birthday", to me. No one looked up or over at me. There was no cake. Just the girls, making an effort of sorts to wish me good cheer. It was an inhibited sort of singing which I shyly acknowledged with reciprocal inhibition. An out of sorts sort of boy who still didn't know quite where he had landed and was as far adrift as he had ever been from purpose or reason, a boy now turned 18 who had buried all his pop dreams deep down and was living from pay packet to weekly pay packet. The music mags had started to refer to something they interchangeably called glam rock one week and glitter rock the next. And here was I at the birth of the new movement spooning the stuff into tiny plastic tubes for retail sales at Christmas.

To compound the emptiness of my going-nowhere life, I took to having a bath late on Saturday nights and then when everyone was in bed I'd to listen to the ether tide flowing back and forth. Roger Wallis on Radio Sweden. Disparate jazz signals. Kid Jensen or Baby Bob Stewart on Radio Luxembourg. Stewart's theme tune *Image* by Alan Haven reeked of desolation and melancholy. I loved it. There's something about those darkest hours. So secret and intimate. You could be the only one listening. The only one out there. Just you and that signal reaching across time zones. Stations barely there. I'd recently read John Wyndham's *The Day of the Triffids* and there's a bit fairly far on in that novel where the narrator describes his fruitless search on a battery-operated radio for signs of survivors. "There was something pip-pipping away around 42 meters" he says. "Otherwise nothing." It's an image that stayed with me. An electromagnetic landscape where life was always out there somewhere, no matter how faint, no matter how mysterious, the source unknown and unlocatable, pip-pipping away.

Signals from Ankara, Prague, Peking, Saigon, Moscow. Spectral whispers float in and out. On the 42-meter band, and on 16 meters, 31 meters and 49 meters too. In a bare lightbulb-lit room in West Berlin or Budapest or Baldock, an agent is writing down the numbers. Somewhere out there a marionette is spinning, a music box key turns tight and a ballerina twirls. A song plays distorted like the world is on a warp. Some old wartime warbler croons in an echoing ballroom from a long ago. A holy man chants. You can hear the cavernous acoustics of a temple. His prayer compresses to

Morse beats. Stations drift in and out. Like thought does. Stations behind stations behind stations like star-cluster constellations beyond infinite shifting constellations. Behind every layer of sound another layer. There is no such thing as silence on the radio. Even when there are no stations to be heard, there are ionospheric crackles and static and hum. Somewhere in the ether it always sounds like Christmas. Somewhere a jazz trumpeter weeps the night. A final muted note fades and a time signal chimes 2 am. A station fanfares a call sign. Could be East European. Could be Arabic. The night frees me from now. All this time to disconnect. The static comes in torrents again. The soundwaves corrugate and shift, sifting the signals, orchestrating the elemental, turning all music into surf music. All pop tunes and show tunes and atonal blare is doomed missions in a meteor storm. A jamming signal surges again. Force Nine. Moderating later. Another song submerged in a sea of white noise. I drown in early morning ether sleep.

All I Want is Out of Here

Chapter 8

WALK IN THE NIGHT (BA-DOO-BA-DOO-BA-DA)

The Cold War was played out in many arenas, on my short-wave radio, in satellite technology and the space race, in basketball and track-and-field athletics, in *Callan* on the TV, where spies could be traded like raw meat, and were as dispensable as pawns on a chess board. An equally gripping piece of Cold War drama spanned my final period of traipsing aimlessly and my first few weeks of factory work. It took place during July and August at the Laugardalshöll Sport Centre in Reykjavik, Iceland, where defending World Chess Champion Boris Spassky played the charismatic and intense title challenger, American wunderkind Bobby Fischer.

Billed as a battle of competing ideologies, the subsequent 21-game competition took chess into the realms of high art, tempered by interludes that were pure Theatre of the Absurd. I used to stay up late at night waiting for the latest twists and turns, and more often than not, to see if the eccentric Fischer had bothered turning up at all. The competition stuttered and staggered on through a series of bluffs and double bluffs, seasoned with subterfuge and paranoia on both sides. Fischer initially haggled over the fee and TV rights, and asked repeatedly for the TV cameras to be turned off. Spassky's Soviet team, suspecting that Fischer was using electronic mind-control devices, had the front rows of spectators removed and the hall swept for bugs. Fischer didn't attend the opening formalities. Spassky ultimately conceded defeat by phone rather than by coming to the hall. It was spellbinding stuff.

I have a dim and distant memory of a curious five-minute programme called *Chess Masterpieces* that ran for a short while on Anglia Television on Sunday lunchtimes. Broadcast in the early 1960s and sandwiched between the religious homilies and the fertiliser ads, salient moments from a match between two famous Grandmasters would be played out via a series of crude stop-start animations narrated by an authoritative voiceover in a clipped English accent. "Petrosian. Knight to King's Bishop Four," he would intone, and a white knight would levitate shakily with all the primitive technical finesse available at the time. Tal or Vera Menchik or Bent Larsen would offer their countermove, and a particular classic chess manoeuvre would be illustrated. I used to love the names of the key exponents. I assumed Tal was Persian. I imagined him wearing a bejewelled turban and a third eye as he gazed thoughtfully at the pieces, but he turned out to be Russian like all the others.

There were often chess puzzles in the back of the Sunday papers too. Dad would sit with our pocket chess set and try to work them out. "Tal. Checkmate in four moves. Can you see how it's done?" I had a rudimentary grasp of the game but I was never remotely in Dad's league. One evening, playing out of my skin I managed to hang on in there and prolong the game well past my usual capitulation time. It hurt my head to concentrate that hard and to try and think that many moves ahead. Despite this monumental effort on my part, when the endgame came it was swift and brutal, and it occurred to me that Dad had been toying with me just to prolong the contest. It was one of those occasional clarity moments where I realised the gulf between my modest efforts and what could be classified as expertise was insurmountable.

Similar bursts of insight would subsequently inform a range of abilities – playing the guitar, playing snooker, achieving the full lotus position, reverse parking – but at 17 the fundamental complexity of chess was another of those Gurdjieffian lightning-bolts of insight, a brief glimpse of the unknowable. As in Gurus, as in Grandmaster. I loved the balletic majesty of the game, as displayed in all its myriad equations. Petrosian sacrifices Pawn. White Queen's Castle to Queen's Rook Three. Black Queen takes White Rook. It was mental jousting at its finest. Martial Arts for the Mind. Intellectual Ju-Jitsu. The symmetry of the language was as beautiful as any set of dance instructions. The Sicilian Opening. The Sicilian Defence. Queen's Gambit Declined. The Poisoned Pawn Variation. The Pas de Deux of repetition and counter-play. Adagio. Solo variations. Coda. Endgame. As in espionage, as in chess.

One morning, before I went to work, I turned on the telly to watch the highlights from the previous night's Olympic Games. Over a shot of the athlete's village in Munich David Coleman was chatting quietly, so I went into the kitchen, made my sandwich and filled a Graham Young-resistant flask of tea. When I returned to the living room Coleman was still talking over the same shot of the Olympic village. Stark concrete façade. Low hesitant voice. Serious measured tones. Not like the garrulous and excitable Coleman at all.

Telly in the morning was still a novelty then. At the Tokyo Olympics eight years earlier, it had been even more of a novelty. Live athletics and a less than pristine picture. Helmut Zacharias and his *Tokyo Melody* theme music. The medal-winning endeavours of Lynn Davies, Ann Packer and Mary Rand. And Coleman too of course. Always Coleman. A sporting fixture all of his own throughout my youth. And here he was now talking hesitantly, gravely even, about what might be occurring in real time behind that stark concrete façade. There was graver still to come. That night we all went to bed thinking the captured Israeli athletes had been freed and the terrorists rounded up and captured. Everyone woke up the following morning to the full horror of what had actually happened and to the new bleak reality of the 1970s. Light-hearted cartoon depictions of hostage takers ("Take me to Cuba" – hi-jacker in aeroplane cabin holding banana instead of gun) disappeared from the newspapers overnight.

Elsewhere, out of necessity and for sanity's sake, the cartoon view of reality prevailed. When Series Three of *Monty Python's Flying Circus* began in October 1972, I readily assimilated it into my lysergic armoury. It was as much a countercultural text to me as any Underground mag, as much a tripper's manual as *Alice's Adventures in Wonderland*. Monty Python was Underground comedy for Underground people and more progressive than any concept album. Plus, the Pythons looked hipper than any rock band. Series Three was their *Forever Changes*, their *Rubber Soul*, their *Electric Ladyland*, their *Wheels of Fire* (studio version). The track listing offered a nod to the immortals. *Whicker's World*, *The Money Programme*, Anne Elk's *Theory on Brontosauruses*, Sam Peckinpah's *Salad Days*, Mr Gumby, Mr Pither's *Cycling Tour of the North Cornwall Area*. All were woven into the fabric of my outlook.

The exchange in the cycling tour where Mr Pither is gently woken by his mother and thinks he has escaped the Russian prison (Pither: So, it was all a dream. Mother: No, no dear, this is the dream, you're still in the cell.) remains for me one of the most mind-expanding moments in the history not just of British comedy but of British philosophy too. Whatever programme came on immediately after Monty Python always required considerable psychological adjustment and an intense debriefing as the viewer was eased back into what passed for reality in the straight world. A Pythonesque worldview bled into almost everything else I watched, blurring the boundaries between the mainstream and the bizarre – and it was often in the mainstream where you found the most bizarre.

An episode of the *Rolf Harris Show*, which ran almost concurrently with Monty Python Series Three, featured the host trying to paint Ken Dodd while Dodd was posing on an uppity horse which seemed intent on proving the maxim: "Never work with children or animals." Harris used to loom up right into the camera lens at the end of the show, mugging endlessly as the closing credits rolled. I became transfixed by his grotesque antics, the way he had to stand there gurning away until someone said "Cut". There was a beer advert from around the same period that had a similar hallucinatory effect. A group of men sat in a pub acting out the kind of stilted tableau of enjoyment that only bit-part actors working towards their Equity card can, while a voiceover extolled the virtues of the beer they were drinking. At the end the camera lingers a little too long and in surreal close-up on the man at the end of the table. The others are laughing but he is over-acting so much that he appears to be having a stroke, his expression contorting into paroxysms of distress. I became obsessed with the advert. I sometimes imagined him sobbing uncontrollably, face pressed to the beer-stained table once someone had shouted "Cut!".

Old telly was a foreign country. They did things differently there. Nothing was as tightly edited as it is now. There were frequent longueurs, jolting jump cuts, incongruous splices. Anyone of my generation who was versed in the one-take shaky-scenery televisual lingua franca of the time would have recognised the incongruities. In his book *Exotica: Fabricated Soundscapes in a Real World*, David Toop used *Lassie* as an example of what he called "the strangeness of old television". Aside from the logistical problems caused by having a dog convey the dramatic narrative, Toop also points out the jarring juxtapositions between soundtrack and plot. "The music shouts 'Look out! Bad things on the way! Right now!'", he says.

"More often than not the scene then switches to an inert landscape or a tepid verbal exchange between two humans." Similar incompatibilities could be observed in *Rawhide* or any of the 1950s and 60s TV Westerns that were still being shown in the early 1970s. Over the opening credits of *Champion the Wonder Horse*, Frankie Lane, in that baritone prairie yodel of his, sang "Like a streak of lightning flashing cross the sky/Like the swiftest arrow whizzing from a bow" at the same time as the less than thunderbolt stallion came gingerly trotting down a rocky incline.

TV music possessed a vocabulary all of its own. I initially became familiar with the wheezing duet of ocarina and mouth organ not through *Pet Sounds* but via the incidental music to *Deputy Dawg*, where those instruments would play on a ceaseless loop completely unrelated to the action, stopping and starting at random regardless of whether the characters were engaged in a mad dash to the hen-house or lazily chewing the fat on the porch of the sheriff's office.

The programmes for schools I watched on rainy mornings when I couldn't be bothered to hitchhike were often augmented by the made-to-measure jazz and folk moodscapes of library music. The jazz they sometimes featured was not discernibly different from what I heard on Charles Fox's programme *Jazz Today* on Radio Three, while the action in school dramas was often punctuated by reflective and melancholy acoustic folk interludes. Similar keening motifs were much used in *The Wednesday Play*, and featured in *Take Three Girls* – where Pentangle provided not only the opening theme but much of the incidental music too. Also omnipresent was the innovative computer-modulated audio of the BBC Radiophonic Workshop. The Workshop's distinctive brand of homespun futurism could be heard on everything from school maths programmes to the news jingles and station idents of the expanding BBC local radio network.

****

The glow from the Pilgrims Inn cast lightning-bolt reflections on the River Ouse and I was awestruck. Did those lights always zig-zag like that? Purple and yellow? Mauve and chartreuse? Did they even have yellow in the olden days or was it a trick of the light? "Gah! Do you get it? Trick of the light." Nobody got it so I went back to gliding around the bar as if on trolley wheels, gnawing my imaginary carrot through pretend rabbit teeth and wondering what was going on. Curiouser and curiouser. Must stop saying that.

The bar was crowded. It was Saturday night and nobody was taking any notice of me. Punters supped in slo-mo. Loud of shirt and mouth. I couldn't understand anything anybody was saying above the hubbub-ha-bub-ha-bubbly. Words left spit traces in the air. Dickie Dangerfield glanced over at me with the face of a concerned parent. There was little he could do to alleviate the situation but he was good enough to indicate that my drink had been spiked by his friend Fally and everything settled down like fizz in a glass after that.

The first I knew that something was amiss was when I began restlessly patrolling the pub, spouting Alice's wonder words through chewy mumbles. Initially I was just thinking it, then I was thinking I was saying it. Then I knew I was saying it. Lewis Carroll, well he just knew, didn't he? I mean, he-just-knew. Everyone at our table was glaring at me. "It isn't a children's book. Not when you really get into it." I don't know who I said it to. It just came out. Fally's mate George leered into my face.

"Is it trippy, man?"

Fally looked on, satisfied with his night's work. Fish-bait maggots wriggled from George's acne-scarred visage.

"No, it's frothy, man!" I replied and reached out to touch George's frothy face. Yarghh! Get it. Frothy, man, like the head on the beer and the foamy ocean bow of the Pilgrim Ship as it slips anchor and ploughs on through uncharted waters westward into the Bedford night. It all links up if you think about it. Toot-toot. Man overboard!

That did it. Dickie walked me outside. Oh yeah sorry. I tried to explain. It was the Mayflower, wasn't it? And maybe I shouldn't have sat at the bar holding a Tia Maria like it was a pint and laughing in an unshaven way like we were back in the Bewley Brothers days of late last winter – although I was hanging out with different dwarf men then of course. And maybe when Dickie politely asked me what I wanted to drink I shouldn't have stared for so long at the optics before finally saying "A BLUE ONE!" in a loud voice. And one other thing. I thought I recognised someone in there. An old schoolfriend supping in the galley with all the slaves in a row-ho-ho with a bottle of rum. He may have only been painted on a backdrop but if it's a reasonable likeness they can still make that stick in court, can't they Dickie? I was babbling like a fucking lunatic.

Dickie made sure I didn't stray too near the water's edge. He steered me to the river bridge, then left me to the elements. I wandered round town for a bit. Past the furniture store with the curved glass frontage where Danny, Veronica, Harriet and I sought comfort and refuge against the penniless evenings before the inevitable policeman would move us on. On up the High Street, past E.P. Rose's, soon to become Debenham's. Past the Cadena, where we used to sit eating pancakes and making cat's cradle with affectionate fingers. Past Kerry's, windows all grilled up, the counter in darkness. Past St Peter's Square where Harold MacMillan delivered his famous "You've never had it so good" speech (which I didn't know then). Past the prison where Hanratty was hung. (Which I did.) Venturing into "Black Tom", an area of town named after an 18th century highwayman, and past a small pub with old men supping silently before I spooked myself and turned sharpish back towards better-lit pastures.

Striding purposefully but with little direction ("Eight miles a day. It's bound to show but I don't know how.") I dolly-drifted and detoured all over town. Approaching the Windsor pub in Silver Street I could see a gathering ahead of me and paused on the other side of the road to observe. Three or four of the old Irish regulars were remonstrating with the landlord on the pavement outside. He had obviously thrown them out and they were passionately and with as much sobriety as they could muster imploring him to let them back in. So he did. I heard him say, "C'mon then, gents. Behave yourself now," in a kindly voice, and they all shuffled back into the bar like a chastised line of saintly sinners. Bedford looked beautiful to me after that.

The cocoa smell wafted across town from the Meltis chocolate factory on Elstow Road where Mum had been a typist before she got married. It met the hoppy stench from the Charles Wells brewery midway on the breeze. Having accomplished an uneven circumnavigation of the town centre, I carrier-pigeoned back towards The Pilgrims Inn. It looked stately and palatial from the river bridge with the thick gloopy waters of the Ouse oozing by. Plate-glass windows. Everyone illuminated inside. Gaudy baubles and neon writing warping on the water. A rich syrup treacling down from the night sky. This I shouldn't wonder was the actual sweet green icing flowing down all the way from the MacArthur Park days. I wanted Dickie to see it as I saw it and thought I should venture back into the bar and find him, but no sooner had I considered that, than the night bent further out of shape and it started to rain: a soft plastic-coated sort of rain that made everything glisten with a petro-chemical sheen. The pavement went plastic, all the shopfronts went plastic, the big red brmm brmm bus going by, that went really plastic. And all this time the sweet green icing continued to settle on the Pilgrims Inn, curling in Mr Whippy formation, like a huge conical hat.

A saxophone swelled up ahead of me. It came from the Pilgrims' jukebox. It spoke to me of my longing. It spoke to me of my need. Junior Walker and the All Stars. *Walk in the Night*. Ba-doo-ba-doo-ba-da. Calling out to me. The long languorous notes of that tenor drawing me closer. Icing dripping down the plate glass. Everybody sparkling inside the pub. To the left of the long bar was a small dance area, more of an empty space than a dance area, but the girls commandeered it as their little bit of territory. I stood outside on the riverside towpath and watched them shimmer and twirl. Coats on chairs. Bags on the floor. Concentrating on drifting away. Energy aura visible in lipstick rays and powder clouds. Physical meditation. Motor city magic. Dharma soul. Karma soul. Mantra soul. Ba-doo-ba-doo-ba-da. Tessa and Harriett where are you in the plastic-coated Bedford night? Where am I? Where is anybody? Why couldn't –

****

Forgetting that I'd volunteered to work a Saturday morning (8 till midday – time and a half), I'd done a Friday-night microdot and turned in for work the next day with a considerable Ready Brek afterglow. Bill sat me at the gift-wrap bow machine and handed me a wedge of wriggly, spiderish ribbon. I fed the material in as best as I could and watched as it threaded and spooled and danced its merrily rainbowed way through the machinery. When I closed my eyes, I could see a multi-coloured negative of the entire mechanism imprinted on my brain. Mr Bechstein's son Simon was put in charge for the morning and had a very free and easy approach to supervision. There was just me, Bill, three of the tinsel-machine girls (one of whom Simon obviously had an eye for) and a smattering of women at the packing benches. Simon had brought in some chestnuts and decided to roast them in one of the industrial machines that was normally used to heat and seal shrinkwrap. He promptly forgot about them and only remembered when loud popping noises started going off. The unmistakable odour of burnt shell permeated the shop floor for the rest of the morning.

There was plenty of Saturday overtime on offer in the weeks leading up to Christmas. The factory's peak production period was in fact high summer and was just concluding when I started work there, but there were always last-minute Christmas orders to complete as shops ran out of stock. Dad was putting in a bit of overtime too at Vauxhall Motors, and one night after his long, extended working day I casually asked him if they'd had a big order come in. He let me know in no uncertain terms that I knew fuck all about factory procedure and large-scale production. Did I really think that someone had phoned up mid-afternoon and said: "Can we have 30 more Vauxhall Vivas by Friday? We've got customers waiting." In his tone I detected a growing disdain for the way I was pissing away my young life like this. Nothing further was said but I got the message.

An assistant storeman was taken on to help Ron with his general duties. His name was Maurice and I'd occasionally seen him about town, usually in a suit. In fact, I think I used to deliver his Daily Mail when I had a paper round. Maurice, it turned out, had been made redundant from a decent clerical position in an office. He was exactly the kind of white-collar casualty I'd read about in that newspaper article where men left the family home each morning too proud to tell their wives they'd lost their job. Maurice's own pride, he told me, forbade him from accepting hand-outs from the state. Rather than claim the unemployment benefit he was entitled to he had taken menial work "until something more suitable turns up".

One thing Maurice was singularly unsuited to was warehouse work. He was good at checking order forms, collating invoices and suchlike, but not so hot on the manual labour side of things. He was medium height, slightly taller than me, and at least a couple of stone heavier but he appeared to have no upper body strength whatsoever and struggled every time he bent down to pick up all but the lightest of packages. One day I watched as Ron and a delivery driver humiliated him, throwing boxes full of goods along a line which I was then supposed to stack on the lorry. Ron and the cuntish delivery guy deliberately kept speeding up, throwing the boxes too fast for Maurice to catch and jeering loudly each time he fumbled and dropped one. Maurice attempted to keep up a jovial demeanour as he underwent this ritual, but I could see the hurt in his face and I despised my workmates for doing that to him.

Virginia Plain was in the charts. David Bowie had followed up *Starman* with the sexually ambiguous *John I'm Only Dancing* and for the first time in ages I felt like I wanted to be part of the general expression of things again. Out there was a better world than in here, where the highlight of some people's day seemed to be slinging boxes into a van and humiliating workmates who were down on their luck. Kevin Ayers and assorted pals had recently performed a two-and-a-half-week stint of late-night shows at the Hampstead Theatre Club under the name Banana Follies. Ayers compared it in an interview to the Dadaist Cabaret Voltaire (the first time I had encountered the legendary Zurich club), but I couldn't go because I was an unskilled wage slave in a factory. Earlier in the year I would have thought nothing of setting off into the night without any idea as to how I was going to get home from Hampstead at 2 am. Now I was rising at 7 o'clock every morning and clocking on and clocking off like an obedient little serf. I hadn't been to a gig since I'd sat on the waste ground in Ladbroke Grove watching anonymous hippies doing their thing for free. Even if you include the jam sessions at Fisher House in Cambridge I hadn't been to more than half a dozen gigs all year. My entire active cultural life seemed to have ground to a halt.

I hadn't visited Kerry's for months either, and when I did I discovered there had been a few changes. For starters, Bowie's Deram album and the Ambrose Slade LP had finally disappeared from their prominent position at the front of the 49p sale rack. The big change, though, was that Clifford had left. Danny said someone had seen him selling INK outside Texas Instruments – or it might have been Black Dwarf outside Vauxhall Motors. His final bequest to Kerry's had been to order ten copies of Chicago's *Quadruple Live* album which sat proudly unsold in their huge boxes on the top shelf behind the counter, and where indeed they remained for several years after. I don't know if Clifford ever carried out his threat to spike Adrian's tea with acid, but I do know that lysergics weave their magic in mysterious ways, and a year or so later I read in the local paper that Adrian had relinquished his managerial duties at Kerry's to go off and manage Alvin Stardust.

Clifford's replacement behind the counter was a surly, dark-haired soul boy called Simon. One day he was keeping a watchful eye on the 10p sales rack and I had no choice but to pay for a couple of Harvest singles. *Butterfly Dance* by Kevin Ayers and *Can't Get Off the Planet* by Pete Brown and Piblokto!. The shop was quiet, so I got him to play them both. "What do you think?" I asked as I handed over my 20p. "Stroker's music," he replied, meaning wanker's music. I'd just met my first dyed-in-the-wool soul snob.

Kerry's is also where I first encountered Fally, the guy who spiked me, along with acne-faced George and several more of Danny's new mates. They would congregate at the far end of the counter, monopolise the record deck and lock earnestly into conversation with Simon about the new soul imports that had arrived in the shop. Danny, Dickie and their newly acquired crew started going off up North at the weekends to all-night dances. They talked about it like it was a religious experience for them. The epiphany didn't seem to impinge on Danny's other music tastes. He still bought Jefferson Airplane, Hot Tuna and Papa John Creach albums. He still loved John Sebastian and Quintessence, although the latter to a far lesser extent now that Shiva and Maha Dev had left the band.

Dickie had undergone a cultural transformation too. He'd always been an odd fish and never easy to summarise, but the kid I'd first encountered at 13 carrying a copy of Paul Oliver's *Story of the Blues* compilation under his arm had now become far less cerebral in his lifestyle choices. "What do you think of this one?" he'd ask as Fally flipped over a new import to check out the B side. Loads of the stuff Fally played sounded great to me. The charts at the tail-end of 1972 were starting to fill up with fantastic soul records. *Back Stabbers* by The O'Jays. *Lookin' Through the Windows* by the Jackson 5, *Here I Go Again* by Archie Bell and The Drells, *I'll Be Around* by the Detroit Spinners, *Keeper of the Castle* by The Four Tops.

Soul music became the soundtrack that choreographed my winter nights. I still associate all those records with Bedford and that period of my life. The Pilgrims Inn jukebox was probably the best in town, full of rarities that never appeared on any pop chart. Likewise, the stuff that the soul boys listened to in Kerry's. "I'm going to sell this one for £2," said Fally one Saturday, pulling out a choice single from a pile he'd just bought. This, at a time when singles still retailed at less than 50p. "Who decides it's worth two quid?" I asked. "Who would you sell it to?" "You create your own market," he replied. He was the first person I ever heard say that. A man ahead of his time was Fally, a man who clearly understood the concept of added value. "You should come with us," Dickie said to me on more than one occasion, eager that I should experience for myself the buzz of a Friday night up North, pilled up and dancing to this obscure music someone was prepared to pay two quid for. I said I'd think about it.

One Saturday evening in October, the Radio One *In Concert* programme featured the Kevin Ayers *Banana Follies* show. Kevin, Archie Leggett and remnants of the Whole World gang performed numbers from the revue. I can't be sure but I think it was the same Saturday that we sacrificially burned the old pub Joanna in the garden. All my acid Saturdays seem to bleed into one around that time. I sat on the front doorstep on an unseasonably warm evening and listened as Lol Coxhill and David Bedford performed their party pieces – *Pretty Little Girl* and *Murder in the Air* – as they had done when they were members of The Whole World. Kevin sang rarely aired obscurities such as *'Orrible Orange* and *Hat Song*. Towards the end of the concert he loquaciously dedicated a song "to an English eccentric called Syd Barrett" and I heard *Oh Wot a Dream* for the first time. The effect of hearing one of my two English eccentric heroes dedicate a song to the other sent the earth spinning off its axis. Everything that the pair meant to me was embodied perfectly in the line: "I met you floating while I was boating." Such a warm sunny image to be projecting onto an October evening as tiny starbursts exploded in the night sky and in my head.

– Hello Brendan.
– Is that you Rob? How are you?
– I'm tripping.
– Where are you?
– In the phone box on Bromham Road. It stinks.
Giggly spittle.

– I'm thinking of forming a group, Brendan. I've thought of some names.

– Come on round.

– Such as Volcano.

– Sounds a bit hard rock. What else?

– Magic.

Just saying it cast a spell.

– People might expect too much of you if you call yourself Magic.

Pow! The phone line fizzles and the receiver explodes into a thousand logic particles, showering the call box in plastic membrane. Let's make this a movement now. Ban all groups that can't live up to their name. That's Curved Air fucked for starters. I would have gone on with this train of thought if the money hadn't run out.

Waded a long way through oil-slick gutters. All those people who write to the local newspapers to complain that the streets are getting dirtier. They're right. The pavements stick to the soles of your feet like chewing gum. I'll be wearing concrete slabs by the time I get to Brendan's. On the way I thought some more about my Magic group. Advertising campaign in the music mags. How it would look on posters. Appropriate font. No, screw that. Do away with the conventional. Conjure it in sky writing and sod the budget. Brendan's logic voice dry and clear bringing me down.

– People might expect too much of you.

Then I remembered what he'd said about Volcano.

– Sounds a bit hard rock.

Slow fuse burning. Had to hide my face in someone's garden topiary just to muffle the cry-laugh.

When I got to Brendan's he was having an argument with his parents. Something about nothing but obviously everything to them. He left me standing in a hallway as big as my house, slumping and unslumping against a wall that was the colour and texture of congealed custard.

Scared that it might consume me, I contemplated death by quicksand custard while Brendan and his parents continued berating each other loudly in the dining zone. The raised voices showed no sign of playing themselves out and I came down a little off my trip. How can you hate your parents like that? No matter how many run-ins I'd had with mine I couldn't build up that degree of loathing. I certainly couldn't talk to them how Brendan was now talking to his Dad. He'd have walloped me from sideboard to settee.

That's the thing about the working class. Your Dad was Inspector Barlow and all the school Beaks rolled into one – that assumed unspoken authority invested in the parent. There's little room for negotiation on that score. It's partly why I couldn't go the extra generation-gap mile like the hippies did. They didn't want to be their parents and half the time I could see why, but it seemed to me that out of that hatred for the old order they built an entire culture in their own image, based on little more than not wanting to be a bank clerk or barrister like Daddy. I didn't want my Dad's life either, but then neither did he.

In his front room with ornaments and plushness and proper high-fidelity, Brendan says: "Do you like Jack Bruce?" "Yes I –" Tells me where you can buy tickets to a waterfall but I already know. Brendan has been doing this since he turned me on to Ginsberg's *Howl* and made me listen to Frank Sinatra lyrics. He asks me how often I take acid and there is a hint of censure in his voice. "Once you get into something..." I say, quoting the Rolling Stone Syd interview for the first time in a while. "It's hard to get out of it," he concludes like a school teacher slamming down a desk lid. Brendan doesn't take acid. I'm not aware that he takes anything at all but like everyone else, like me, like all of us, he has an irritable unpredictable side. He hangs out with Dickie quite a bit and they share a certain sardonic worldview. He plays me *Hot Rats*. Side One. All the way to the grand piano flourish at the end of *Son of Mr Green Genes*. "I love this bit," I say, so he takes the needle off the record with just seconds to go, seemingly just to spite me. On my acid trip it seems like an omen. You don't get to decide how it ends. I overthink the incident all the way back into town.

Back at the bus station Steve Danbury looms up like a bad dream. Another of the Bedford heads who hang around the windswept alleys and alcoves. Another false prophet come to claim me as I wait for the last bus. Back in 1969, which seems like a century ago, my classmates and I were lounging around one lunchtime when he and Carl Taylor crossed the school playing fields. We watched as they traced the arc of the perimeter fence and disappeared into some windbreak conifers. Periodically a trail of blue-white smoke emerges. Eventually so do they. The smoke has an unusual pungency as it drifts downwind to where we sit, agog and intrigued. When they re-emerge from their hiding place Steve seems to walk with a moon bounce. Carl is excited, elbows jabbing as he gestures, like he's trying to fly or something. They giggle drift past us and the smoke smell clings to them, leaving a tantalising trail marked Out of Bounds. It was the first time that I'd knowingly seen someone smoking dope. The fact that it was being done on school premises by two fifth-formers, who couldn't care less as they would be leaving soon, only added to the cool cachet.

That was then. Steve Danbury emerging from a school hedge backwards after smoking his strange brew in the Out of Bounds. Like me he never stayed on at school. Now he's making a hazy beeline along the bus station bays because I'm the only one there. The wind whips up rubbish and herds it into guttered corners. His smile smirk says "I know you, don't I?" but his eyes seem uncertain and it doesn't matter anyway. Just another bus-station encounter in the debris-driven night. Lays it on me. Slow babble of dumb talk. I don't know if he's stoned or just talks that way now. I humour him with as much tolerance as I can muster. Polite in my disdain.

Just the right side of undetectable. He drifts away. He drifts back again.

– I know the answers.

– All of them?

– Yeah?

I'm not inclined to ask but he's going to tell me anyway.

– Reality is a distant light dying away.

– I'll remember that.

– You won't. You should read *On the Road* by Jack Ker-

– I have.

I hadn't. I just wanted him to shut up.

– Then you should know. Like I know. It's all a trap man. The system. Jobs. It's all a con. Gotta live the life man. Got to live the life.

To my further dismay he whips out a mouth organ. Essential accessory for every bluffer who doesn't play guitar. It's either that or the Jews harp for which I blame Medicine Head. Steve Danbury wails the flatland blues and I his captive audience must suffer. Where's the bus? Or anybody?

Brendan Brotherson.
Reality Checkpoint.
Late 1972.

Tuesday November 21st. I'm watching *The Old Grey Whistle Test*. Bob Harris introduces a group called Sparks. They look buttoned-up and unprepossessing but they perform two numbers, *Girl from Germany* and *No More Mr Nice Guys*, that turn my head around. The former has an unshowy monotonous beat, not ploddy 12-bar monotonous, Velvet Underground monotonous. Monotony with intent. The keyboard sound is a bit Velvet Underground too, but toytown Velvets not avant-garde atonal Velvets. The singer's high register swoops and swoons and sighs all over and under and around the beat, and breaks into a charmingly alarming falsetto in the chorus. His vibrato has a trace of Marc Bolan and the backing vocals sound like Steve Took off the old Tyrannosaurus Rex records. There's even a bit of whistling.

The band play it subversively, knowingly, artily straight, like they are in on a joke that the rest of us are not yet party to. There is a surface politeness to the whole thing but there's an undertow too, like they could go full-tilt outrageous at any moment. The second number, *No More Mr Nice Guy*, is hard-edged, nagging and insistent, full of dramatic crescendos and faux heroics. The singer gives vent to a demented tooth-baring yelp as he sings a kind of chorus coda, but it's hard to tell what's meant to go where because the verses sound like hooks and the choruses sound like admonishments. That insistent Velvet Underground piano is there again, underpinning everything. They sound like a cutesier and more tuneful Alice Cooper. Afterwards Bob Harris said something faintly disparaging and clearly didn't know what to make of them. Neither did I but they impressed the fuck out of me. I didn't hear them again for 18 months but I filed them away in my memory. Heard once but not forgotten. Other voices. Other pop possibilities.

Another night, late November, again blitzed by acid I walked to the edge of Bedford to the very last bus stop by the very last house where the town ends and there is nothing but darkened pastures out there. I tried to hitch but nothing stopped. Suspicious motorists seemed to slow down, check their reflections in my dilated pupils then drive on into the inky blackness. Earlier, further back up the road, outside Dame Alice Harpur School in Cardington Road, I felt an unsettling presence behind me. I turned around and two policewomen on foot patrol stood there. I suspect they had been there some time.

– Oh, I'm sorry. I thought you were traffic wardens.

I thought this would adequately explain my rudeness. The little person who sat at the back of my head and remained straight on such occasions whispered instructions.

– Don't blow it Rob. Don't blow it. Don't offer to dance around the maypole with them or offer to pass on Steve Danbury's answer to life.

I'm tripping my sparks off. I want to share the universal love of big church with them. I want to shout THROW AWAY THE PSYCHIC HANDCUFFS MAN! My wild eyes are clearly spilling out everything bar the formula for diethylamide 25. The policewomen merely ask me where I'm going and send me on my way. Had the dialogue lasted a few seconds longer I would have been in big trouble. Even during that brief exchange I felt a sudden urge to question their credentials. These traffic wardens will stop at nothing to move you along when it's a maximum of one-hour parking, loading-bay only.

I get to the bit where Bedford ends and wait for cars to compete for my sparkling passenger-seat personality and my inner wisdom. But there's nothing. Just the cold blue sodium of the street lights and silent road. I started thinking how great it would be if you could send your instructions in by telepathy and a bus, a bus with your name on the front, came when you called. I tried it out to see if there was method to my madness. Cleared my throat.

– Coo-eeee bus.

That should do it. Not too shouty. Just enough audibility to carry back into town on the breeze. I watched my words trace a path all the way back to the bus station, down Harrowden Road, London Road, over the railway bridge, past St Johns station, round the one-way system, past college and County Hall, down St Mary's Street, over the river bridge, past the empty market stalls, the burger stand and the late-night Christian converters, past Bedford Modern school and the town library, through the shopping arcades and precincts, all the way back to base, where my driver, upon instruction, would put away his newspaper, start up his engine and respond to my call.

– Coo-eeee bus.

As if by magic an outline appeared in the distance. Unmistakably a bus. A single decker, fully lit-up, number as yet a blurry hieroglyph. The shape drew nearer. Stopping at stops. After a while I could clearly make out the passengers, counting how many got on and off. The bus got larger and closer, swelled up like a bright green blimp. Soon be on it. I watched and waited and waited and watched as it leaned into a curve, and where the road forks right and left it sped off right leaving me left. It passed the cavernous airship hangars of RAF Cardington, chugged over a hump-back bridge and on off up a steep hill till it was a distant light dying away, then a dot, then gone.

It got like that. Everything.

Back at work on Monday morning, stacking flat-pack cardboard in a corner, Mr Bechstein approached and asked me if I might want to consider working in the office. "You're a bright lad," he ventured, even though I'd provided scant evidence to back up his claim. "I see from your form that you've got O Levels. Do you want to work on the factory floor for the rest of your life? There's a clerical job going if you want it. Some days will be quiet. Other days will be so busy your feet won't touch the ground. We'll train you up and by the time you're 23 you could be earning…"

He was acting out of kindness and generosity and had my best interests at heart. Like Dickie with the Northern soul I said I'd think about it. And what I thought about it was this. I instantly projected a vision of myself in my early 20s. I'd be standing in a local pub with some mates. I'd be wearing a truly horrible shirt that would be tucked in to some equally awful trousers. For some reason I fixated unduly on the shirt, a real cheap and nasty affair, gaudy print motifs, blue on white, electric-shock fibres, the type you could buy off the cheap rails in Harry Fenton. I saw myself in the bar, forming a semi-circle of drinkers with my mates. I'd be nicknamed Brainbox on account of my impressive haul of school certificates and my propensity for an expanded vocabulary and "all that weird music he listens to". "Oh, there he goes again, typical Brainbox," they'd say as I supped my disgusting ale. I'd have the makings of an impressive beer gut too, like some of the lads of my age that I saw around town. Mr Bechstein had reached out to me and offered me a route out of unskilled labouring and all it did was panic me and cause me to have future flashes of a young man trapped by circumstance. I pondered this scenario for the rest of my working day, and concluded long before clocking-off time that I had to get the fuck out of there.

I poured all this out in desperation one night when I was round at Brendan's house. Dickie Dangerfield was there too. In my memory Brendan had just bought Bob Marley's *Catch a Fire* album and was trying to convince me that it was better than all that skinhead shit I used to like at school, even though it just sounded like slightly reggaefied rock music to me. But *Catch a Fire* didn't come out till months later, so that must have been another conversation we were having further on down the line. Let's say for local colour's sake that it was Little Feat's *Sailin'*

Shoes instead. I told Brendan and Dickie that I felt trapped and that I had really fucked up my life, how everything had gone off the rails since last winter and now I was trapped in this dead-end job.

"What do you want to do?" asked Brendan.

"What I really want to do is go back to college."

"So, write them a really creepy letter?" said Dickie. "See if they'll let you back in again. Just say, 'I realise the error of my ways and I'll be a good boy in future, blah blah blah'." Dickie didn't have to do that and, in some ways I'm still surprised he did. He was already in a casual relationship with Methadone and pursuing a lifestyle that was never going to lead in any way back to formal education, but he was willing to suggest to me that I should give it another go. In fact, he insisted.

I'd been living on my instincts for the first half of the year. In the second half, once I ran up against the buffers I hadn't known what to do. It simply hadn't occurred to me that I could opt back in to the education I'd truncated so hastily the previous December. My horizons had narrowed to such an extent that I'd couldn't imagine doing anything other than dead-end menial work in order to get by. But it was precisely that menial work which convinced me that I did need to find a way back in, and the way back in was the very thing that I had turned my back on. Working in the glitter factory had drained all my hidden reserves, most of my creativity, virtually every last vestige of imagination. Time crawled at a deathly pace from the moment I clocked on to the moment I clocked off again. "Write them a really creepy letter," said Dickie, so I did. I sat down with pen and paper and explained that a sharp dose of unskilled factory work had convinced me of the value of qualifications, and that I was eager to resume my studies. I can't remember what else I said in the letter but that much at least was heartfelt. A couple of weeks later I received a reply inviting me in for a chat. I left the glitter factory at lunchtime, saying that I had a dentist appointment, and hitched into Bedford.

The Principal, Mr Davies, the man who first interviewed me when I was still at school, had left. He'd been replaced by a younger, less crusty appointee also called Mr Davies. Also in attendance was a new Vice-Principal, another name and face unknown to me. I basically repeated what I'd said in the letter and didn't make any attempt to ingratiate myself. Both men heard me out in silence. The Vice-Principal leaned by a window ledge and cast doubtful looks whenever I met his eye. Mr Davies seemed more benign, he even nodded sympathetically a couple of times. There was a considered pause when I finished talking. "I have to say that we get a few requests like this," he said in a deep Welsh baritone, "and I also have to say that it very rarely works out." "Most just leave again," added the Job's comforting VP. But Mr Davies had obviously picked up on my barely concealed desperation, and he read my sincerity correctly. He said that I could start in January if I liked with the proviso that if I mucked things up this time there would be no third chance. "So, I'm on trial basically," I said with perhaps a little more truculence than was called for. "Oh no," said the entirely agreeable Mr Davies, who could have rescinded his offer there and then had he so wished. He must have seen in me something that I probably still couldn't see in myself at that time, someone who was worth handing a lifeline. All this while, his Vice-Principal stood by that window ledge giving me a look that suggested he didn't trust me as far as he could spit.

It only occurred to me afterwards than the small matter of me distributing acid on the fifth-floor had never been raised. It also occurred to me for the very first time that perhaps the information had never been passed on to anyone higher up the managerial chain. The letter I had hastily intercepted and stuffed into my pocket back in January made no mention of it. It just said that I had left college of my own volition or sentiments to that effect. I later discovered that the lecturer who had stumbled upon my illicit activities had also since left, so it's possible nothing further was ever said. Or perhaps Mr Davies and his Vice Principal did know – the VP's expression during my interview certainly suggested he did – and that I was in fact just another in a long line of beneficiaries of a lenient further-education system that opened its doors to all kinds of deviants and drop-outs and rejects in those far-off halcyon days of half a century ago.

After spending the first half of the year deceiving my parents into thinking that I was attending college I was now hesitant about telling them I was going back. I stood in the kitchen doorway as Mum served up the evening meal. All my spiritual soul-searching and band-seeking and winging it came down to this one nerve-wracking moment in the kitchen. Fate, fate, her steak and kidneys on my plate. "Mum, I've got something to tell you." I must have been nervous because in the long pause that followed she said, "What's up boy? You've gone as white as a sheet."

I didn't realise until that moment just how much of an intolerable emotional burden my whole situation had become to me, but there was an immense release of pent-up relief when I heard myself saying the simple words: "I'm going back to college." Mum's first reaction was a practical one. "I shall miss the keep," she said, disappointed about the money I'd no longer be providing from my pay packet. "I'd better let the Family Allowance know," she added, balancing the books as usual, practical eye as always on the purse strings. Four young mouths to feed and just Dad's housekeeping money to spread out over a working week. "You're doing the right thing, boy," said Dad when he got home from another day's grind at the car-production plant.

The week I handed in my notice at the glitter factory there was a piece in Melody Maker about Led Zeppelin. Written by Roy Hollingworth, the MM journalist who had covered Syd Barrett's ill-fated appearance with Stars at Cambridge Corn Exchange, it began with an exasperated manifesto cry on behalf of the macho tendency. "If you really wanna hear a rock'n'roll band, wipe off that silly bloody make-up and go and see Zeppelin," he grunted. The piece was one long testosterone snarl on behalf of the bollocks-out, real-music brigade. There was a lot of it about at the time. In my final week at the glitter factory I snuck a few tubes of glitter out each night as ammunition for the new culture war that lay ahead. We also had the best-decorated house in the street that Christmas. When I went out at night I would dab a tiny amount of glitter on my face and go about my business with a sparkle. The look was subtle and only visible in a certain light. I liked to keep people guessing like that. Within a few months, androgyny would be virtually compulsory for anyone in possession of a modicum of cuteness. I needed to be prepared.

My hair had grown out sufficiently from its Martian suedehead crop for me to consider getting a new look. I had no more idea of where David Bowie got his Ziggy cut than where Marc Bolan bought his girls' shoes, but I took a train up to London, sought out the poshest looking stylist in Kensington High Street and paid the most I'd ever handed over in my life for a haircut. I took the 1967 Bowie album on Deram along to give the hairdresser an idea of what I wanted. I actually preferred that cut to the Ziggy one. It was more of a mod cut with a high parting, bouffantish in the way mod boy-girls wore it when that was the style. What I got from a delightfully attentive salon boss was a kind of hybrid of the Deram album cover and the cut Bowie had modelled on the front of Melody Maker back in January. I knew nothing of the Kansai Yamamoto photo in Vogue, the original inspiration behind the Ziggy cut. Nor was I aware of Bowie's stylist Suzi Fussey and her Schwarzkopf Red Hot Red with 30-volume peroxide, or how she'd used Gard anti-dandruff treatment to set her Ziggy creation in shape. The science and the back story were unknown to me. All I knew was that I didn't want to walk back into college looking like the same guy who had been kicked out a year ago. My main ambition over Christmas, apart from avoiding *My Ding-a-Ling* and Little Jimmy Osmond on the radio, was to keep my hair set just so.

It was Christmas Day morning and I was watching *The Point!*, Harry Nilsson's charmingly weird cartoon film on BBC2. I turned to my sister, apropos of nothing, and said: "I don't know if this has been the best year of my life or the worst." The comment displayed an untypical degree of prescience and self-awareness for someone who had just turned 18. A year earlier I'd soured everyone's Christmas Day and a few days later my younger siblings had watched me walk out of the door with a boxful of LPs, threatening never to return. Some role model. Now here I was watching Harry Nilsson's cartoon fantasy which he'd dreamed up on acid and gifted to the world as an album, a book and a film. It seemed a good place to settle temporarily as I mused philosophically about the 1972 I'd just had. The best of times or the worst of times? A little from column A, a little from column B, I guess.

My parents invested a lot of time and energy encouraging their kids not to end up "working on the dustcart" (us boys) or "Woolworths" (my sister). If my year off-radar taught me anything it's that you can't just drop out. Without a safety net there's nothing to catch your fall. You just keep on dropping. I wasn't yet sufficiently clued-up enough to see how all this would play out further down the line – how the middle-class, well-heeled drop-outs I subsequently encountered could usually, at their convenience, drop back in again at a later date. Nor had I seen enough then of what happens to working-class kids who buy into the whole hippie dream and then find themselves at the bottom of the heap without recourse to a rescue plan. At 17 I had glimpsed just enough to sense that the dream itself was flawed on multiple levels, particularly if you didn't have the funds to sustain yourself. All my ideas about escaping ran up against the fiscal buffers that year. The only place you could escape to with any degree of success was inside your own head.

It was the same with my religious quest. Circumstances and wherewithal denied me the opportunity to go and live with Barry and Eve in their Clapham Common ashram, or sit at the foothills of the Himalayas and suss out the cosmos. I rationalised I could still carry the ashram on my back and do all that at home (or wherever I chose to call home), should I so desire. And that's essentially what I did from then on. Never mind yin and yang and macrobiotics – which I never truly figured out anyway. In the end I was more inspired by the cartoon cosmology on the sleeve of a Gong album than I was by ensuring that I chewed my long-grain rice 50 times before swallowing. And that's how it remained throughout my teens and early twenties. One-part Buddhist punk, one-part piss-taking cynic. Willing to dive into the mystic, but retaining the sanity-preserving capacity to laugh at the cosmic absurdity of it all.

Cue *17* by Jethro Tull. Roll end credits.

Afterword

Some time in the 1990s, or it could have been the early 2000s, given the fallibility of mid-life memory, I was in the Record and Tape Exchange bookshop in Notting Hill Gate when I spotted a copy of the third edition of Nicolas Saunders' *Alternative London* on the shelves, the very edition I'd once owned and long since dispensed with. For old time's sake I bought it and welcomed the survival guide back onto my own bookshelves as an aide mémoire. I had to go down to Putney after that, and from there made my way into central London by train. Just outside Waterloo the engine halted and waited for a red light to change. In that compulsive fidgety manner that some of us display I took the copy of *Alternative London* out of my bag, carefully peeled off the price label and put the book away again. It can't have been in my hand for more than 30 seconds. As the train moved off again, I got up and made my way to the doors where an oldish hippie-looking guy stood waiting to get off. He leaned in almost conspiratorially, like he was about to sell me drugs. "Couldn't help noticing you were looking at the old *Alternative London* there," he said wistfully. One quick glimpse of that distinctive orange and yellow cover was all it took. He told me he used to street-sell it back in the day. I précis-ed for him, in the brief time we had, what the book had once meant to me and what I had gained from it. It was just a simple shared moment by a train doorway – an old head and a former apprentice reminiscing – and then we went our separate ways. As we all did. As everyone I've mentioned in this book did.

I went back to college in January 1973, dressed in high-waisted trousers, a red-and-black-striped public-school blazer which I'd found on Portobello Road market and sandy brown cord Hush Puppies. My Bowie haircut held its shape for a couple of months before collapsing like a soufflé. It grew out again into a style more reminiscent of a Spider from Mars than Ziggy. Within a couple of weeks of starting back at Tech, a student came up to me in the toilets, pushed his face ascloseasthis and screamed POOF! Some kids in the back row of one of my O Level retake classes muttered the same under their breath. I obviously gave off a certain "Is he or isn't he?" vibe, something the new influx of public-school drop-outs in the Mezz warmed to immediately. We bonded via unwritten codes. These were as subtle as the tiny grains of glitter on my face that only sparkled in a certain light. The Mezz was still the same in-between place it had been when I left. For all us in-betweenies that spacious canteen, midway between the ground and the first floor, was our cat walk, our Salon. One morning soon after I returned to college, someone from the Drama Society came round trying to drum up recruits for their next production. He stood at the table adjacent to mine where three of the Bedford Modern School drop-outs were holding court. "No thanks," I heard one of them say. "We're Mezz actors." And that's what we all were. Mezz Actors. All of us who were in the process of inventing or reinventing ourselves, all of us in our various stages of becoming. We cohabited on that halfway floor between floors where identity was up for grabs and guessing was the game.

Books furnish a room and learning furnishes a life. All that reading I'd done in my "gone missing" year – the Burroughs, the poetry, the Zen, the sacred texts, the profane texts – formed the bedrock of my strategies for the next several years and held me in good stead. What had at first seemed inchoate and shapeless and random constituted a pretty formidable alternative curriculum by the time I was 18. And that was just the start of it – the beginning of a life-long journey that brought me to this point here. The books I read then became my building blocks, all part of an intuitive self-improvement programme as I dedicated myself to knowing more than I did yesterday or the day before that. During my previous brief college sojourn, I was still carrying a lot of refusenik baggage from my schooldays, but I wised up considerably during that 12-month absence and hit the ground running when I returned to Tech. In five indifferent Grammar-school years plus a solitary term of further education, I'd amassed a grand total of three O Levels. After that I never failed at anything academically again. Failed at plenty else, sure, but once I'd learned the rules of intellectual engagement there was no stopping me.

I reined in my leisure pursuits moderately. I still enjoyed the occasional acid trip when the opportunity presented itself – the microdots during that period were the product of the Operation Julie gang up there in the Welsh hills and were pure god drops – but I kept leisure time and work strictly separate. I still displayed evidence of an unruly intellect, a character trait I retain to this day, but if I didn't like Plan A I always made sure I had a Plan B. If I didn't like a book on the English A level curriculum I asked what I might read instead. The Metaphysical Poets for the unfathomable Jane Austen was a good swap. If I didn't like an essay question I made up my own. I exasperated my English lecturer, a tolerant old scouser called Russell Woodward who had come out of retirement to teach us passionate, bright young Mezz actors. He rode a 500CC motorbike, and knew all the old Liverpool comedians like Ken Dodd and Ted Ray. He allowed me untold leeway, cut me more slack than you'd find in a coal yard and warned me I'd have to find my own research sources if I opted to study Marvell, Donne and Herbert instead of *Pride and Prejudice*. Which I did. "Robert already had an undergraduate approach to his learning," he wrote approvingly in one of my end-of-term reports, which for the first time since Junior school were not abysmal.

The crucial thing is I knuckled down and did my work. You make it easier for them if you're a pest AND you don't work. It's harder to censure you for mildly hedonistic indiscretions if you're a model pupil as well. I learned that much. And if this book has an underlying moral, beyond the astral traveller's tales, the mishaps, happy accidents and chancy encounters, then it's that. You have to get your education from somewhere, even if it's not from the officially sanctioned and approved sources. You have to fill your head with something, otherwise the system will fuck you over double the amount that it would do anyway, even if you do possess a pocketful of pass grades. The machine can find all kinds of novel new ways to mangle your head, chew you up and spit you out. But you still have to do your learning, even if it involves, as it did in my case, veering temporarily off radar, taking refuge in provincial libraries and making up the syllabus as I went along.

Culturally, 1973 was just like 1972 only more so. TV was still full of extrasensory magic and absurdist interventions. Within weeks of returning to college, I was at home watching the telly one lunchtime when *Pebble Mill at One* was invaded by Welsh-language protesters. They took the microphone from the show's genial host Bob Langley and proceeded to propagandise in Welsh for the next half-hour. There was no attempt to take the programme off-air. The cameras carried on rolling and at the end of their peaceful protest they just handed the microphone back to genial Bob. It made the papers the next day.

Meanwhile the full-scale hippie invasion of Schools Programming continued unabated. Thanks to a joint initiative between the Inner London Education Authority and the Greater London Council a show went out during 1973 featuring Dandelion recording artists Tractor, who offered weekly guitar and drum tuition. Ron Geesin provided electronic music for maths programmes. Jazz and folk remained ubiquitous on everything from schools drama slots to *Play for Today*. In my recollections of that era, "schools-programme jazz" now constitutes a genre in its own right. The miners' strike and the three-day week meant that we often sat in unheated, unlit classrooms in our overcoats, and became unavoidably politicised simply by virtue of our circumstances. I listened to a lot of Radio Moscow, whose news broadcasts framed the entire conflict in classical Marxist terminology, the presenters in their stern Pravda voices talked unceasingly about the ruling class and the proletariat. You didn't get that with Reginald Bosanquet and Sandy Gall.

In October 1973 I went to see Faust supported by Henry Cow at Cambridge Corn Exchange. It remains one of the best half-dozen gigs I've ever been to. I was so blown away by Faust that I came home and listened to an hour of shortwave interference before I could sleep. At around the same time *Man About the House* started on ITV and Richard O'Sullivan deposed Rolf Harris as king of the closing-credits muggers. I continued to view everything, from awful TV sit-coms to the gaudy excesses of glam rock, through a shimmering prism of acid. Telly was still in black and white but everything else played out in hyper-real, neon-lit, candy-coated multi-colour.

I was flicking through Melody Maker one day. The Glitter Band had started having hits of their own and now here they were being profiled on the esteemed pages of the MM. I was less than fascinated by their music and still repelled by the odious Gadd, but I was an inveterate consumer of pop trivia so I was semi-digesting the profiles just to see what groups they'd all been in previously. I wasn't even bothering to match up the band members with the previous experience, just skim-reading across the columns. I reached the names Black Velvet and Heaven and looked up to the top of the page and there was Pete, the drummer I'd met in Stockwell, queuing up to be one of life's encyclopaedia salesmen – or not as it turned out. Pete who invited me back to his Brixton flat, as we walked, talked and dreamed our pop dreams. Pete who was never in when I phoned after that, having evidently found his own dream gig to live large in.

Episodes from that limbo year have criss-crossed my life ever since, sometimes flickering by in the briefest of encounters: a tune heard, a poem read, a conversation half remembered, a layby glimpsed in the half-dark. Occasionally reminders loom up at the most unexpected moments. I didn't think about 1972 for years. I was happy to move on. Life propels you forward at a frantic pace at that age. You rarely dwell, or pause to look back even for a moment. There is always something new to adore or be cynical about. Now I think about that period of my life quite often. It crosses my mind whenever I look at the books on my shelves, the volumes that – unlike Alternative London – I didn't discard as soon as I felt I no longer had any use for them. The *Some of IT* compendium, *Poems of Solitude* from the Late T'ang Dynasty, the Penguin *Children of Albion* anthology. I still have them all, along with many other books and records that have followed me from town to town, rented room to rented room, shelf to makeshift shelf. Mementos that had been savagely tossed aside during the impetuous purges of youth were eagerly reacquired whenever I chanced upon them as other people's cultural cast-offs in charity shops and at boot sales. Most of those LPs and singles I took to the David's Bookshop warehouse in Letchworth gradually returned to my collection (and I still mourn the ones that didn't).

That Year Zero strategy becomes unsustainable once you begin to realise that you are the indelible sum of your parts. At some point between Tech and Polytechnic I adopted Ian Pinner's bus-station caff line on the Mersey poets. "You grow out of them, don't you?" I said to a fellow Poly student with the seasoned pomposity of someone "who already had an undergraduate attitude". She didn't think you do grow out of them, actually, and told me so. And after a while I didn't think that either. Or rather I did, and then I grew back into them. Some things are cultural constants. Other are subject to periodic renegotiation. Paul Green's *This View from Above* disappeared into a box-load of miscellany and would re-emerge every few years, whenever I sorted and sifted.

I kept waiting for *This View from Above* to get bad in the same way that a lot of stuff got bad once the scales of impressionability fell from my eyes. The majority of the stoned poetry and rabble-rousing rhetoric in the Underground press for instance. A fair amount of hippie crap in general in fact. But the Paul Green book never did turn to crap. In fact, as the years went by the tone of those poems only seemed to grow more distinctive and alluring. Green's voice joined Syd Barrett, Spike Hawkins and Pete Brown in the select pantheon of people I aspired to write like. When the growth of the internet began to make the past readily accessible in previously unimaginable ways I went searching for Paul Green, just to see if he still walked among us.

After several false starts and dead-end trails, I e-mailed the wrong Paul Green who put me in touch with the right one. In April 2002 I was given an address in Peterborough and wrote to it, explaining to the poet just how much his irregular verse had meant to me. You and Syd Barrett mate. You and Syd Barrett. I'm still prone to fan gush when the mood takes me. Back came a kind and generous reply which began: "Thank you for your letter. Without further ado I think I can say it was one of the most surprising letters of my life..." With hindsight Mr Green thought his early efforts were "either rash or brash, but at the time of their writing, were innocently wild". As eulogies to youth go that's up there with the very best. Rash, brash and innocently wild. Weren't we all?

Books and records come and go. People aren't so easily replaced, lapsed friendships not so readily resumed. The memories of those who flit across these pages remain with me. Some are here and some are missing as the Pet Shop Boys song would have it. I sup with the ghosts of remembrance every time I evoke their names. I spoke to Syd Barrett on the phone in the summer of 1973. I'd returned to the glitter factory for vacation work and blagged a brief and bizarre conversation under the boss's nose, telling him it was a local call. Syd was being represented by the Circle Agency at the time and full of the armour plated confidence of youth I phoned them and asked if I might interview Syd for Terrapin magazine. They gave me a London number and the unmistakeable voice of Syd answered. "You'll have to talk to X" (name lost in the mists of time), he replied. I didn't know if this meant that he was now fetching X or what, so I waited. I could hear someone – I assume Syd – pacing about a room. There was no further response, and after a few minutes I got the message and hung up. Oh, wot a dream that was.

I interviewed Kevin Ayers in a Brixton bar in 1996 for a Soft Machine feature I was writing. "I spent my entire late teens waiting for you to become famous," I half-jokingly chastised him. "It's like I said in that song *Stars*," he replied. "If you want to be a star start shining, stop whining. That was a message to myself." We talked of Gurdjieff and Madame Blavatsky and the 40-something me regularly had to pinch himself that this conversation too wasn't part of the extended dream sleep that precedes the revelatory awakening. For the same feature I interviewed Daevid Allan at the Glastonbury home he was renting at the time. I told him about the letter I once sent. He said he had a trunk full of such correspondence back home in France and had always made a point of trying to answer such soul-searching enquiries as my own. Interviewing Pete Brown for my Syd Barrett book, *A Very Irregular Head*, I mentioned casually that when I was starting out the only other writer whose sense of elision gripped me as much as Syd's was Spike Hawkins. "Oh, I think Spike knew Syd," he said and went to fetch his address book. A few weeks later I was sitting in Spike's flat, listening to the man himself reminisce about time spent with Syd Barrett. Connections lead to connections. Wheels within wheels. The dot-to-dots all join up and make a shape. The jigsaw puzzle pieces fit. Eventually.

As for the quartet of girls Danny and I met on that Bedford Bus Station bench in October 1971, I lost touch with them all for a bit when I went back to college. I saw Harriet just the once, at a party soon after I returned to college. I was amiably high. She was genial and amused at my antics. I bumped into Veronica occasionally as she was going out with

Danny, but saw less of them both as time went by. Veronica confessed to me one day that she dreaded Danny and Dickie coming back from their Northern club soirées. The speed comedowns and jittery exhaustion, gently nursing Danny back to something approaching health before work on Monday, it took its toll.

Dickie Dangerfield, meanwhile, maintained a robust aversion to employment. He continued to urge me to come to the soul nights with them, but I was too busy getting my academic shit together, and warning bells always rang when he described a typical club night out. I know that if I'd immersed myself in that culture I probably wouldn't be recalling that period in tranquillity now. I remember standing in Kerry's with him one day when Roxy Music's new single *Pyjamarama* was playing. He was making a strong case for them being the most original band on the planet right now. He also told me he'd gone off the Stones, and thought the rot set in with *Tumbling Dice*. He remained as critically astute as any of us. Soul boy George wasn't so lucky. He of the "Is it frothy man?" drink spiked night in the Pilgrims Inn would regularly cadge money off me if he saw me around town. "Do you know him?" said a couple of college-girl friends in horror as he made a bee-line for us one evening as we waited for a bus. His trampish demeanour and indifference to personal hygiene repelled them. "Smelly George", his mates called him. Smelly George came out of the Pilgrims Inn one night, emboldened on pills and booze, and decided it would be a good idea to swim to the other side of the Ouse. The river is very wide at that point and has deceptive and deadly undercurrents.

Danny reappeared in my life after a gap of nearly 25 years when he recognised himself as the unspoken other in a piece I wrote for Mojo magazine about seeing Syd Barrett's Stars at Cambridge Corn Exchange. We caught up on the intervening years in a series of lengthy phone chats and dwelled on matters both weighty and ephemeral. In particular I remember him mentioning "all those boxes of records I've hauled from house to house". He evoked it beautifully, all the enduring artefacts that come to define us. He got in touch again when I was diagnosed with and treated for cancer in 2005. He remained as funny, sharp and irreverent as ever. He summarised a recent reunion with the old soul crowd as "everyone looks the same except that they all have huge heads now". I haven't spoken to him in a while but I occasionally receive spam e-mails suggesting his account has been hacked so I assume he's still around. His ex-wife Veronica reappeared equally surprisingly in my life when she found me on social media. She lives in the USA now and from her profile pic still looks pretty much how I originally remember her, same Cheshire Cat smile, same twinkle.

After I'd I completed my A levels I took another year out to work and play before I went to Bristol in 1975 to start my degree. It was a very different kind of gap year this time. Three of us rented a flat in Bedford above a takeaway opposite the Tech college. It became a bit of a rendezvous point for every passing deviant and wastrel we knew. What happened above the takeaway stays above the takeaway. As well as Pete, one of my best mates from college, the other rent paying occupant was Randolph, an ex-public schoolboy who had forsworn a promising talent as a classical pianist to become an ice-cream man. Randolph's father had been the architect responsible for the design debacle of County Hall, the same County Hall that began sinking the moment it was built. Randolph is the reason I know the full story. As well as having an esteemed father of local fame and notoriety, Randolph was also going out with Tessa – no-bullshit, booble-bath Sheffield Tessa. Still as funny, still as formidable. Michelle was a regular visitor to the flat too. As well as just generally hanging out, she would often bring her boyfriend up to borrow a spare bedroom for purposes of sexual intercourse. Veronica informs me that Michelle has recently retired after rising to a position of prominence in the field of education. That's Deputy Headmistress to you.

Our Bedford landlord, Tony, was a well-respected member of the local "Italian business community". If we ever complained to Tony about the crack in the wall that let in rain, or the unsafe state of the fire escape at the back of the flat, his response was always the same. An aggrieved shrug followed by "Eh, I let you bring girls up here, don't I?" The inference was "and don't think I don't know what else goes on up here". In keeping with our liberal visitors' policy, the downstairs entry door out onto the street was invariably left unlocked. Steve Sangster and Eugene often used to sit on the bottom steps, taking refuge from the winter weather, gouging away until the latest fix wore off. The pair of them were in a bad way by 1975. Steve was no longer the sparky guy who had sold us acid that October Sunday by the bus station. When I was doing my A levels he often sat in the Mezz, nodding out, of us but no longer with us, incapable of playing any part in the pageantry. I wasn't there the day he came in at lunchtime, took a plate and spoon from the canteen counter and helped himself to a portion of slops from the discarded dinners bin. A girl I knew threw up at the sight of that.

One foul rainy Tuesday evening Tony came up for the rent. "Eh," he gesticulated towards the door. "I just kicked a couple of junkies off your steps. Fucking lowlife, eh?" When Tony had gone we crept warily downstairs. There was no sign of Eugene but we found Steve, battered and bleeding on the bottom step. He wearily accepted our offer of water and a flannel. I'm not even sure he knew where he was. A few weeks later he fatally overdosed in the Mezz toilets. Some of the more impressionable junior members of the local hippie fraternity came out with sentiments along the lines of "It was what he would have wanted," and "The Mezz was like a second home to him", but I just thought it was fucking sad. What a waste of a life.

A few years later I heard through the rumour mill that Tessa had been diagnosed with cancer. I only pieced the story together slowly from what friends of friends had been told, but gradually I learned that it had been a virulent and invasive form of the disease, which at one point had entailed amputation in a vain attempt to stem the spread. I still know little more than that, other than the fact that Tessa didn't make 30. The exact details are too gruesome for me to contemplate even now. I can still hear the way she said "booble bath".

In 1983, after my first marriage ended, I was briefly living back in the old homestead and working in Bedford. I was passing the Harper Suite shopping centre one day when a tall bearded guy walked by. He was flanked by two elderly people that you could have taken to be his grandparents. As he passed he offered a tentative smile, like he recognised me from somewhere but wasn't really sure if it was me. I was a good way further down the road when I realised it was Dickie Dangerfield. I suddenly remembered that he had elderly parents and had been an only child. I recall him telling me that at school. Dickie had cast an increasingly forlorn figure as the 1970s progressed. There would be the occasional news snippet on Page 5 of the local paper about a Richard George Dangerfield who had been found staggering along some village B-road and when apprehended by the police was found to be in possession of Class A drugs. Dickie disappeared from my radar once I went off to Bristol Polytechnic in 1975. That passing glimpse in Bedford, eight years later, was the last time I ever saw him.

In one of the last phone conversations I had with Danny, when I was recovering from cancer, he filled me in on the intervening years. Danny and Dickie were always the closest of buddies, and their Northern soul days, and nights, were eventful. Danny told me they were beaten up once, not by strangers, but by the very mates who used to gather in Kerry's to listen to the latest imports. I wouldn't have lasted five minutes in that kind of company. I was always too knowing and mouthy by half. You wouldn't have needed to add amphetamines to the mix for that to get combustible. I'd often wondered how such a roughneck crew tolerated the long-haired, methadone-dabbling Dangerfield. Now I partly knew. Hippie Dick, they called him, affectionately I hope. I didn't have my Northern Soul epiphany till the early 1980s. Indeed, it was only when I started seeing references to the all-nighter phenomenon in the music mags in 1974 that I realised retrospectively what Danny's Bedford crew were all part of. I don't remember any of them using the term Northern Soul at the time. I never met people like that again until I moved to Manchester at the height of the rave period, same scally tendencies – same full-on hedonism, shit jobs if they had jobs at all, same quasi-religious devotion to the music.

I mentioned to Danny that I'd always been grateful to Dickie for convincing me that I should go back to full-time education. Someone had to tell me that and I'm still surprised it was him of all candidates, the boy least likely to sign up for night classes. Danny told me Dickie had a pretty rough time of it later on. They lost touch when, after his own "chequered period", as Danny euphemistically put it, he got his shit together, remarried and found his way back into gainful employment.

On a whim, during a period of work that involved long-distance driving, Danny looked Dickie up and took him down to the West Country for a bit of a break from his drudge life. He told me that when he'd turned up at Dickie's house – he was still living with his parents in the Bedfordshire village where he grew up – Dickie's bedroom looked the same as it did when he was 16. "Porn mags under the bed. Hendrix poster on the wall." Down in the West Country things didn't go well. At breakfast in the B&B Dickie got his works out on the table, became loudly abusive to a party of Japanese guests, and all but got them slung out of their accommodation. "I think he was on the rent for a while, as well," said Danny as the story got progressively grimmer.

On another whim, in 2004, Danny decided to look up his old pal again. This time there were no porn mags under the bed and Hendrix poster on the wall. The garden was overgrown and there was a For Sale sign up outside the house. Danny learned that Dickie's elderly parents had died, in 1996 and 2000 respectively, and asked a neighbour what had happened subsequently. The neighbour told Danny that after Dickie's Mum had died, he had put his own affairs in order and left what worldly wealth he had to Battersea Dogs' Home. Dickie died in 2004, aged just 49.

At school I remember he went to see the Woodstock film before any of us. He couldn't believe that Hendrix was just standing there, playing *The Star-Spangled Banner*. From the soundtrack he assumed, like we all did, that Hendrix must be writhing around and throwing shapes, simulating intercourse with his Stratocaster. No, said Dickie. He just stood there, full of grace and beauty, the violence flowing from his guitar strings not his posture. I can't imagine Dickie dancing at soul nights and doubt if he did. I can see him thumbing through the record boxes though. I'll always be able to see him doing that.

My parents lived long enough to see me get a degree and form a band but not long enough to see me have a book published (at 38, I just sneaked in before the dreaded "40 and still not published"). Dad died of a heart attack in 1980 aged 53. Mum died of cancer aged 50 the following year. "He's going to be a writer, aren't you boy?" she said, that sunny afternoon in the back garden. Not long before she died we were talking about this and that, and the subject of my troubled year came up, obliquely. "We saw you hitchhiking one morning when you should have been at college," said Mum. "We were just going into Biggleswade and you were on the other side of the roundabout. I said, 'Shall we pick him up and ask him where he's going?' Your Dad said, 'No, leave him to work out whatever it is he's going through'."

All those times I left the house fooling no one but myself. They probably knew, or at least strongly suspected, all along.

Victor George Payne and fuller in the face Grandson. 1982.

Grandad outlived them all. His wife, his youngest daughter, his son-in-law all pre-deceased him. He witnessed the mass unemployment of the 1980s and I saw the anguish in his face as he remembered the years of the Depression. "I thought those times would never come again," he said. Despite it all, he remained hearty, resilient and tough as old boots. When I was younger, and used to pop round to see Grummar of a summer's evening, he would often be sitting on a bus-stop bench with all the other old boys, nattering and watching the world go by. One by one those old boys vacated the spot to go to another place, until eventually there was just Grandad left, alone with his memories. Always a keen gardener, he only gave it up when it became too arduous for him when he was in his late 80s. "Comes hard, boy," he said to me. A master of understatement.

One day in 1991 I was taken aside to a quiet room in Addenbrooke's hospital in Cambridge to be told he had inoperable bowel cancer and that they were sending him home. The inference was that he was not expected to survive for many more weeks, a few months at best. He lived for another four years. During my occasional visits in that twilight period he began to experience those vivid flashbacks to youth that many elderly people slip into. One day, remembering his turbulent time in the fields in the early 1920s he said, almost as an aside, "and my mate Archie said the proletariat are going to take over". I'd never heard Grandad use the word proletariat in his life, nor was he ever likely to – unless it was the name of a horse he had backed to win the 3.15 at Kempton Park. He was remembering the immediate aftermath of the Russian Revolution, rekindling a spark of hope that had once spread from field to field and farm to farm in rural Bedfordshire. In that small utterance I heard big history and the long reach of the 20th century, a collective folk memory echoing down the ages, and now passed on to me, seated in an armchair in the cramped modest living room of his council bungalow.

Compared to such immensity my gone-missing year was just a single cross-stitch in the tapestry, an insignificant detail easily missed. Perhaps one day I'll be recollecting in reverie such magnified moments of a young life, recalling how Grantchester Meadows felt underfoot on a spring morning, what strong tea tasted like in a greasy-spoon caff, reciting the words that first came alive as I read and read and read in a municipal library, clambering high into a lorry cab, uncertain of my destination, reaching over to slam a heavy door and setting off for who knew where, "curving past cares".

I still don't know if it was Nick Drake. I know it was me though. A version of me anyway.

Printed in Great Britain
by Amazon

11112108R00149